COMPUTER-AIDED LEGAL RESEARCH (CALR) ON THE INTERNET

ocre record

Second Edition

COMPUTER-AIDED LEGAL RESEARCH (CALR) ON THE INTERNET

Second Edition

Craig B. Simonsen

Christian R. Anderson

Pearson
Prentice Hall
Legal Series

PEARSON
Prentice
Hall

Upper Saddle River, New Jersey 07458

Library of Congress Cataloging-in-Publication Data

Simonsen, Craig B.
  Computer-aided legal research (CALR) on the Internet / Craig B. Simonsen.
     p. cm.
  Includes bibliographical references and index.
  ISBN 0-13-119774-6
  1. Legal research—United States—Computer network resources. 2. Legal research—
United States—Automation. 3. Information storage and retrieval systems—Law—United
States. 4. Internet—United States. I. Title.
KF242.A1 S56 2006
025.06/34 22   2005018666

Director of Production and Manufacturing: Bruce Johnson
Senior Acquisitions Editor: Gary Bauer
Editorial Assistant: Jacqueline Knapke
Consulting Editors: Enika Schulze and Nancy Blanchette/Athena Group, Inc.
Senior Marketing Manager: Leigh Ann Sims
Managing Editor—Production: Mary Carnis
Manufacturing Buyer: Ilene Sanford
Production Liaison: Denise Brown
Production Editor: Judy Ludowitz/Carlisle Publishers Services
Composition: Carlisle Communications, Ltd.
Senior Design Coordinator: Christopher Weigand
Cover Design: Kevin Kall
Cover Printer: Phoenix Color
Printer/Binder: Hamilton Printing

Chapter One is adapted from, "Assessing the World from a Computer: The Internet," from Linda Furlet and
John Gurdak, chapter eight, Computer Applications for Legal Professionals, 9th edition, Dallas, Pearson
Publications Company, 1999. Used with permission. In Appendix D information on "netiquette" from "The Net:
User Guidelines and Netiquette," found at www.fauedu/netiquette/net/elec.html, copyright © 1998, Arlene
Rinaldi and Florida Atlantic University, is used with permission.

Computer-Aided Legal Research (CALR) on the Internet is designed as a textbook for classroom use. The
information contained herein is intended only for educational and informational purposes.

Pearson Education LTD.   Pearson Education Australia PTY, Limited
Pearson Education Singapore, Pte.   Ltd Pearson Education North Asia Ltd
Pearson Education, Canada, Ltd   Pearson Educación de Mexico, S.A. de C.V.
Pearson Education–Japan   Pearson Education Malaysia, Pte. Ltd

10 9 8 7 6 5 4 3 2 1
ISBN 0-13-119774-6

Foreword

When I graduated from the Indiana University School of Law in 1986, the Internet was not a tool available to lawyers and paralegals. In fact, attorneys and paralegals generally did not even have PCs on their desks. In those "good old days," we spent countless hours in law libraries and courthouses tracking down relevant laws, regulations, cases, histories, guidance, and other documents relevant to the practice of law.

How the Internet has changed everything! These days, most information relevant to the practice of law is available right from our desktops. Legal decisions are still available through the LEXIS® and Westlaw® legal databases, but those databases are accessible over the Internet as well. In addition, innumerable Internet Web sites exist offering attorneys and paralegals access to everything from state and federal laws and regulations to administrative agency guidance. In fact, some "official" versions of government publications are available only through the Internet. With so much information available on the Internet, a succinct guide to legal and factual research on the Internet is essential.

Computer-Aided Legal Research (CALR) on the Internet is a wonderfully clear, jargon-free guide to Internet legal resources. Chapter 1 offers a helpful overview of the Internet, including an interesting history of the origins of the Internet. Chapter 2 through Chapter 8 discuss relevant issues for conducting research on the Internet, including what to search, where to search, and how to search on the Internet. The textbook not only identifies hundreds of Web sites where interesting information can be found, but also describes ways Internet searches should be phrased and conducted in order to obtain the most relevant information. Not all sources of Internet information are the same!

Chapter 9 through Chapter 25 provide information on Internet sources and sites for specific practice areas. The textbook literally offers an A to Z discussion of relevant Web sites. As an environmental attorney, I found Chapter 15, Environmental Law Internet Sources and Sites, particularly helpful and have bookmarked many of the referenced Web sites on my Internet browser. The practice area chapters are relevant both to seasoned practitioners in the particular area of law and to those who may be learning the area for the first time.

The four appendices are also extremely valuable. Appendix A discusses Internet terms, concepts, and acronyms in an easy-to-follow format; Appendix B describes essentials of the domain-name system; Appendix C provides an index to Internet domains; and Appendix D provides a guide to "netiquette," or the proper use of the Internet. The appendices, along with the Index, are extremely easy to use.

The textbook also corresponds well to the American Association for Paralegal Education (AAfPE) "Model Syllabus: Legal Research and Writing and CALR." The model syllabus and this textbook should be considered integral resources for paralegal training. Use them both to maximize your ability to tap into the boundless resource known as the Internet.

Eric E. Boyd, Partner
Seyfarth Shaw LLP
Chicago, IL

Brief Contents

Pearson Legal Series

Pearson Legal Series provides paralegal/legal studies students and educators with the publishing industry's finest content and best service. We offer an extensive selection of products for over 70 titles and we continue to grow with more new titles each year. We also provide:

- online resources for instructors and students
- state-specific materials
- custom publishing options from a Pearson Prentice Hall representative; visit www.prenhall.com

To locate your local Pearson Prentice Hall representative, visit *www.prenhall.com.*

To view Pearson Legal Series titles and to discover a wide array of resources for both instructors and students, please visit our Web site at:

www.prenhall.com/legal_studies

Contents

Chapter 2
Research on the Internet: Using Site
Addresses and Directories   27

Chapter 3
General Internet Resources and Tools   35

Chapter 4
Essentials of Research on the Internet: Search Engines   59

Chapter 5
Legal Research (Sources) on the Internet   69

Chapter 6
Searching in Legal Databases on the Internet   79

Chapter 7
General Sources of Topical Internet Resources
93

Chapter 8
Evaluating Internet Resources and Information
97

Chapter 9
Administrative Law Internet Sources and Sites
105

Chapter 10
Alternative Dispute Resolution Internet Sources and Sites   111

Chapter 11
Bankruptcy Law Internet Sources and Sites   115

Chapter 12
Business, Contract, Corporate, and Securities Internet Sources and Sites   119

Chapter 13
Criminal Law Internet Sources and Sites   125

Chapter 14
Elder and Aging Law Internet Sources and Sites   131

Chapter 20
International Law Internet Sources and Sites   177

Chapter 21
Labor and Employment Law Internet Sources and Sites   183

Chapter 22
Litigation, Personal Injury, and Tort
Internet Sources and Sites   187

Chapter 23
Occupational Safety and Health Law
Internet Sources and Sites   193

Preface

The AAfPE Model Syllabus

This textbook has been prepared to complement and to correspond to the "Model Syllabus: Legal Research and Writing and CALR" (Syllabus), prepared by the American Association for Paralegal Education (AAfPE). The textbook provides in-detail instruction in computer-aided legal research (CALR) on the Internet and many hours of hands-on practice through computer laboratory projects.

Acknowledgments

This project involved a huge investment, including lots of time, thought, and patience (mine and others!). My immense thanks go first to the God of the universe, who has gifted me with the skills, ability, and the opportunity to work on this book. Very special thanks also to Nancy and Kevin for allowing me to invest myself in this project.

Thanks to Christian R. Andersen as a contributing author. His chapters have added to the overall depth and technical sophistication of the book. Thanks to Linda M. Furlet, whose technical and writing skills nicely round out the whole work. Thanks to Lyonette Louis-Jacques, whose chapter on legal research on the Internet brought to this book a law professor's perspective on the subject. Thanks to Elizabeth E. Kirk, whose work on evaluation of Internet resources brought to this book a law librarian's critical analysis of this medium. Thanks to Eric E. Boyd for preparing the thoughtful foreword.

Particular thanks to Katherine A. Currier, J.D., Konnie G. Kustron, J.D., and Dr. Robert N. Diotalevi, LL.M., for their thoughtful reviews and comments on a preview copy of earlier drafts of this book. Kudos especially to Ms. Currier, whose detailed comments were instrumental in the shaping of this work.

Thanks also to Susan Hyser, Attorney and Westlaw® Account Manager, and to Westlaw® for review and comments on one of our chapters, for contribution of Figures and an Internet research scenario, and for provision of complimentary passwords, which facilitated chapter research and reviews and discussions in this work.

Thanks to the whole Pearson/Prentice Hall editorial and production team for all of their assistance on this edition. Finally, special thanks to Enika Pearson Schulze, Pearson/Prentice Hall Consulting Editor, and to Nancy Blanchette for their outstanding work on this book. Enika's constant support and encouragement, along with her energetic approach to publishing timely, quality textbooks, is a credit to her and a boon to the profession.

Special thanks to the reviewers of this text: Labron Shuman, Delaware County Community College, Media, PA; Kent Kauffman, Ivey Tech State College, Fort Wayne, IN; Taylor Morton, Legal Education Consultant, Altadena, CA; Thomas Goldman, Bucks County Community College, Newtown, PA; Robert Diotalevi, Florida Gulf Coast University, Fort Meyers, FL.

Authors and Contributors

Craig B. Simonsen is a senior litigation paralegal at the Chicago office of Seyfarth Shaw LLP. He had been an adjunct instructor for the paralegal studies program formerly at Mallinckrodt College in Wilmette, Illinois, and has taught continuing education seminars for the Roosevelt University's Lawyer's Assistant Program in Chicago, Illinois. Mr. Simonsen received his M.A. (1985) in history from Northeastern Illinois University and has a lawyer's assistant certificate from the Roosevelt University program. Mr. Simonsen has authored other Prentice Hall Legal Series titles, including *Essentials of Environmental Law* (3d ed. 2006) and *Essentials of the Internet* (2002). He also authored the *Environmental Law Resource Guide* (Clark Boardman Callaghan 1995), a paralegal practice series deskbook. Mr. Simonsen has also authored numerous Blackboard CourseSites and textbook companion Web sites for various legal studies titles, including *Introduction to Law: Its Dynamic Nature* (2005) by Henry Cheeseman, for Prentice Hall. Additionally, Mr. Simonsen was the featured speaker on Internet research and resources for the Lake Michigan States Section of the Air & Waste Association in April 2005 and on environmental law at the 2005 Annual Convention of the National Federation of Paralegal Associations (NFPA). He has also authored numerous articles on environmental law and litigation support appearing in the *NFPA Reporter* and *The Paralegal*. Mr. Simonsen is founder and past chairperson of the Illinois Paralegal Association's Environmental Law Section.

Christian R. Andersen is a senior intellectual property paralegal who has been working in the area of intellectual property since 1987. He is currently employed by a large international corporation as the senior paralegal of the intellectual property section. Mr. Andersen has been involved in all aspects of intellectual property, including prosecution; maintenance; and enforcement of patent, copyright, and trademark rights. One of his primary responsibilities is the review, analysis, and approval of all forms of media ad copy for the corporation. Mr. Andersen graduated in May 1984 with a bachelor of arts, *magna cum laude*, English honors program, from California State University, Northridge, and obtained his paralegal's certificate in 1987 from VTI Institute for Paralegal Studies. Mr. Andersen has served as the chair of the intellectual property section (1993–96) and as the chair of the community service committee (1994–95) for the Dallas Area Paralegal Association and has served on the International Trademark Association (INTA) committee of the U.S. Trademark Office (1994–95) and the meetings committee (1998–2001). Mr. Andersen is the author of *Essentials of Intellectual Property*, also a Prentice Hall Legal Series title.

Linda M. Furlet is a consultant and publisher of electronic systems. As president of the electronic publishing firm of Furlet Publishing Services, she has designed computer applications and online documentation systems for numerous banks and financial services companies throughout the United States. She has written, edited, and indexed numerous publications in the computer and income tax fields and has lectured on the theory and application of indexing in the online help environment at national conferences. She also creates online help and documentation systems for a major tax accounting software company. Ms. Furlet holds a B.A. from Trinity University. She is coauthor and editor of *Computer Applications for Legal Professionals*, 9th ed. Prentice Hall 2000, also a Prentice Hall Legal Series title.

Lyonette Louis-Jacques is a naturalized American citizen originally from Port-au-Prince, Haiti, but educated mostly in the United States. Immediately following her graduation from the University of Chicago Law School (JD) in 1986, she began work at the University of Minnesota Law Library, where she taught courses on American as well as foreign and international legal research. Ms. Louis-Jacques is the cofounder of INT-LAW, an electronic conference for the discussion of issues related to foreign, comparative, and international legal (FCIL) resources. Ms. Louis-Jacques is a member of the Committee on Electronic Technologies (CET) of the American Society of International Law and the author of a guide to law-related electronic mailing lists and Usenet newsgroups.

Elizabeth E. Kirk is the electronic and distance education librarian at the Milton S. Eisenhower Library (MSEL), The Johns Hopkins University, in Baltimore, Maryland. As electronic and distance education librarian, Ms. Kirk develops and coordinates the Eisenhower Library's efforts to improve support through information resources and services and works to create partnership relationships with the Homewood Schools and other academic units, with Hopkins affiliates, and with appropriate external agencies. Her primary task is to mainstream MSEL support for distance and electronic education. Ms. Kirk also designs, develops, and implements entrepreneurial projects for the Sheridan Libraries in the areas of electronic and distance education information services and personal research services. One recently launched project is Regents College Virtual Library, an electronically based library service for Regents College of Albany, New York. Ms. Kirk has also served as an adjunct faculty member in the Johns Hopkins University Division of Education, where she taught a graduate course entitled "Integrating Technology into the Adult Classroom."

The Constantly Changing Internet

The author acknowledges that the Internet is a constantly growing, changing thing. That said, the author has attempted to include Internet links that will be stable and unchanging. Examples of such are http://www.ibm.com and http://www.osha.gov. The pages are not unchanging, but the URL addresses will probably remain the same in the foreseeable future.

Readers are encouraged and requested to submit to the author any Internet links referenced in the book that are "broken" or ineffective. The author would also be happy to receive links that readers believe would be appropriately listed in the volume but are not currently included. New resources are constantly coming on line, and the author certainly may have missed some!

The author will list corrected and submitted links on the book's corresponding Internet page on the publisher's Web site (http://www.prenhall.com/legal_studies/index.html). Please submit suggested new or broken links to the author at paralegal_studies@prenhall.com.

Introduction

The Internet is technologically a global network of connected computers–like a LAN (local area (or small) network), except it is a world-wide network of networked computers. It quickly became a popular tool used by research professionals in business, education, government, marketing, and by the public at large. Statistically, the Internet is one of the fastest-growing areas in computing today. With enormous data resources (electronic files containing data, programs, images, etc.), e-mail (electronic, computer mail), e-commerce (a Web site set up for the particular purpose of promoting commerce), and e-messaging (two or more computer users connected through the Internet and sending instantaneous or live messages between one another), the Internet is ablaze with activity.[1]

This textbook will prepare aspiring legal professionals to maximize the value of the Internet. To individuals, the innate value of this preparation is in a lifelong knowledge and skills set that will prepare them for employment and the marketplace. The innate value to employers is in increasing the functionality and use of high-end, powerful, personal, and networked computer systems by professional legal staff.

More than a basic knowledge of the Internet and trained research skills are imperative for effective computer-aided legal research (CALR). Computer-aided legal research is defined simply as the use of computers to automate the search for legal and factual information. That said, having an education in what sources contain what information is essential for CALR practitioners.

For instance, if we think in terms of a physical library, understanding which library rooms to look in, which card catalogs to look at, and which shelves to look at can significantly increase the researcher's likelihood of finding responsive documents. It is similar for the Internet researcher. If a CALR researcher knows which Web site (an address or location that is on the Internet) to go to (e.g., the U.S. Department of Transportation's Web site) and which directory (a site on the Web that catalogs or categorizes Web sites by subject and indexes the sites, often providing a brief description of their content) to go to (e.g., Docket & Regulations), and which regulations to look at (e.g., Title 49 of the *Code of Federal Regulations* (Transportation)), the researcher has a good likelihood of finding responsive documents.

This textbook presents a comprehensive review of the knowledge, tools, search skills, and methodology necessary for legal professionals to excel at CALR on the Internet. But more than that, it provides students with practical hints and research scenarios throughout so that students may experience CALR research firsthand.

---

[1]Readers are encouraged to consult Appendix A: Internet Terms, Concepts, and Acronyms for words and phrases that are unfamiliar and undefined in the text.

Chapter 1 provides a detailed review of what exactly the Internet is, including where it came from and how it works. It also reviews several hot topics and legal issues surrounding the Internet today. An important point is that much of the information and many of the documents found on the Internet are available nowhere else. Conversely, many of the documents available for free on the Internet would otherwise be available only to those willing and able to pay for them. Practically, then, the Internet provides the legal professional with powerful and inexpensive resources and tools for doing all kinds of CALR projects, which this textbook seeks to exploit.

The scope of information available on the Internet is extraordinary. Research methods and illustrations for researching on the Internet are provided in Chapter 2 through Chapter 7. Chapter 2 looks specifically at Internet addresses and Internet directories and their uses. It provides tips and examples of searching out and locating known (or guessed-at) Web site addresses. It also reviews the most common Web site tools, such as site directories, keyword indexes, and site-specific search engines.

In Chapter 3, numerous examples of Internet resources and tools are provided to illustrate the variety and the quality of Internet information available. The chapter provides detailed listings and addresses to

- Search engines, directories, and virtual libraries
- Databases (nonlegal)
- Useful resources
- Government sites—federal
- Government sites—state
- Government sites—municipal
- Traditional legal research database (commercial) sites
- Selected legal service provider sites
- Legal professional reference sites

The search engines (Web programs or services that allow database queries for keywords and then return matching Web sites and documents), directories, and virtual libraries (Web sites that are set up for the specific purpose of collecting and disseminating particular types or groups of documents and information) provide a wealth of pre-indexed materials and keyword and phrase access to millions of documents. Google™ is one of the best-known search engines.

Internet databases (collections of related information or documents) also provide a wealth of pre-indexed materials with keyword and phrase access to millions of documents. America's Job Bank (http://www.jobsearch.org) is an example. Useful resources covered include sites like The Acronym Finder (http://www.acronymfinder.com) and *Introduction to Basic Legal Citation* (Legal Information Institute 2003 ed.) by Peter W. Martin at http://www.law.cornell.edu/citation).

The government sites—federal, state, and municipal resources—provide government-related resources and tools. Examples include the following. The *Congressional Record Index* (http://www.gpoaccess.gov/cri/index.html) provides keyword searchable access to the full text of the *Congressional Record*. The *Federal Register* Daily Table of Contents (http://www.access.gpo.gov/su_docs/aces/fr-cont.html) provides immediate access to today's rules, proposals, and notices published by federal agencies. Several years ago, lawyers and the public alike would have to wait days and weeks before the paper copy of the *Federal Register* would finally arrive in the mail. The Daily Table of Contents provides mirror-image (pdf (Portable Document Format)) copies the day they are published!

The traditional legal research database (commercial) sites listed include vendors like LexisNexis® (http://www.lexis.com) and Westlaw® (http://www.westlaw.com). Traditionally, lawyers needed to have specialized computers provided by the vendor or PCs equipped with the vendor's proprietary software to search the vendor's legal database. Now, anyone with a PC that is connected to the Internet can access and search the legal research database (commercial) sites.

The selected legal service provider sites include vendors such as Kroll Ontrack Inc. (http://www.krollontrack.com) and TrialGraphix (http://www.trialgraphix.com). Kroll provides document image database services capable of organizing and searching millions of documents. TrialGraphix provides litigation support and trial services. Its graphics work very well with juries, and its presentation software displays the graphics electronically so that witnesses can manipulate and work with the graphic images.

The legal professional reference sites provide links to professional association Web sites such as the American Bar Association (http://www.abanet.org) and the National Association of Legal Assistants (http://www.nala.org).

Chapter 4 reviews Internet search engines and illustrates their usage. In this chapter, we discuss the pitfalls and potholes into which researchers may fall while searching the Web. For instance, researchers must have a good sense of what it is they are searching for. Having "sort of an idea" of approximately what is wanted will lead to millions of search hits, with few being what is really needed. In addition, there is so much data "out there" on the vast Internet that a researcher will see a lot of junk mixed with the diamonds.

In Chapter 5, a law professor and law librarian illustrates the vast legal resources available on the Internet. Literally hundreds of Internet pages of legal interest are listed and described in this chapter.

In Chapter 6, the several common computer-aided legal research (CALR) databases are reviewed. The use of CALR databases over the Internet is illustrated, and the various systems are contrasted.

Chapter 7 introduces many topical and practice area Internet resources and provides links to general sources and sites for topical materials.

Chapter 8 provides "Evaluating Information Found on the Internet,"© a useful resource for legal research professionals. With the mountains of data available over the Internet, if only a few pebbles can pass the evaluation for quality assurance, then that is that. A research professional must be able to analyze and distinguish Internet material—the good from the junk.

Chapter 9 and all of the following chapters are the topical, practice area chapters. The introductions to the topical chapters serve as a summary for anyone unfamiliar with the practice area. More than a summary, though, the chapter on intellectual property is a comprehensive overview of copyright and trademark protections. The topical, practice area chapters list and describe specific topical resources and tools. These topical lists are not complete lists on each topic, but each is a starting point and a list of useful sites for researchers working in these particular areas.

As an aid to readers, Appendix A lists Internet terms, concepts, and acronyms and provides definitions and illustrations. In Appendix B, the essentials of the domain-name system are presented. Appendix C lists domain-name suffixes, so that researchers will always know, at least generally, from what site the data came. Appendix D provides useful information on so-called "netiquette."

CHAPTER 1

The Internet

Linda M. Furlet

SUMMARY

This chapter introduces and delineates what exactly the Internet is and where it came from. The chapter puts the Internet in historical context and explains how the Internet is used by lawyers and other members of the legal community. Finally, it discusses legal and hot topics relating to the Internet.

OBJECTIVES

- The student will be equipped with the historical and technological background necessary to have an understanding of where the Internet came from.
- The student will learn about what the Internet is and what it does.
- The student will be introduced to how the Internet is used by lawyers and other members of the legal community.
- The student will be introduced to some of the legal issues and hot topics that surround the Internet.

What Is the Internet?

The **Internet** is the global **network** of computers that communicate using a common language. It is similar to the international telephone system—no one owns or controls the Internet, but it is connected in a way that makes it work like one big network. Over thirty million people have **e-mail** access to the Internet, and most of those use other facets of the Net too.

What is the Internet? It is a network, a loose organization, a public forum, a mailbox, a business tool, a library, a software shop, and a newspaper.

With permission, Chapter One has been adapted and updated by CRAIG SIMONSEN and LINDA FURLET from Chapter Eight of COMPUTER APPLICATIONS FOR LEGAL PROFESSIONALS, 9/e by JOHN A. GURDACK and LINDA FURLET. ©2000 Pearson Prentice Hall.

Origins of the Internet

The Internet that exists today began in 1969 as an experiment of an agency of the U.S. Department of Defense. The agency connected various defense department computers, defense contractors, and universities doing defense research into a classified network that accomplished two things. First, it enabled users to share expensive computing resources, which saved money; and second, it gave the Defense Department a network upon which to test various methods for keeping military networks operational in times of war. If one network was knocked off line (by a nuclear attack), the other networks could still work and communicate with each other. The National Science Foundation (NSF) then created the idea of a vast network with other scientific research centers and educational facilities so that ideas and research could be more easily accessed and exchanged.

To manage this huge project, the government created an organization called the Advanced Research Projects Agency (ARPA). Later this new network was called the **Advanced Research Projects Agency Network** (**ARPANET**). Once the researchers figured out a way to connect the computers, they needed methods of making them communicate via a network language. The first language to come out of this was **Transmission Control Protocol/Internet Protocol** (**TCP/IP**). Throughout the 1970s and early 1980s, the network grew and portions of it were declassified. During the same period, other, separate networks were established to link university researchers and scientists.

In 1986 the National Science Foundation established its network, **NSFNET,** to allow researchers across the country to share access to a few expensive *supercomputers* (the fastest and most powerful types of computers for scientific applications). Quickly thereafter, the various separate research networks began hooking to NSFNET and, in effect, to each other. In 1990 the original Defense Department network was retired. Eventually the resulting **internetwork** was linked to the various internetworks abroad and today's global Internet congealed from many separate parts.

Since then, the Internet has continued to grow steadily. Most major universities in the world are connected to the network, as are most U.S. government agencies. Business quickly discovered the network. Most of the larger law firms in the United States have established direct connections to the Internet, with their own place on the information superhighway. There is no way to gauge how many are connected through a commercial access provider. However, as of 2001, it was estimated that 42.2% of the total U.S. adult population (over age eighteen) were regular Internet users.[1]

Since the early 1980s, when the government began to share its network technology with the world, there has been growth on a scale that is hard to imagine. To put it into better perspective, in the early 1980s there were only 213 registered hosts on the Internet. By 1986 this number had risen to 2308 hosts. By January 1995 there were more than 4.85 million registered hosts. This num-

---

[1] *The Internet Economy Indicators*™ *at* http://www.internetindicators.com/facts1.html (Apr. 11, 2001).

ber does not include personal computers (PCs) that were accessing the Internet but merely includes the number of **servers** that make up the Internet.

The Internet Facilitates Data Communication

Primarily, the Internet provides a means for *data communication*. Data communication is the process of transmitting data from one computer to another via conventional communication **links** such as telephone lines. This allows information to be shared by many users. Data communication is especially useful if the person wanting the information is far from the computer that stores the information.

The successful implementation of data communication is the same as the implementation of any other computer application; the appropriate hardware and software are needed. A basic understanding of data communication hardware and software, primarily relating to the Internet, is essential.

Hardware for Data Communication

Data communication hardware provides the means by which computer data, in the form of electronic signals, can travel between computer devices. The basic hardware elements of a data communication connection are

- a **host** (or **server**) computer,
- a data transmission device (like a **modem**),
- communication lines (such as telephone lines or cable),
- a data reception device (like a cable modem), and
- a client (or user) computer.

There are several different ways to communicate data. For instance, data can be sent between computers on a **local area network (LAN)**. The computers in that instance are equipped with LAN cards that allow them to transmit and receive data traveling through cables that connect the computers.

Historically, one of the most useful and widely used methods of data communication over the Internet was called **telecommunication.** Basic telecommunication hardware consists of a host computer, the host computer's modem, a client's receiving modem, a client computer, and telephone lines in between—hence, the name "TELEcommunication."

Telecommunication was performed by the following process. A host computer's data storage device (such as a disk drive or hard drive) contained information that a remote user (or client) desired. The host computer first read the data from its storage device, then transformed and transmitted that data via a modem. The modem had to transform the data for transmission over telephone lines.

Computer data signals are digital, consisting of discrete "on" and "off" pulses of electricity. In contrast, the telephone system predominantly used analog signals, consisting of a continuous stream of electricity that varies in intensity. The host's modem was able to transform digital data signals into an analog form for transmission over telephone lines. The client's modem then transformed analog signals back to digital.

Software for Data Communication

For data communication to be performed, the host and the client computers needed to use the same communication **protocol.** Communication protocol is a machine language by which computers communicated with one another. Because changing the communication protocol of a mainframe computer was a monumental task, it was much easier to require each client computer to conform to a host's protocol. A law office that communicates with a **computer-aided legal research (CALR) database** has to adjust the protocol of its computer to match the host's software communication protocol.

Both the host computer and the client computer require data communication software. The software sends and receives data through an interface port. For telecommunication, a modem is hooked up to the interface port, such as an interface board or a serial port on the computer. Communication software runs in the same manner as any other PC software. The communication software controls the operation of the modem and adapts the client's protocol to that of the host computer. With the newest generation of PC communication software, the process of setting up the proper protocol is fairly easy. LEXIS® and Westlaw® communication software are good examples of CALR data communication software.

These sophisticated data communication programs have additional functions such as data capture and **offline computing.** Data capture or **downloading** is the ability to receive data from a remote source and to store it in a local device. Downloaded information can also be used or incorporated into computer spreadsheets, database management systems, and word processors. The opposite of downloading is **uploading,** which transmits data from the user's computer to the host computer for storage. *File transfer* is the process of downloading or uploading files. Offline computing is the ability to process data, such as composing queries, while not communicating with a host computer. The time spent communicating with a host computer is called *connect* or **online** time. Offline computing can be a valuable function when a user is accessing a computer service that charges for online time.

Many databases for legal and general information research bill for online time. Offline computing allows a user to minimize the amount of online time. Naturally, the less time spent on line, the lower the user fee.

Internet Browsers

To access the Internet, the researcher must use an application called a **browser.** The two most widely used browsers are **Netscape® Navigator®**, published by Netscape Corporation, and **Microsoft® Internet Explorer®**, published by Microsoft Corporation. Both the Microsoft® Internet Explorer® and the Netscape® Navigator® browser facilitate searching, finding within documents, viewing, and downloading or uploading information on the Internet. A screenshot of the Microsoft® Internet Explorer® is shown in Figure 1-1.

Both browsers offer many "extras" to their users. For example, using either Netscape® Navigator® or Microsoft® Internet Explorer®, a user can hold a real-time conference with other users over the Internet, including sound, collabo-

Figure 1-1 Microsoft® Internet Explorer®.
Reprinted with permission. Copyright © 2004, Microsoft.com.

ration on work files, and text-based chat. Also included are integrated readers for e-mail and **Usenet newsgroups** (this describes a set of machines that exchange articles tagged with one or more universally recognized labels, called *newsgroups* or *groups* for short).

Internet browsers use electronic **addresses** called **uniform resource locators (URLs)** to locate and identify information. A URL describes exactly where a particular piece of information is. The Internet browser interprets the **Hypertext Markup Language (HTML)** (a fairly simple Internet programming language) that makes up a Web page and assembles it for viewing on the client's computer screen. Different browsers interpret HTML differently. Because of the varying interpretations, a user viewing Web pages through one browser may see a slightly different page from the page presented through a different browser.

How Do Lawyers Use Data Communication?

Lawyers are especially interested in information processing. Often the required information is not easily available and must be gathered from an outside source. With the creation of public **databases,** any user can now access vast quantities of information. These public databases are convenient, fast, and relatively easy to use.

Without leaving the office, a researcher can use a personal computer to connect to a public database. Once a researcher is connected to a database, the researcher can search for what seems like an infinite volume of information. A search in an electronic database can save countless hours of manual research time. These databases also allow for printing or downloading. More extensive information about databases and searching is available in the following chapters.

Online Legal Research Databases

Online legal research databases provide researchers with extensive libraries of case law, statutes, and other legal source material. Most of this information is stored in full-text format, allowing for comprehensive queries. For instance, a query can be formulated to search for all cases by the New Jersey Supreme Court containing the words *dog, bite,* and *liability.* Then the excerpts or the complete text of each case can be viewed, printed, or downloaded. For a more in-depth discussion about searching legal databases on the Internet, see Chapter 6.

Nonlegal Databases

Research performed by legal professionals is not limited to legal issues. Often the investigation of facts and factual information is critically important. Thousands of nonlegal databases contain information on every imaginable subject, including full-text copies of periodicals, newspapers, and newsletters. The quantity and substance of information stored in public databases are rapidly increasing as demand grows for computer research.

Newsgroups

Internet **newsgroups,** through Usenet networks, allow "electronic discussions" to take place concerning a particular subject or interest. It is a discussion, conceptually, in which information and opinions are shared with people all over the world. Within each newsgroup **discussion group** are articles on a given subject. Usenet newsgroups allow readers to reply to articles read and to publish (post) articles for others to read.

E-Mail

E-mail, that is, electronic computer mail, allows the user to write messages on a computer and then to transmit the messages to another computer so that the addressee can read the message on another computer. E-mail allows users to skip the process of printing messages on paper (as in letters or memoranda) and then hand-carrying them to an addressee (by a courier service or U.S. Postal Service). E-mail, conceptually and typically, saves paper, time, and energy.

Web Sites for Marketing

Attorneys and law firms, like corporate and government entities, are actively creating and updating **Web sites** that reflect their practices and interests. These Web sites often contain attorney biographical information, practice categories, newsletters and advisories, success stories, **pages** of links, and representative client lists. Many attorneys and law firms are finding that potential clients and employees review and evaluate their Web sites.

The Internet as a Network

The Internet allows people from nearly every country and from many different walks of life to correspond with one another, to do research, and to find information. Physicians use it to heal, journalists use it to report, researchers use it to find information, and everyday folks use it to do everyday things.

The computers that constitute the Internet come in just about every size, shape, and type. They are spread all over the world—in every continent, including Antarctica. According to the Internet Society, a volunteer organization, the number of computers on the Internet is almost doubling every year.

Most of the computers on the Internet do not exist simply to be part of the Internet. They are actually the computers used every day by governments and their agencies, universities, research organizations, corporations, libraries, and individuals. Because each computer is on the Internet, however, its users can take advantage of some of the information stored on many of the other computers. Each computer's users can also exchange messages with the users of the other computers.

The computers on the Internet can talk to one another because they are networked; they are connected so that they can exchange information with one another electronically. On the Internet, connections take many different forms. Some computers are directly connected to others with wire or fiber-optic cables. Some are connected through local and long-distance telephone lines, and some even use wireless satellite communications—the same types used today for some long-distance phone services and cellular phones—to communicate with other computers on the Internet.

To summarize, a network is made up of two or more computers that are connected so that they can exchange messages and share information. An internetwork is two or more networks that are connected so that they can exchange messages and share information. The Internet is the world's largest internetwork. It includes computers hooked together in networks, those networks hooked together in internetworks, and those internetworks hooked together in still bigger internetworks. There are over 50,000 networks within the Internet today. Because the Internet is an internetwork, each computer is not necessarily directly connected to every other computer. In other words, any computer on the Internet can talk to any other, but the message may have to travel through several other computers on its way there.

The Internet as an Organization

Although most people talk about the Internet as if it were some giant singular entity, it really is not. No single entity or organization controls it. Computer owners control their computers. The Massachusetts Institute of Technology (MIT) controls its computers, the Library of Congress controls its computers, the University of Pisa controls its computers, and so on.

Many discrete organizations on the Internet have their own rules concerning which types of activities are allowed on their computers and which are not. These rules are called *acceptable-use policies,* and usually they are not enforced very carefully. No single set of acceptable-use policies covers the whole Internet.

Nobody controls the Internet; people simply join up and participate. The Internet resembles a neighborhood where people communicate because they are able to; but they have not established a formal organization with rights, rules, and leaders. Just as each computer on the Internet is under its owner's control, some networks that make up a large part of the Internet are controlled by their owners. For example, as previously noted, the Internet today arose, in part, from a project called NSFNET, a network of researchers and universities created by the National Science Foundation and therefore funded by the United States. The NSFNET and other federally funded networks that are part of the Internet set their own acceptable-use policies. But again, although government and industry control pieces of the Internet, nobody controls the whole, nor is anybody likely to do so soon.

Because of the lack of central control, different resources on the Internet require different steps and skills, which makes using the Internet difficult. Software companies are working on better software to make the Internet (or parts of the Internet, anyway) appear as one smooth system to its users.

Efforts are underway to smooth out the wrinkles between the many networks run by federal agencies and to link them to the entire academic and research community, forming one, high-speed network. This early step in the creation of the information superhighway effectively puts much of the policymaking power for a big slice of the Internet under U.S. government control. Looseness is the Internet's blessing and its curse. Because traditionally the Internet has been open and free, it has evolved on its own into a giant resource that probably never could have come about if any one government or large corporation held the reins. Because nobody is in charge, the Internet is inconsistent and sometimes difficult to use. As people use it to access different computers and services, they find that not everything operates the same way on the Internet. There are some general rules that people follow—a sort of traditional *Internet etiquette.* See Appendix D. These rules are very general and are loosely followed, if at all.

Although no single group really controls the Internet, there are groups that influence it. Two volunteer groups, a council called the Internet Architecture Board and a technical advisory team called the Internet Engineering Task Force, work together to enforce minor rules to keep the whole thing working, such as deciding which kinds of communications languages should be supported by the network. Although the Internet includes many different types of computers and networks, it cannot work unless everybody observes a few basic rules in their underlying communications technologies. These volunteer groups develop rules to keep the Internet running smoothly.

People who want to use the Internet but cannot access it through computers at their company or school have to pay a commercial service provider for access to the Internet. The Internet itself is free and open to all (although there are many fee-based services, such as LEXIS® and Westlaw®, on the Internet), but some people have to pay a service provider to open the door.

The Internet as a Public Forum

Several of the most important Internet resources enable users to exchange information in an open, public way. These resources provide a forum where users can write and post messages for other users and read messages posted by others. In that sense, these resources play the open-air-exchange-site role played by a coffeehouse or other public meeting place. These *coffeehouse resources* actually come in several different types, each of which is used differently.

Each coffeehouse resource typically handles a specific topic or area of interest. Because these resources are divided by subject, users can easily find messages related to their interests and can post messages where the messages will be read by people who share the users' interests. For example, a user interested in the Central Intelligence Agency (CIA) can read messages about the CIA in the resource that covers it. The user can also respond to or comment on those messages or write messages for other CIA buffs to see. There are hundreds of these resources, including topics on computers, freedom of information, disabilities, gun control, film and television, AIDS, law, employment, nutrition, and architecture.

Even though they are divided by subject, the coffeehouse resources can become overcrowded. They can pile up hundreds of messages, which makes keeping up with them or finding any particular message difficult. Often, people who use these resources have access to a special computer program that helps them find messages on a particular topic. They can instruct the program to sort through the messages and show only the messages that match a very specific interest. This helps people find what they are looking for quickly without having to wade through an overwhelming pile of messages. Users can also browse through messages looking for something of interest.

Different types of Internet resources fill the coffeehouse role, with each type used differently. Many such resources fall into one of two major types: newsgroups and mailing lists.

- *Newsgroups* (sometimes called *Usenet newsgroups* or *network news*) are more sophisticated (and more difficult to use) in the ways they enable their users to work with messages. Newsgroups are available for a huge range of topics: the professional, the personal, and the unusual.
- *Mailing lists* (also known as *discussion lists*) are simpler and usually based on professional topics. **Mailing lists** send all messages related to a particular topic directly to the user by e-mail. **Subscribers** to a mailing list

can also send in their own messages, which are then sent out to everyone else on the list.

Many of the rest of the Internet resources that serve the coffeehouse role are grouped under the name *bulletin boards*. Although they all share a category name, each bulletin board works a little differently. These resources offer Internet users a way to get the answers to questions when they do not know whom to ask. A paralegal looking for a particular resource can post questions about research techniques on an Internet resource for paralegals. Other paralegals will read the message, and those with an answer or a tip will post replies. Scientists and scholars use this capability to exchange news and information about important topics, from fusion to fat cells.

The Internet as a Mailbox: E-Mail

Without question, the most-used Internet facility is e-mail. Many people obtain Internet access just to have e-mail capabilities. A screenshot of a Microsoft® Outlook e-mail message screen is shown in Figure 1-2.

Traditionally, all that could be included in an e-mail message was words. However, with the worldwide use of graphical computing environments, people now include documents, pictures, video clips, and sounds in e-mail messages.

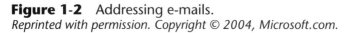

Figure 1-2   Addressing e-mails.
Reprinted with permission. Copyright © 2004, Microsoft.com.

Everyone who uses the Internet has a unique Internet name, called an address. An e-mail address consists of three parts:

1. the user's name,
2. the "@" sign (crucial!), and
3. the **domain** (the host computer, usually a commercial access provider or a university, business, etc.).

Virtually every federal agency, Congress, and the White House all have e-mail addresses. A worker in the White House named Larry Pumpernickel, for example, might have this e-mail address: lpumpernickel@whitehouse.gov. The e-mail shown in Figure 1-2 is addressed to someone@aol.com.

The e-mail address provides all the information required to get a message delivered anywhere (to any domain) in the world. When an e-mail address is incorrect in some way (the system's name is wrong, or the domain does not exist), the mail system will bounce the message back to the sender, much the same way that the U.S. Postal Service does when you send a letter to an out-of-date address. Remember, computers are very literal. Every character you press (or do not press) will be relayed exactly the way it is typed. A bounced-back message will include the reason for the bounce; a common error is addressing mail to a nonexistent account name.

While there are **directories** that list e-mail addresses on the Internet, not everyone is listed in a directory. The best way to locate an e-mail address is to ask that person. More and more, professionals are listing their e-mail addresses on their business cards and letterheads, along with their telephone and fax numbers. Why? Because e-mail is a means of communication, just like the telephone and fax.

No two Internet users have the same address, so to send a message to an Internet user anywhere in the world, all the sender has to know is the address of the recipient. The sender types up a message in the e-mail program, logs on to the Internet, types in the address, and sends the message on its way.

In theory, the message should arrive at the recipient's computer almost instantly; after all, it is traveling through wire at nearly the speed of light. However, there is not always (if ever) a straight line between any two computers on the Internet. The message may have to pass through a number of networks and computers before it reaches its destination; and it could get held up, temporarily, anywhere along the way. Eventually, however, the message is delivered to the addressee's computer.

The most useful feature of e-mail is the way in which it enables users to work with the messages. They can instantly send a reply to a message they have received. They can forward a message to someone else (perhaps a person who can answer a question the message asks). They can print the message. Senders also have e-mail options. They can send the same message to one or many recipients at once.

The use and preparation of e-mail involves the following steps:

- Prepare the text. This can be done on line or off line.
- Dial up or otherwise connect via cable or direct satellite link to the e-mail service. The use of an **Internet service provider** (**ISP**) such as **America Online**® is necessary for this.

- Type in the user authorization code, such as the user name and password. This prevents unauthorized access and facilitates billing for the service. This is called *signing on*.
- Transmit an existing message, or prepare new messages.
- Check for any waiting e-mail stored in the mailbox.
- View any waiting messages, save them to the local computer, or print them out.

E-Mail in the Legal Profession

Remember how overnight mail revolutionized the business world? E-mail is instant mail. In the legal profession, speed and reliability in the delivery of a letter, brief, or other written communication are often critical, especially in a multistate or international practice. There is probably less chance of losing mail in an electronic system than in the traditional mail delivery system.

Law offices benefit greatly from the use of e-mail. E-mail can expedite negotiations, litigation, and delivery of work product to the client. The possible uses of e-mail are limited only by the imagination of the user.

Take the following example: contract negotiations with a multinational corporation.

> Your law firm represents a client in New York who has negotiated a purchase contract with a chemical company whose home office is in Holland. At the closing, the seller requests some additional terms. The terms are drafted and easily added to the contract using the firm's document processor. The seller reviews the contract and says that he must clear the added terms with his home office in Holland before he signs. Either the closing can be postponed, or the contract can be instantly transmitted to Holland via e-mail. Once the contract has been reviewed, an e-mail response can be sent back to New York.

Any kind of document can be delivered by e-mail. It may even be preferable to send someone an e-mail message than to make a phone call. No longer do you have to play "telephone tag." Trying to track down that elusive coworker? Send an e-mail message. It is up to the law firm staff to realize the usefulness of e-mail and to apply this powerful tool in the practice of law.

The desire to communicate is the essence of networking. People have always wanted to correspond with each other in the fastest way possible, short of normal conversation. E-mail allows people to write back and forth without having to spend much time worrying about how the message actually gets delivered. As technology grows closer and closer to being a common part of daily life, the need to understand the many ways it can be utilized and how it works, at least at some level, is vital.

Employee E-Mail

Most people believe that their e-mail is private. That is true to a point, but when you compose e-mail on an employer-owned computer system, using employer time and sending it out via employer connections, it is no longer private e-mail. The privacy of employee e-mail has been litigated many times, and the courts have ruled overwhelmingly that an employer has the right to read employee e-mail and that employees have no reasonable expectation of privacy. Some cases have involved employees using employer e-mail to look for other employment, to pass on employer trade secrets and proprietary information, or to harass or threaten people. In these cases, the employer was held to have a right to read employee e-mail and the employee had no recourse.

E-mail is now considered an acceptable form of communication and, as such, is discoverable in litigation. In the Department of Justice case against Microsoft®, the software giant's e-mail retention hampered its defense, as numerous old e-mails came to light contradicting sworn testimony by witnesses. In the independent counsel's investigation of President Clinton, more than one witness had computers seized and searched for old e-mail.

Because of the Microsoft® case, many companies have adopted a retention/destruction policy for old e-mail. After a certain period of time, all e-mail backups on the network are destroyed. This makes it difficult to prove a paper trail; so in order to keep thorough records, users must now revert to printing documents out and placing them in files. Printed documents, of course, continue to be fully discoverable.

Most companies have strong anti-sexual-harassment policies in place. E-mail containing jokes that are sexual or racist in nature, even between coworkers, can be considered to violate these policies and are often grounds for termination. The rule of thumb is: Be careful what you write in e-mail.

The Internet as a Business Tool

The use of the Internet for business has sparked much debate. No doubt, given the increasingly global business climate and the great extent to which big companies rely on computers, the Internet looks like a great vehicle for national and international business communication. It is certainly cheaper and more flexible than building a private, global computer network from scratch.

There are, however, reasons that business use of the Internet has been heavily restricted through the years. Much of what is now the Internet began as an experimental research network for the Defense Department; evolved into a project of the federally funded National Science Foundation; and is now evolving into a new, federally sponsored network of government agencies and academia, dubbed the **National Research and Educational Network (NREN).**

Simply put, the U.S. government has sunk a lot of money into the domestic parts of the Internet and is sinking still more. Taxpayers are generally agreeable about money spent "in support of research or education," which is what the NREN portion of the Internet is chartered to do; but ugly arguments sometimes ensue when large corporations are permitted to use a tax-subsidized network for the benefit of their own bottom line.

Beyond that political issue is a philosophical one. Although the Internet has always had business users of a sort (after all, many of the principal users of the Internet in its formative years were defense contractors), some users have come to think of the Internet as a big co-op, the world's largest community garden and pitch-in lunch. They believe that the lack of central control of the Internet and the exclusion of mercenary corporate interests are what kept the network healthy, growing, and pure. They want the Internet preserved as a forum for scientific and social inquiry and global exchange, a vehicle for the public good, not private profit.

Still more problems arise in doing business on the Internet, including the fact that the precise laws and policies regarding copyrights, monetary transactions, international currency conversion, taxes and exchange, privacy, and security have yet to be ironed out to everyone's satisfaction. Thus, the rule for the parts of the Internet subsidized by government has long been "no commercial traffic," as described by the NSF's acceptable-use policy for its NSFNET, which by itself comprises a big chunk of the Internet. Many smaller government and academic networks have similar policies; and, even beyond these networks, there has been a traditional discouragement of commercial activity. Business users, like anyone else, have always been welcome to use the Internet for research; but when they begin to use it to send their purchase orders from sales offices to headquarters, or as an e-mail system for the overseas marketing staff, or as a junk mail delivery system, Internet purists cry foul.

Yet, the commercialization of the Internet has been exploding for many years. The policies restricting business activity have been little enforced, despite the grumbling of some purists. In 1991 some of the government restrictions on commercial use were lifted. That opened the door for a dozen networking companies to set up their own major sections of the Internet to support commercial traffic while working around the NSFNET and its no-business policy. A few examples? In addition to the obvious examples of onscreen advertising and e-mail, businesses already use the Internet to

- sell real estate, books, concert tickets, handmade dolls, and flowers;
- provide credit reports, legal services, consulting services, and customer support; and
- publish newspapers, newsletters, and magazines that can be read on the computer screen and are paid for by reader subscriptions, advertising, or both.

In an extraordinary development, the NSFNET was retired at the end of April 1995, with almost no visible effects from the point of view of Internet users. Now, in its place, there is a fully commercial system of networks that have been erected where a government-sponsored system once existed. At the end of the last century, the **e-commerce** market, as it is known, was estimated to be more than $1 billion in annual revenue.

The Internet as a Library

In fact, the Internet is many libraries, numbering in the many thousands, all over the world. Among the earliest and most avid users of the Internet were colleges and universities. Many have their whole computer network tied into the Internet, including the computerized card catalog for the university library. These schools use the Internet to operate interlibrary loan programs. When a student or professor requests a book that is not in the stacks, the library can locate the book at a branch campus, another university, or even at a public library or private research collection and can have it sent from there. Of course, the university pays for that privilege by making its own collection available to all the other libraries from which it borrows. All this interlibrary networking leaves many public, private, government, and academic catalogs accessible to any Internet user. Curious readers can plumb the collections of the great universities to find exactly the material they are looking for. The choices include public and private libraries and specialized libraries for medicine, law, and other subject areas.

Thousands of libraries are on the Internet, including many public libraries. Some libraries allow people to order a title over the Internet to be delivered by mail. For those that do not, Internet users can usually go to their own local university or public library and ask a librarian to make the request.

No matter how users finally get their hands on the desired book, the value of the Internet is that it lets users find the book, no matter where it is stacked. To help, there are bibliographic indexing services on the Internet that list where materials on certain subjects can be found. In the information age, there is another kind of library. The text of reports, papers, and even whole books can be (and usually is) stored in computer files. Here is where the library resources on the Internet shine. Literally millions of files of information are available on the Internet that savvy users can locate and then copy right over the Internet from the distant computer to their own, where they can read the information on their computer screens or print it on a printer. Next to e-mail, this is the most often used and most valuable resource on the Internet. It allows researchers (or the merely curious) to acquire the latest and most detailed information about every topic imaginable. In fact, much of the information available this way may not be published in any book; the Internet offers people access to information that is unavailable to them in any other way.

As more and more computers today acquire multimedia capabilities, more material has appeared on the Internet to serve those machines. Although most of the computer files on the Internet contain only text (which users can read by opening the files in a document processing program), a growing group holds pictures, video, and sound. You can, in fact, find entire books in computer files on the Internet, in many different places. Perhaps the best known source is *Project Gutenberg*, a volunteer project to transfer important reference works and works of literature to computer files and make them widely available. Already, through Project Gutenberg, people can copy from the Internet anything from Shakespeare to *Roget's Thesaurus*, to *Moby Dick*, to the *Book of Mormon*, to the CIA *World Fact Book*.

Much more is available now, and still more is on the way. Among other electronic book providers on the Internet is the Online Book Initiative (OBI).

The Internet as a Software Shop

If computer files containing books can be copied across the Internet, so can files containing anything else, including computer software. People find software in several different ways on the Internet. When they find it, they can copy it to their computers and use it there, just as if they had bought it at a software store. People often post on the Internet software they have written, much as they would post a message for others to read. That software can be copied and used by others. Some software companies also make their products available on the Internet to paying customers.

Software available through the Internet comes in three basic types

1. **Freeware** is absolutely free of charge and available to all. An example is the Adobe® Reader® software, which is available free to anyone who cares to download it from its maker (http://www.adobe.com). A screen-shot of the Adobe® Reader® freeware is shown in Figure 1-3.
2. **Shareware** is offered on a "try before you buy" plan. Users can copy the software and try it out for free, but they are instructed to send a nominal fee (usually $10 to $50) to the programmer if they intend to use the software regularly. Jumbo!® (http://www.jumbo.com) is an example of a shareware provider.
3. **Commercial software** over the Internet is the same as the packaged software sold in stores (but without the box) and is offered by the same commercial software companies. Commercial software requires payment up front; typically, the user must supply a credit card number before copying the software files.

Software is available on the Internet for almost any type of computer and for almost any purpose: business programs, personal programs, games, and so on. Among the most popular programs found on the Internet are tools that help

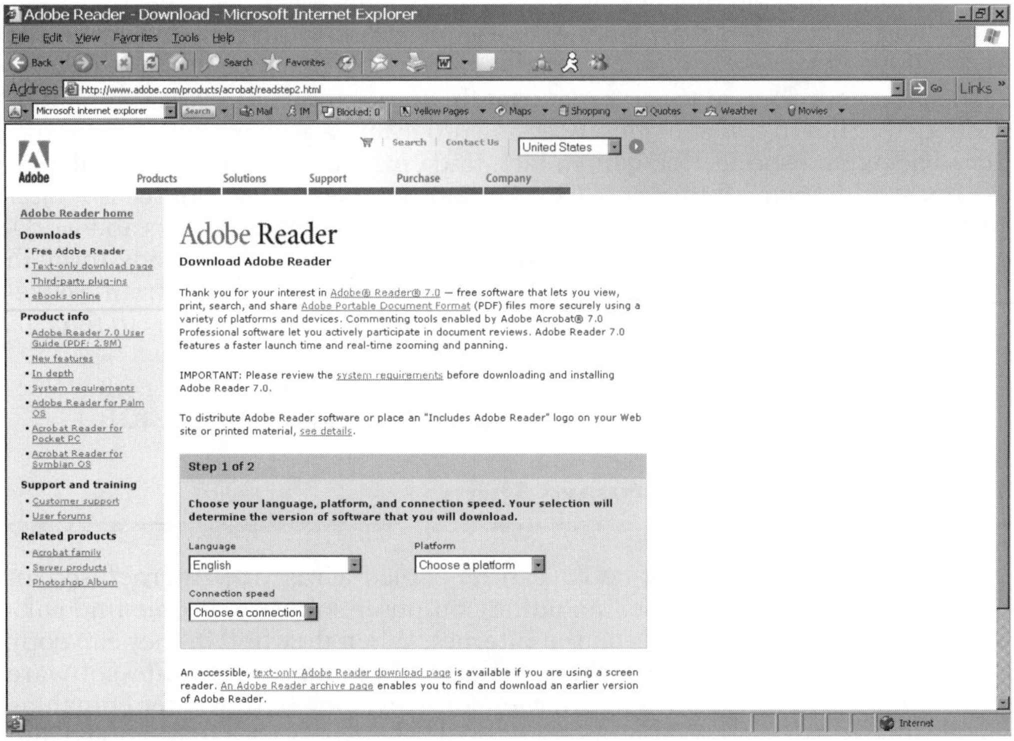

Figure 1-3 Freeware on the Internet.
Adobe® Reader® product screen shot reprinted with permission from Adobe Systems Incorporated.

people use the Internet more easily or effectively. Often available as freeware, programs such as Microsoft® Internet Explorer® help people use the Internet.

The Internet as a Newspaper

The Internet has become the premier vehicle for delivery of news. Online resources keep Internet users abreast of the latest events in every country from Afghanistan to Zaire. Sometimes, these services are the best (or only) way to get current and complete information about a particular region. During the Soviet coup attempt in 1991, a small e-mail company in Russia provided the only way to get news into and out of the region. Through e-mail, that company served news through the Internet to CNN and the Associated Press and, of course, to others on the Internet.

Internet users can tap into resources that supply up-to-date news and discussion on every imaginable topic. In addition to the various country- and region-specific resources, others supply news about environmental events, sports, global and national politics, party politics (separate groups for Democrats, Republicans, Libertarians, and the like), civil rights, the economy, and much more.

In addition to what the coffeehouse resources offer, there are actual newspapers, magazines, and newsletters that users can access through the Internet and read through their computer screens. Some are scholarly or scientific journals, but a growing number are general-interest consumer publications. Some were created just for the Internet, but some are special electronic versions of publications that are also available in print.

All the major news networks maintain Web sites that are kept current with the television news. For example, during the climactic vote in the Clinton presidential impeachment trial, Internet users watched the vote in "real time" with a Web window that showed the tally changing second by second. During the 2000 presidential election, users were continuously updated as to the changing vote tally in Florida.

Using these resources, Internet users can acquire more timely and more detailed news about their areas of interest than they could ever find in the national broadcast or print media. Perhaps more important, in many cases they can respond to the news, add to it, or ask questions about it.

Internet Languages

The Internet and Internet browsers have their own languages because they operate on the Transmission Control Protocol (TCP) and the Internet Protocol (IP). While most legal professionals never have to use these languages directly, they make use of many of them indirectly every time a user accesses the Internet. The major Internet languages are

- **Hypertext Markup Language (HTML):** The language in which all Internet pages are written.
- **Java™:** A language created by Sun Microsystems, Inc., that allows the user to create interactivity over the Internet.

- **Virtual Reality Modeling Language (VRML):** A growing language used to create virtual reality worlds. In the future, Web pages will most likely only be used after flying to a place in a virtual world and accessing a document from a virtual book.
- **Extensible Markup Language (XML):** A superset of HTML; Extensible Markup Language allows the user to tag various parts of a document with user-defined tags and extends the HTML language for greater flexibility and reusability.
- **Common Gateway Interface (CGI):** A category of languages, including PERL, a language used to manipulate text files with information in them. It also provides a direct link to **Unix** commands. Unix is the operating system used on most Internet servers. PERL is the most popular CGI language in the world today.

Gaining Access to the Internet

There are many methods for accessing Internet service providers (ISPs). Most providers furnish local telephone numbers to dial to log on to the Internet using a modem. In addition to modem access, there are special modems called **integrated services digital network (ISDN)** modems.[2] These modems require a special connection service from the local telephone company. Integrated services digital network modems use *channels* to establish connections with the Internet. There are two main channels: Channel A and Channel B. Both channels can access 56 kilobits per second individually. When using an ISDN modem, users have the option of turning on the second channel to double the access rate to 128 kilobits per second.

The ISDN lines (the connection from the local phone company) also have one interesting and very powerful feature. Users may access the Internet on Channel A while having a conversation on Channel B using a normal telephone. This can be very cost-efficient for small businesses, because it affords both a connection to the Internet and a second phone line at the same time. At the office, your company may have a **direct connection** to the Internet. This would simply be an ISDN modem hooked up to the network somewhere, or a T1 or T3 line connection. These are extremely fast and are usually reserved for large companies.

Direct connections to the Internet are widely known as *cable lines* or *direct satellite links (DSLs)*. All of these forms of Internet connections also support "wireless" connections, which require the installation of a *wireless router*. The wireless router is essentially just an electronic box or board that the cable or direct satellite is plugged into. Once the wireless router is plugged into an Internet connection, a laptop computer with "wireless" capability (a wireless board or card installed) can access the Internet without being directly hooked up to a cable or satellite dish connection.

---

[2] To be exact, these are not really modems. Modems have to convert information through "modulation." Integrated services digital network "modems" do not convert information. Data traveling to ISDN modems are pure digital information requiring no modulation, which is partially responsible for the faster transfer rates.

Legal and Ethical Issues and the Internet

Although it has been around since the early 1970s, the Internet did not become important in commercial and everyday life until the mid-1990s. Once it became a viable commercial delivery system, it exploded in popularity. However, the law failed to keep up with its growth and the Internet has become the focus of a number of legal and ethical problems in the last few years.

Jurisdiction

No one owns the Internet. Transactions take place in a nebulous place called "cyberspace," and no one can pinpoint exactly which governmental entity has jurisdiction over cyberspace. If a transaction takes place between two individuals in cyberspace or a crime occurs in cyberspace, where exactly can it be said to have occurred? While some governments take the position that jurisdiction is present at the physical location of the offending party, it becomes difficult to prosecute if the offender is located in Texas, with one set of laws, and the victim is located in California, with another set of laws.

For example, in most states, it is illegal to sell wine via mail order. A few states, however, consider this to be a legal act. So, if a seller in Washington State, where it is legal, sells wine over the Internet to a buyer in Texas, where it is illegal, has a law been broken? And, if so, where is the jurisdiction? It is the Texas law that has been broken, but the offending seller is located in Washington.

Sales and Use Taxation

Because the Internet has no legal jurisdiction, it also has no taxing jurisdiction. The Clinton Administration declared a three-year moratorium on Internet taxation to allow e-commerce time to grow. However, it has grown at such a furious rate that state and local entities are now complaining about declining revenues from sales and use taxes. President Bush indicated that he favors an extension on the moratorium on Internet taxation. He also favors a permanent ban on all Internet access taxes.

A bookseller in one state does not usually charge sales tax on an item shipped to another state. The buyer is supposed to pay the state a use tax equal to the sales tax that would have been collected if the item had been purchased in the home state. In practice, however, very few buyers ever pay the use tax. While this complaint is not new and has been voiced in the past with regard to interstate mail-order and phone-order purchases, the far reach that the Internet gives e-commerce merchants has state and local comptrollers concerned that tax revenues will continue to decline.

The only means that comptrollers will have to collect use tax from buyers is to obtain lists of purchases from online sellers. With the enormous proliferation of online commerce, it is unlikely that any one local or state jurisdiction will be able to impose Internet taxes. However, a national sales tax would cure the taxation problem. Predictably, neither sellers nor buyers want any kind of

Internet tax, but with millions of tax dollars going uncollected, it is likely that the new century will see a broader sales tax in place for e-commerce.

Income Taxation

The Internal Revenue Service (IRS) has enthusiastically embraced the Internet; and the IRS Web site, located at http://www.irs.treas.gov, is one of the most useful governmental **sites** on the **World Wide Web.** On this site, users can obtain information, download up-to-date forms for printing on a local computer, and make payments on line. Electronic tax filing has become very popular as more people file their taxes with the use of tax preparation programs, and the IRS has responded by promising faster refunds for those who file electronically.

The proliferation of person-to-person sales on the Internet has, however, also created an enormous underground economy. Many people sell items such as books, records, and collectibles on line through personal Web sites or through auction sites such as eBay Inc., and the sellers are not subject to any governmental oversight. While the IRS frequently visits sellers at a flea market or hobby show, it has no means of tracking the millions of personal sales made through the Internet every day.

Most sellers do not realize that their profits (the price paid by the buyer minus the price initially paid by the seller to acquire the item) are taxable income, and most do not track their transactions or pay income taxes on their profits. For many people, this new underground economy has become quite profitable because it is essentially tax-free. While the IRS has not yet devised a method of tracking individual sales, it is likely that "power sellers" who sell hundreds of items a day, even if they are selling their record collections from their garages, will find their transactions under scrutiny.

Regulation Versus Free Speech

Internet publishing falls under the First Amendment protections, but from the first recognition that the World Wide Web was an open forum for anyone to post anything, governments have tried to regulate the flow of speech on the Internet. Several laws in the United States have been passed and signed (most notoriously, the Communications Decency Act), only to be struck down by the Supreme Court as infringing unnecessarily on free speech and the free press. Other countries such as Singapore and Germany have enacted regulations to keep the flow of Internet pornography from reaching their borders. With information traveling electronically, however, a pornographer in a country with liberal laws can send illegal materials to a minor in a country with stringent laws. Very little can be done to stop this.

Pornography is not the only free speech issue. If a person defames another by publishing falsehoods on a local bulletin board, the damage is local and the injured party can probably not prove substantial damages; but, if the defaming information was posted to the Internet with a potential audience of millions, the potential damage becomes much greater and so does the liability of the offender. Even some presidential candidates who have found themselves the target of parody and satire on the Internet have reacted by calling for greater regulation of the Internet—although, if the parody were to be printed, it would clearly be protected under the First Amendment.

A free society with free flow of information will always find that, no matter what the venue, forbidden or dangerous information will find its way into the public arena. Most people were shocked to discover that information for building bombs was easily available on the Internet. Actually, the information had been in the public domain for over twenty years; the only thing that had changed was the Internet ease of obtaining the information. What a disgruntled person might have once had to work hard to find out can now be downloaded and printed with a few keystrokes. The challenge of free speech and its responsible use will continue to be a major issue for the Internet.

Defamation, Libel, and Slander

Consider, for instance, defamation. The term *defamation* refers to a false statement made about someone or some organization that is damaging to his, her, or its reputation. For a statement to be defamatory, the statement must be published to a third party and the person publishing the statement must have known or should have known that the statement was false. The law of defamation is complex, as it has been determined by numerous court decisions rather than one national statute. In addition, a claim of defamation is subject to a variety of defenses, such as the First Amendment and the defense that the statement was true.

Libel and slander laws protect an individual against the dissemination of falsehoods about that individual. To be actionable, the falsehood must injure the individual's reputation or subject the individual to hatred, contempt, or ridicule. The individual can obtain monetary losses as well as damages for mental anguish.

Rights of Publicity

Several areas of law deal with the right of the individual to control image and reputation. The right of publicity gives the individual the right to control the use of one's name, face, image, or voice for commercial purposes. For example, Ford's advertising agency tried to persuade Bette Midler to sing during a Ford television commercial. She eventually refused. Ford then hired her backup singer. The performance of the backup singer was so similar to that of Bette Midler that viewers thought Bette Midler was singing. On the basis of that confusion, Midler sued and won $400,000 in damages.

If you intend to use preexisting material from television or film, you may also have to deal with the rights of members of the entertainment unions to get "reuse" fees. These unions include the Writers Guild, the Directors Guild, the Screen Actors Guild, the American Federation of Musicians, and the American Federation of Television and Radio Artists. Under the union agreements with the film and television studios, members of these unions and guilds who worked on a film or television program have a right to payment if the work is reused.

Fraud

One of the largest areas of commercial growth on the Internet has been online auctions. Online auction sites, headlined by eBay Inc., now account for a sizable portion of Internet traffic and have become the main venue for Internet sellers to offer their merchandise to prospective buyers. On any one day, millions of items are offered for auction by sellers who deal directly with the winning bidders, paying only a small percentage of the sale to the hosting auction site. While most auctions go smoothly, there are inevitably criminals who take advantage of a popular means of making money. Several people have been arrested for offering nonexistent items for sale; buyers who won the auctions and sent money orders in good faith have received nothing in return. Fraudulent sellers prey upon the desire of the buyer for the merchandise and consider that a buyer who really wants something is less likely to ask questions.

Another area of fraud is the misuse of credit card numbers. Secure Sockets Layer (SSL) technology is in use by most legitimate sites that sell merchandise and offers strong protection against credit card number theft through the use of encryption. (You can tell if a site is SSL-encrypted if it mentions its "secure server" and if a small lock icon appears.) However, many eager Internet buyers do not always buy on SSL-encrypted sites, and many send complete credit card numbers through e-mail. Although the vast majority of Internet credit card transactions are successful, a number of buyers have found that their numbers were diverted and stolen.

Because e-commerce is here to stay, we can expect to see development of even stronger secure technology in the next few years. Several auction sites have started offering buyer's insurance so that a buyer is protected up to a certain dollar amount against defrauding sellers, and several large online sellers offer to reimburse any buyer whose credit card number is stolen on their sites.

Linkage

A growing area of concern in cyberlaw is the illegitimate use of linkage. While the Internet is built on the use of **hyperlinks,** which allow users to jump from page to related page with the click of a mouse, a new twist on defamation and fraud has been found with the use of illegal hyperlinks.

An illegal hyperlink occurs when one site is linked to another with no apparent reason for the linkage. This does not include the ubiquitous My Favorite Links found on many personal **homepages,** but usually occurs when a shady or illegal business is attempting to link to a legitimate business to siphon business, embarrass the legitimate business, or use graphics and other materials on the legitimate business's server without paying for it. This is jocularly called "bandwidth robbery." Because businesses pay for the amount of hits or traffic on their Web sites, if a bandwidth thief links to graphics on a site so that they appear on the thief's site, it is essentially causing the legitimate business to incur extra expense and load on its server.

Another variation of linkage theft occurs in the use of meta keywords, or **metatags.** Metatags appear in the header of HTML pages and are used by the various **search engines** to locate and categorize Web sites. If you have a Web site devoted to the *Titanic*, then you would probably place the following HTML tag in the header of your page:

```
<META NAME="KEYWORD" CONTENT="Titanic shipwrecks disaster iceberg">
```

Since most search engines categorize Web sites and return search results based on the contents of metatags, all that is necessary to steal traffic from a popular Web site is to view the metatags in the source code of the popular HTML page and copy it into the other HTML page. The search engine will then read the copy page and rank it along with the popular page when returning results on a search to a user.

Spam

One of the worst by-products of e-mail has been **spam**[3] mail. This is bulk e-mail. Like bulk postal mail, it generally is commercial in nature. Unlike **snail mail,** however, millions of e-mails can be sent at one time for virtually no cost. While spam appears to be relatively harmless, causing the average user to spend a few seconds deleting it from the e-mail inbox, it actually has a very negative effect on the Internet. When millions of e-mails are sent to people at one time, the cumulative effect is to clog the internetworks and slow down the transmission of legitimate Internet traffic. Just as first-class mail sometimes seems to vanish in a sea of bulk mail, legitimate person-to-person e-mail can be delayed if the system becomes clogged with frivolous e-mail.

Another problem with spam is that a great deal of it is pornographic in nature. Because it is sent to millions of names at a time, the chance always exists that a minor will read it. While most adults will just delete it, a child may be lured into clicking on a hyperlink inside the e-mail and be routed into a pornographic site.

Still a third problem with spam is that much of it concerns fraudulent moneymaking schemes, such as Ponzi and pyramid schemes. Writers of chain letters have discovered that it is much less expensive to send out chain e-mails than it is to mail letters through the U.S. Postal Service (where chain letters are illegal). Chain e-mails are no more legitimate than their paper cousins and should be deleted immediately.

Malicious Behavior: Hacking and Computer Viruses

In the past few years, as the Internet has grown, it has become a playground for malicious behavior. Numerous sites have been "hacked" (broken into) by pranksters who, in most cases, have merely published a mocking replacement Web page that disappeared as soon as their work was discovered (usually

---

[3] Hormel Foods Corporation, the commercial manufacturer of the edible SPAM®, has stated: "You've probably seen, heard or even used the term 'spamming' to refer to the act of sending unsolicited commercial e-mail (UCE), or 'SPAM' to refer to the UCE itself. . . . We do not object to the use of this slang term to describe UCE, although we do object to the use of our product image in association with that term. Also, if the term is to be used, it should be used in all lowercase letters to distinguish it from our trademark SPAM®, which should be used with all uppercase letters."

within minutes). Among the victims have been the Pentagon, the FBI, the State Department, and even some commercial sites.

While most ordinary users are not worried about being hacked, they can be affected by a growing problem of computer viruses passed around the Internet. For years, the newsgroups have been breeding grounds for computer viruses; but, in recent years, viruses have been written that exploit security holes in popular programs such as Microsoft Word and Microsoft Outlook. One virus, the Melissa virus, caused the victim to unknowingly send out e-mails to everyone in his or her Microsoft Word and Microsoft Outlook address book. Melissa brought numerous corporate networks down before it was stopped. Other viruses exploit the common placement of programs on a local fixed drive to delete or damage files.

While e-mail itself cannot contain a virus, the attachments often can. Users should be wary of opening any attachment that comes to them from an unknown person, because it may contain a virus that will bring down the recipient's computer.

The Future

In *A Brief History of the Internet*, the authors ask:

> The most pressing question for the future of the Internet is not how the technology will change, but how the process of change and evolution itself will be managed. . . . [T]he architecture of the Internet has always been driven by a core group of designers, but the form of that group has changed as the number of interested parties has grown. With the success of the Internet has come a proliferation of stakeholders—stakeholders now with an economic as well as an intellectual investment in the network. We now see, in the debates over control of the domain name space and the form of the next generation IP addresses, a struggle to find the next social structure that will guide the Internet in the future. The form of that structure will be harder to find, given the large number of concerned stakeholders. At the same time, the industry struggles to find the economic rationale for the large investment needed for the future growth, for example, to upgrade residential access to a more suitable technology. If the Internet stumbles, it will not be because we lack for technology, vision, or motivation. It will be because we cannot set a direction and march collectively into the future.[4]

DISCUSSION QUESTIONS

1. In what year did you first use the Internet? For e-mail? For research?
2. What elements of Internet history do you recall? For instance, when, if ever, did you first place an order using a Web site?

---

[4] Barry M. Leiner, Vinton G. Cerf, David D. Clark, Robert E. Kahn, Leonard Kleinrock, Daniel C. Lynch, Jon Postel, Larry G. Roberts, & Stephen Wolff, *A Brief History of the Internet, at* http://www.isoc.org/internet/history/brief.shtml.

3. Do you feel it would be appropriate to pass legislation limiting the amount of spam e-mail that can be sent? If so, how would you define what is "spam" and what is legitimate e-mail? What about a "newsletter" to all of the client contacts for your law firm?

4. Given that the Internet was established by the Defense Department for security reasons, and given the post–9/11 terrorism environment, should the Internet be accessible by everyone, or would it be better to keep it private and secure from outside persons (and their viruses)?

PROJECTS

1. Make a list of what hardware you would need to access the Internet from your home.

2. Make a list of the software you would need to access and make full use of the Internet from your home.

3. Research the elements for any news concerning the Internet taxation issues discussed in this chapter.

CHAPTER 2

Research on the Internet: Using Site Addresses and Directories

SUMMARY

This chapter reviews the use of Internet addresses for finding and searching for information and documents on the Internet. Internet addresses are reviewed, along with the most common Web site tools. Finding unknown Web sites is illustrated, and Internet directories are listed and reviewed.

OBJECTIVES

- The student will be pointed in the direction of known information.
- The student will be introduced to the most common Web site tools.
- The student will learn to search for and to find particular Web sites.
- The student will be introduced to Internet directories and their uses.

Sources of Internet Information

The Internet is in many cases for the research professional the best source for information and documents. As Jerry Lawson[1] explains:

- Currently, most of the information on the Internet is free.
- The extent and quality of the best resources on the Internet are rapidly increasing.
- Government agencies, universities, businesses, and law firms are all adding to the store of useful information available on the Net.

There are many methods for locating information on the Internet. Surely the easiest scenario is one in which the site address is known. Next, Internet **directories** provide hyperlinks to prereviewed and indexed sites and information of all kinds. Finally, running queries in some of the Internet search engines is a way to locate substantial documents and information on the Internet that would otherwise never be found. This chapter reviews the first two, while Chapter 6 discusses in greater detail working with Internet search engines.

---

[1] JERRY LAWSON, THE COMPLETE INTERNET HANDBOOK FOR LAWYERS 52 (1999).

When the Site Address Is Known

Finding documents and information on the Internet when the site address is known is a best-case scenario. This is a situation in which a researcher knows from knowledge or experience that the information sought is located at a particular site. In this case, the researcher just types the Internet address into the Web site address line of the browser software.

If the information or documents needed pertain to or originate from a particular publisher, such as the federal government, then the easiest way to obtain that material is to just go to the publisher's site. These days, chances are pretty good that the information or documents will be found on the publisher's site.

Types of Search Tools

Once connected to an Internet Web site, a researcher may have multiple avenues to locate needed and useful information. These avenues typically involve

- topical directories,
- keyword **indexes,** and
- site-specific **search engines.**

These Internet search tools can be helpful in sifting the "wheat from the chaff" in the mountains of data on the Internet. Before beginning, though, the researcher must have a good sense of what is being searched for. If a researcher is looking for "I'm not quite sure what," then no one (including the assigning attorney) should be surprised if it is not found.

Internet Research Scenario: The Site Address Is Known

Consider a case in which the client has learned that the U.S. Occupational Safety and Health Administration (OSHA) plans to visit its grocery warehousing facility in the next few days. Posit that it has fairly new safety personnel who have not gone through such an event before.

In this example, government information such as agency policy, guidance, directives, and regulations is required. The best place to look for this information is on the OSHA Web site. The OSHA Web site is a good example of a government Web site with effective search tools to assist the researcher—including topical directories, keyword indexes, and a site-specific search engine.

TYPES OF SEARCH TOOLS

Site directories are catalogs or listings of linked topics related to a particular Internet site.

Keyword indexes are links to other Web pages concerning a specific topic.

Site-specific search engines are programs or services that allow you to query a site-specific database (i.e., only the pages at this particular site) for keywords and then return matching Web pages.

Site-Specific Topical Directory

At the OSHA homepage, at http://www.osha.gov, there is a decent directory listing, including links for: Compliance Assistance, Laws & Regulations, Cooperative Programs, State Programs, and Safety/Health Topics. A screenshot of the OSHA.gov Web site is shown in Figure 2-1. In this example, directory links under Laws & Regulations (Standards, Interpretations, Federal Registers, Directives) and Safety/Health Topics (Ergonomics) are helpful. Depending on whether the state where the facility is located has an OSHA-approved program, the State Programs directory listing may be necessary for related links.

Unfortunately, many other Internet sites do not offer topical directory listings and indexes. Some may offer links to particular subject matters or to site-specific search engines to locate information; but many, unfortunately, continue to be just a screen full of text about the particular agency, office, or site concerned. Such sites are all but useless for online research purposes.

Site-Specific Keyword Index

On the OSHA homepage, there is a keyword index, listed as the A-Z Index (http://www.osha.gov/html/a-z-index.html). The A-Z Index is fairly common at Web sites, and frequently requested materials and documents are usually

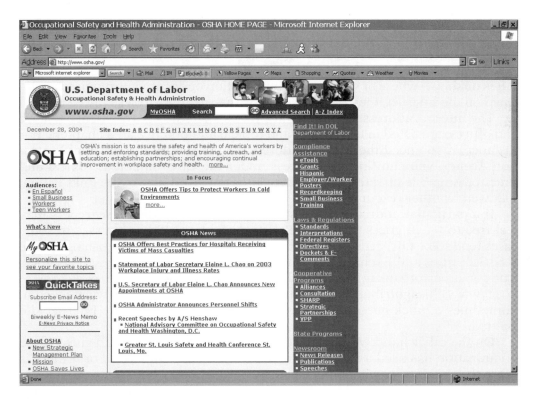

Figure 2-1   OSHA's homepage.

found listed there. Taking the A-Z Index link on the OSHA site takes the researcher to numerous topical materials with A-Z links for jumping to particular topics or keywords. For instance, selecting the *G* link brings the user directly to links for General Industry Standards (1910) and the Grocery Warehousing eTool.

Site-Specific Search Engine

The OSHA homepage also provides the researcher with a site-specific search engine, listed on the main page as Search. In the screen in Figure 2-1, the Internet research professional would type in the Search box the keyword "inspection."

Running that query brings up numerous references, including portions of the *Field Inspection Reference Manual.* Also found were numerous other completely unrelated hits, but a few jewels as well. For instance, the following related hits were found:

- Section 5 - Chapter I. Pre-Inspection Procedures
- Section 6 - Chapter II. Inspection Procedures
- Section 7 - Chapter III. Inspection Documentation
- 1903.4 - Objection to inspection

So, in this example, the information needed may well be entirely available from the pertinent and known Web site.

How to Find a Site Address If It Is Unknown

If it is unknown where or whether the information or documents required are located on the Internet, then one of the major Internet directories may be useful.

The Internet addresses to common entities, including government agencies and offices, are listed in the general and topical and practice area chapters. For instance, if you need the Internet address for the U.S. Environmental Protection Agency, you can find the address under the Environmental Topical and Practice Area Site chapter. Government sites are listed first in the links listing, followed by other resources.

If a particular address is not listed in the directory, then researchers may feel free to try to guess the Internet URL or address. The addresses in some cases tend to be fairly easy. OSHA, for example, is at http://www.osha.gov. The U.S. Securities and Exchange Commission is at http://www.sec.gov. This holds true for other organizations as well. For instance, the *Chicago Tribune* is at http://www.chicagotribune.com. Intel Corporation is at http://www.intel.com. Sometimes a quick guess can save the effort of a search for the Internet site wanted.

On the other hand, Web site addresses can also be difficult to guess if the organization has used a hyphen or an abbreviation of some kind or if there is more than one entity with similar names. For instance, there is a Keystone Industries with the URL address of http://www.keystoneind.com. This entity, though, is not the one that I had set out to find. Instead of a window and screen company, I found a chemical company! The entity I was looking for I subsequently found. Its URL address was http://www.keystone-industries.com.

Internet Research Scenario: The Site Address Is Not Known

When an entity is known, such as British Petroleum, but its URL address is not, the easiest way to locate it is through an Internet search engine. A *search engine* is a Web program or service that allows you to query a database for keywords and then returns matching Web pages. Popular search engines include **Google**™ and **Yahoo!**®.

So, go to http://www.google.com and run a search for British Petroleum. The results we received were: 1,260,000 pages for British Petroleum. The first hit, though, was our searched-for entity: http://www.bp.com.

A screenshot of the Google.com search results page is shown in Figure 2-2.

Internet Directories

Numerous directory Web sites on the Internet provide researchers with an easy way to find all sorts of categorical information. A *directory* is a site that catalogs, indexes, and categorizes Web sites by subject and may also provide a brief

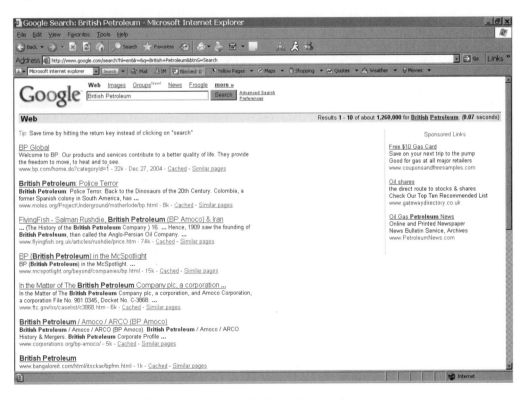

Figure 2-2   Google™ search results for British Petroleum.
Reprinted with permission. Copyright © 2004, Google, Inc.

description of Web site content. Yahoo!® (http://www.yahoo.com) is the most well-known Internet directory site.

The overall scope of free-access Internet directories is considerable. Laura Cohen,[2] librarian at Albany University, recommends several starting points for Internet research through directory sites:

- To explore a large number and variety of sources, try the *Librarians' Index to the Internet* (LII), http://www.lii.org. Supported by a federal grant, a large number of indexers select and annotate Web resources across a broad range of topics. With its extensive but careful selection, objective and useful annotations, and hierarchical organization, LII may well be thought of as the thinking person's Yahoo!®.
- The Argus Clearinghouse, http://www.clearinghouse.net, is one of the highest-quality subject directories on the Internet. It consists of rated collections of recommended sites organized into subject-specific guides. The guide authors are often specialists in the field. According to Cohen, this site is highly recommended for academic research.
- The WWW Virtual Library, http://vlib.org, is one of the oldest and most respected subject directories on the Web. This directory consists of individual subject collections, many of which are maintained at universities throughout the world.
- INFOMINE, http://infomine.ucr.edu, is a large directory of Web sites of scholarly interest. The directory may be browsed or searched by subject, keyword, or title. Each site listed is accompanied by a description.

At the directory sites, typically the researcher will find search tools, such as detailed topical directories and keyword indexes; and many also support site-specific search engines to bring up relevant hits.

CONCLUSION

In conclusion, remember that the researcher must have a good sense of what is being searched for and should use a mix of search tools available at the Web sites to narrow down and find pertinent information and documents. When the Web site address is known, go there first. Otherwise, take advantage of the wide array of directory Web sites to locate needed information.

DISCUSSION QUESTIONS

1. Have you used Internet directories for research before? If so, what for? Was your research successful? Why or why not?
2. How would you determine the Web site address for the U.S. Department of Labor?
3. Think of an example of when an Internet search engine would be more useful than a directory. Why?
4. It seems as though Web site addresses are always changing. Should there be a rule that once a Web address is specified, the creator needs to stick with that Web address? Why or why not?

---

[2] *See* Laura Cohen, *Conducting Research on the Internet, at* http//www.albany.edu/library/internet/research.html. (2000).

PROJECTS

1. Find the Web site address for the White House. Find the Web site address for the Senate.
2. Find the Web site address for the California Environmental Protection Agency.
3. Find the Web site address for General Electric Company.

CHAPTER 3

General Internet Resources and Tools

SUMMARY

This chapter reviews and sets out general resources and tools found on the Internet. It reviews search engines, directories, and virtual libraries; nonlegal databases; useful tools; federal, state, and municipal government sites; commercial legal research database sites; selected legal service provider sites; and legal and paralegal professional reference sites.

OBJECTIVES

- The student will be introduced to the wide variety of resources and tools that are available over the Internet.
- The student will review specific Internet resources and tools that a paralegal and other members of the legal community at large may often refer to.
- The student will be provided with hands-on practice using specific Internet resources and tools that a paralegal and other members of the legal community at large may often refer to.

Resources and Tools on the Internet

The Internet is a global network of networks and is becoming one of the most popular research tools used by marketing, business, education, government, and the public at large. As former U.S. Department of Commerce Deputy Secretary Robert L. Mallett reported, "[I]ndividuals can now access more than one billion Web pages, and an estimated three million pages are added daily."[1] As Justice Stevens noted in his opinion in *Reno v. American Civil Liberties Union*, 521 U.S. 844, 117 S. Ct. 2329, 138 L. Ed. 2d 874 (1997):

> [T]he best known category of communication over the Internet is the World Wide Web, which allows users to search for and retrieve information stored in remote computers, as well as, in some cases, to communicate

---

[1] Press Release, Department of Commerce, U.S. Commerce Deputy Secretary Robert L. Mallett Addresses Electronic Commerce Small Business Summit: Urges Small Businesses to Take Advantage of E-Commerce Opportunities (June 23, 2000) (on file with author).

back to designated sites. In concrete terms, the Web consists of a vast number of documents stored in different computers all over the world. Some of these documents are simply files containing information.

This chapter provides Internet addresses and descriptions of general Internet resources and tools useful to the CALR professional. To illustrate the use of some of these tools, various Internet research scenarios are provided before each main resource category as suggested projects. To go to one of the Web sites listed in the tables that follow, type the Internet address—shown in the left column of the tables under the Web site name—into the prompt or address line of the browser software.

General Internet Resources and Tools

Within each category of general resources and tools, as listed in the tables, the Web site lists are further listed in alphabetical order by site name or description. Users are encouraged to submit other suggested links to the authors at paralegal_studies@prenhall.com.

- Search Engines, Directories, and Virtual Libraries
- Databases (NonLegal)
- Useful Resources
- Government Sites: Federal
- Government Sites: State
- Government Sites: Municipal
- Legal Research Database (Commercial) Sites
- Selected Legal Service Provider Sites
- Legal and Paralegal Professional Reference Sites

1. Search Engines, Directories, and Virtual Libraries

Some of the following search engines, directories, and virtual libraries were previously mentioned in the preceding chapters. Researchers are encouraged to explore all of these search engines and directories to best take advantage of them all.

Internet Research Scenario: Finding Photographs

In this scenario, the litigation team is looking for a graphic or picture that will illustrate to the jury at the trial of a tort case what a golden retriever dog is. The facts of the case involve a vicious attack by a neighbor's dog, which bit a ten-year-old child. To find this graphic or picture we would use the Ditto site, "the leading visual search engine." A screenshot of the Ditto.com homepage is shown in Figure 3-1.

Go to http://www.ditto.com. Type "golden retriever dog" at the Search text box. The query returns many images that are pictures of golden retriever dogs.

Figure 3-1   Ditto homepage.
Reprinted with permission. Copyright © 2004, Ditto.com.

---

1. Search Engines, Directories, and Virtual Libraries

4Anything™[2] http://www.4Anything.com	This site is a subject directory or "network of Web guides" that help, users easily find high-quality, relevant information on line for thousands of topics of interest and Web sites. Each guide helps users focus their searching via a well-organized, highly manageable list of recommended sites for a given topic, along with valuable commentary on each site.
About™[3] http://www.about.com	This is a fairly extensive directory site that consists of over 475 Guide sites. The sites cover more than 50,000 subjects with links to the best

(continued)

---

[2] Copyright © 2000-2004, LIvVE.com. Inc. and its content partners. All Rights Reserved. "4Anything Network," "4anything.com," the "4" in the searchlight beam design, and the "LIvVE" logo design are trademarks of LIvVE.com, Inc.
[3] Copyright © 2005, About, Inc. All rights reserved. A PRIMEDIA Company.

	resources on the Net and the fastest-growing archive of high-quality original content. Topics range from pregnancy to cars, palm pilots to painting, weight loss to video game strategies.
AltaVista™[4] http://www.AltaVista.com	This site is based on "patented technology" that unlocks the vast Internet with its "multidimensional" search to provide immediate access to the richest, most relevant information across the Internet.
Ask Jeeves®[5] http://www.ask.com	This is a "plain English" search tool. Enter questions in plain English in the text box on the Ask Jeeves® homepage, then click on the "Search" button.
The Big Hub http://www.isleuth.com	This megasearch engine tool allows the researcher to select up to ten of the top search engines and directories.
Copernic® http://www.copernic.com	This is a separate software program that installs on your hard drive to function as a meta search engine. It is freeware.
Ditto http://www.ditto.com	This search engine provides an unusual visual mechanism to search the Web using pictures instead of text. Users are directed to the originating Web site on which the pictures are located.
Dogpile®[6] http://www.dogpile.com	Dogpile® uses numerous Internet search engines to compile search results.
Excite™[7] http://www.excite.com	This search engine is "concept" driven. Its results are often good, useful, and sometimes unexpected.
FindLaw®[8] http://www.findlaw.com	This is "the leading Web portal focused on law and government." It provides access to a comprehensive and fast-growing online library

---

[4] Copyright © 2005, Overture Services, Inc.
[5] Copyright © 2004, Ask Jeeves, Inc. All rights reserved.
[6] Copyright © 2005, Infospace, Inc. All rights reserved.
[7] Copyright © 2001-2005, The Excite Network. All rights reserved.
[8] Copyright © 1994-2005, FindLaw, a Thomson business.

of legal resources for use by legal professionals, consumers, and small businesses. FindLaw provides a broad array of features that include Web search utilities, cases and codes, legal news, and community-oriented tools, such as a secure document management utility, mailing lists, and message boards.

Google™[9]
http://www.google.com

This site uses what it terms "a revolutionized searching" process with its patent-pending "PageRank™" technology. PageRank™ capitalizes on the uniquely democratic characteristic of the Web by using its vast link structure as an organizational tool. In essence, Google™ interprets a link from page A to page B as a vote by page A for page B. Google™ assesses a page's importance by the votes it receives. Google™ also analyzes the page that casts the vote. Votes cast by pages that are themselves "important" weigh more heavily and help to make other pages "important."

GovEngine.com[10]
http://www.govengine.com

This is "the premier federal, state, and local government site on the Internet." Although not a search engine, it provides a gateway to searchable government Internet sites.

HotBot[11]
http://www.hotbot.com

"Since its launch in 1996, HotBot has been named the number one search site on the Web in independent reviews from the top consumer-oriented computer and personal-finance publications in the United States. HotBot has garnered these awards by offering Web users one of the most comprehensive and up-to-date snapshots of the Web currently available. HotBot indexes every word, link, and media file on more than 110 million Web documents and refreshes its entire database of documents every three to four weeks. It also allows users to construct sophisticated search queries of its index without previous knowledge of complex search terms and methodologies. Instead, HotBot offers users a simple, point-and-click interface, intuitive

(continued)

---

	pulldown menus, and the ability to use plain English terminology for constructing searches."
The Law Engine!™[12] http://www.thelawengine.com/index.htm	This site provides comprehensive links to primary and secondary legal sources, such as case law, statutes, and current literature.
Mamma[13] http://www.mamma.com	The Mother of All Search Engines®.
MetaCrawler®[14] http://www.metacrawler.com	This site uses numerous Internet search engines to compile search results.
Meta-Index for U.S. Legal Research http://gsu.edu/metaindex	This site provides a good starting place for legal research with links to other helpful sites.
WWW Virtual Library, at Indiana University School of Law http://http://www.law.indiana.edu/v%2Dlib/	In 1992 Indiana University School of Law–Bloomington, was chosen by CERN, originators of the World Wide Web Consortium, to be the host of the Virtual Library. The World Wide Web Virtual Library is a collection of subject-related Web sites maintained by institutions throughout the world, each administering a different subject. An independent committee made up of maintainers of various subject area sites manages the project.
Yahoo!®[15] http://www.yahoo.com	This site is the largest and best-known subject directory. It classifies topics into fourteen categories and then into hundreds of subcategories.

2. Databases (Nonlegal)

Databases freely available on the Internet provide researchers with a vast array of information. These databases can be important in collecting "the facts" associated with particular cases. These sorts of details were previously unavailable without a trip to the university library.

---

[12] The Law Engine!™ is a trademark of Goldberger & Associates. Copyright © 1996-2004, Goldberger & Associates. All rights reserved.
[13] Copyright © 1996-2000, Mamma.com, Inc. All rights reserved.
[14] Copyright © 2005, InfoSpace, Inc. All rights reserved.
[15] Copyright © 2005, Yahoo! Inc. All rights reserved.

Internet Research Scenario: Finding Lawyer's E-Mail Address

In this scenario, we wish to forward a deposition e-transcript (electronic format transcript) to a cocounsel, but we do not know exactly his firm or his e-mail address. For this scenario, use the Martindale-Hubbell Lawyer Finder.

Go to http://lawyers.martindale.com/xp/Martindale/home.xml. At the search screen that opens at this site, fill in as much information as is known about the attorney searched for. For instance, fill in the following:

Last Name:	Boyd
First Name:	Eric
City:	Chicago
State:	Illinois

The resulting search pulls up the following record:

Eric E. Boyd, Partner
Seyfarth Shaw LLP
55 E. Monroe Street, Suite 4200
Chicago, Illinois 60603–5803

At this screen, the database provider allows you to send an e-mail to Eric, but it uses an Internet form through its systems rather than providing the individual's e-mail address. To work around this, follow the link to Eric's law firm, which was highlighted to indicate that it was an active link. At Eric's firm's page, there is a link to the firm's Web site: http://www.seyfarth.com. Now click on that link. At Eric's law firm's Web site, like so many other law firms, there is a link to Attorneys (Our Firm–Attorneys). Follow that link and either search for Boyd in the firm or follow the index to attorneys whose names begin with *B*.

Eric is found, along with his title and e-mail address:

Boyd, Eric E., Partner
eboyd@seyfarth.com

---

2. Databases (Nonlegal)

America's Job Bank[16] http://www.jobsearch.org	"America's Job Bank is the biggest and busiest job market in cyberspace. Job seekers can post their resume where thousands of employers search every day, search for job openings automatically, and find their dream job fast. Businesses can post job listings in the nation's largest online labor exchange, create customized job orders, and search resumes automatically to find the right people, right now."

(continued)

---

[16] Copyright © 2003, America's Job Bank.

CIA's World Factbook http://www.odci.gov/cia/ publications/factbook/ index.html	This is an astounding compilation of facts and figures for countries and regions around the world.
County and City Databooks http://fisher.lib.virginia.edu/ collections/stats/ccdb/	This resource provides access to the electronic versions of the 1988, 1994, and 2000 County and City Data Books, which summarize local (county and city) statistical information.
GuideStar®[17] http://www.guidestar.org	This site makes many thousands of U.S. nonprofit organizations available for searching through the GuideStar® database. Search by charity name, category, keyword, city, state, income range, and employer identification number (EIN). The search results provide the organization name, city and state location, ZIP Code, and a summary of the organization's mission. Reports include the organization mission, programs, goals and results, finances, and leadership. Information about the organizations is derived from the organizations themselves, IRS 990 and 990-EZ forms, and the IRS Business Master File (BMF).
The 'Lectric Law Library Lawcopedia's Historic Court Decisions[18] http://www.lectlaw.com/tcas.htm	This site presents "a selection of famous, infamous, and historically significant constitutional court decisions."
Martindale-Hubbell Lawyer Finder[19] http://lawyers.martindale.com/ xp/Martindale/home.xml	This site allows users to search for particular attorneys or for topical or geographically located practitioners across the country and around the world.
National Atlas of the United States®[20] http://nationalatlas.gov	This site provides the National Atlas of the United States®, which "includes five distinct products and services. In addition to providing high-quality, small-scale maps, the Atlas includes authoritative national geospatial and

---

[17] Copyright © 2005, Philanthropic Research, Inc. All rights reserved.

[18] No one connected with the 'Lectric Law Library, including Sponsors, Advertisers, & Content Providers, necessarily Endorses, Warrants or Approves of any of its material. Also, Library content is NOT meant to provide Specific Legal Advice, or to Solicit or Establish Any Kind of Professional-Client Relationship.

[19] Copyright © 1996-2002, Martindale-Hubbell, a division of Reed Elsevier Inc. All rights reserved.

[20] National Atlas of the United States® and The National Atlas of the United States of America® are registered trademarks of the United States Department of the Interior.

	geostatistical data sets. Examples of digital geospatial data include soils, county boundaries, volcanoes, and watersheds. Crime patterns, population distribution, and incidence of disease are examples of geostatistical data. This information is tied to specific geographic areas and is categorized and indexed using different methods, such as county, state, and ZIP Code boundaries or geographic coordinates like latitude and longitude. These data are collected and integrated to a consistent set of standards for reliability. The Atlas includes easy-to use online interactive maps. You can use your favorite Web browser to display, print, and query custom-made maps. These maps include links to related sites on the Internet for more up-to-date, real-time, and regional data information."
NewsVoyager[21] http://www.newspaperlinks.com/home.cfm	This is a "gateway to your local newspaper."
U.S. News Archives on the Web http://www.ibiblio.org/slanews/internet/archives.html	This site provides links to newspapers in states from Alabama to Winsonson.
USAJOBS® http://jobsearch.usajobs.opm.gov/index.asp	This is the U.S. Office of Personnel Management's Web site. "USAJOBS is the Federal Government's official one-stop source for Federal jobs and employment information."

3. Useful Resources

The variety of useful resources available over the Internet increases every day. These can also be fun.

Internet Research Scenario: Need a ZIP Code

In this scenario, we have a letter to mail but do not have the associated U.S. Postal Service ZIP Code. For this scenario, we go to the U.S.P.S.'s *ZIP Code Lookup*.

Open the Internet browser software, and go to the *ZIP Code Lookup* Web site at http://zip4.usps.com/zip4/welcome.jsp. At this site, simply type in the street

---

address, city, and state, and then double-click on the Submit button. Very quickly, the complete address, including the proper ZIP Code is returned.

Internet Research Scenario: The Conversion Factor

In this scenario, an issue in an international contract case involves the loss of 150,000 liters of petroleum. The research project is to locate a conversion chart that would convert 150,000 liters of petroleum into U.S. barrels. For this scenario use the Google™ search engine.

Go to http://www.google.com. Search for "weights and measures." The resulting search results include: "Conversion of weights and measures, metric conversion." Selecting that link takes the researcher to http://www. convert-me.com/en.

At the Convert-Me.com homepage, there is a link to convert Capacity and Volume. Following that link provides a listing of possible volume measures, with an entry box for placing the value to be converted. Place the known value of 150000 [note, no comma] in the entry box for Liters, and click on Convert. The liters converted to 943.5 barrels.

3. Useful Resources

Acronym Finder[22] http://www.acronymfinder.com	"The Acronym Finder is the Web's largest database of its kind. Here you'll find definitions for acronyms, abbreviations and initialisms about all subjects, including information technology, telecommunications, military, government, and much more."
Area Code Look Up[23] http://www.melissadata.com/lookups/phonelocation.asp	Use this site to look up telephone area codes when you have part of the address. Or try one of these other related sites: http://www.anywho.com[24] http://www.yellowpages.com[25] http://www.whitepages.com[26]
Convert-Me[27] http://www.convert-me.com/en	At this site, a user can easily perform online conversions (e.g., metric conversions) for many measurement systems.

[22] All trademarks/service marks referenced on this site are properties of their respective owners. The Acronym Finder is copyright © 1988-2005, Mountain Data Systems. All rights reserved.
[23] Copyright © 2005, Melissa Data Corp. All trademarks are used as property of their owners.
[24] Copyright © 2005, AT&T Corp. All rights reserved.
[25] In Partnership with WorldPages.com. Copyright © 1997-2004 YellowPages.com, Inc. All rights reserved.
[26] Copyright © 1996-2005, WhitePages.com. All rights reserved.
[27] Copyright © 1996-2005, Sergey & Anna Gershteins.

Court Rules, Forms and Dockets, LLRX®.com[28] http://www.llrx.com/courtrules/	"This site includes links to over 1,400 sources for state and federal court rules, forms and dockets. You can browse to find the resource you need, or search by keyword."
Dictionary.com[29] http://www.dictionary.com	This site is just what it purports to be, a handy electronic dictionary.
Federal Rules of Civil Procedure (2003) by Cornell University[30] http://www.law.cornell.edu/ rules/frcp/overview.htm	The Legal Information Institute of Cornell University's Law School notes that "these rules govern the conduct of all civil actions brought in Federal district courts. While they do not apply to suits in state courts, the rules of many states have been closely modeled on these provisions."
Federal Web Locator[31] http://www.infoctr.edu/fwl	This site provides useful and updated links to U.S. government Internet sites.
FindLaw® Legal News[32] http://news.findlaw.com	This site provides daily updates on topical law news.
Internet Research Tools http://www.afn.org/~afn05660/ search.html	This site provides a wealth of links to search engines, Usenet searches, mailing lists, and phone books.
Internet Legal Research Group™[33] http://www.ilrg.com	This site provides categorized indexes of thousands of select Web sites, in addition to thousands of locally stored Web pages and downloadable files. This site was established to serve as a comprehensive resource of the information available on the Internet concerning law and the legal profession.

(continued)

---

[28] Copyright © 1996-2005, Law Library Resource Xchange, LLC. All rights reserved.

[29] Copyright © 2005, Lexico Publishing Group, LLC. All rights reserved.

[30] This hypertext version of the rules was initially prepared by Peter W. Martin, Legal Information Institute, Cornell Law School. Subsequent updates have been prepared by the LII student editorial board under his supervision, most recently in the summer of 1996. Sources: Digital text taken with permission from U.S.C.S. published by Lawyers Cooperative Publishing Co. Conditions: Copyright in the underlying marked up html and infobase files which implement the editorial and hypertext features of these documents is held by Cornell University. Distribution of this version on the Internet, does not constitute consent to any use of the underlying hypertext markup for commercial redistribution either via the Internet or using some other form of hypertext distribution. Date: Oct. 25, 1996.

[31] Copyright © 1994-2003, The Center for Information Law and Policy.

[32] Copyright © 1994-2005, FindLaw.

[33] Copyright © 1995-2005, Internet Legal Research Group. A product of Maximilian Ventures LLC.

***Introduction to Basic Legal Citation* (LII 2003 ed.) by Peter W. Martin**[34] http://www.law.cornell.edu/citation	"This citation primer is based on the Seventeenth Edition of *The Bluebook.* This document links, point by point, to the disk version of this material held on the LII's Folio Webserver."
iTools™[35] http://www.itools.com/research/	This site has many handy lookup and finding tools. It provides dictionaries, a language translator, shipping companies, listservs, a thesaurus, a quotations database, plus much more.
Legal Lexicon's Lyceum http://www.lectlaw.com/def.htm	This site provides a law dictionary with thousands of definitions and explanations of legal terms, phrases, and concepts.
Meta-Index for U.S. Legal Research http://gsulaw.gsu.edu/metaindex	This site provides a good starting place for legal research with links to other helpful sites.
Microsoft®'s TerraServer[36] http://terraserver.microsoft.com	Microsoft®s TerraServer site presents the earth in a mosaic of photographic imagery with satellite photographs and street maps.
OneLook® Dictionaries http://www.onelook.com	This site is an Internet search engine that finds online dictionaries that contain the word searched for. The actual dictionaries are provided by other Web sites that are listed and linked to by this site in its search results.
Pleading Index http://www.law.fsu.edu/library/faculty/gore/index.html	This is a model index of pleadings, which is useful for students to see how to prepare one. Links are provided to the actual underlying pleadings.
Purdue University Libraries Quick Reference[37] http://www.lib.purdue.edu/eresources/readyref	This site provides links to English, international, acronym, and technical dictionaries; a variety of thesauri; general works on information technology from academic sources and the popular press; a collection of maps and travel information such as recreational areas and currency exchange rates; a wide range of phone books and area codes from around the world; links to the periodic tables of elements and a collection of weights and measures conversion

---

[34] Copyright © 2004, Cornell University.
[35] Copyright © 1995-2004, iTools™.
[36] Copyright © 2004, Microsoft Corporation.
[37] Copyright © 2004, Purdue University. All rights reserved.

	tables; and links to federal and Indiana state documents dealing with government issues such as constitutions, the Declaration of Independence, and census data.
Real Life Dictionary of the Law[38] http://dictionary.law.com	This dictionary contains legal terms in "real-life" (plain English) format.
The Spider's Apprentice[39] http://www.monash.com/ spidap.html	A helpful guide to Web search engines, including tutorials, may be found here.
Supreme Court Bulletin, Legal Information Institute[40] http://www.law.cornell.edu/ focus/bulletins.html	This site provides summaries of Supreme Court decisions delivered by e-mail within minutes of release, along with instructions on how to access those decisions in full text.
Thesaurus.com[41] http://www.thesaurus.com	This site is just what it purports to be: a handy electronic thesaurus.
U.S. Supreme Court Opinions at Willamette Law Online[42] http://www.willamette.edu/ law/wlo/us-supreme/index.htm	"This service provides same-day summaries of certiorari granted, oral arguments, and decisions published by the United States Supreme Court. The certiorari summaries focus on the facts and decision from the lower court. The week prior to oral arguments we provide an outline of the issues presented to the Court as argued in the briefs. The decision summaries provide the holding from the United States Supreme Court and a brief overview of the Court's reasoning."
World Wide Web Research Tools[43] http://www.virtualsalt.com/ search.htm	This is an excellent collection of research sites.
ZIP Code Lookup[44] http://zip4.usps.com/zip4/ welcome.jsp	Use this site to look up a U.S. ZIP Code.

4. Government Sites: Federal

The sophistication and quality of many federal Web sites are very good. Generally, these sites provide at least rudimentary identifying information and a statement of the related entities' purposes and goals. The better sites provide comprehensive indexes and directories to related documents, laws, regulations, policies, forms, and other materials.

Internet Research Scenario: Printing U.S. Postal Service Package Labels

In this scenario, we have a package to mail and we wish to use the Priority service. For this scenario we go to the U.S. Postal Service's homepage.

> Open the Internet browser software, and go to http://www.usps.com. At this site, follow the link to "Click-N-Ship®! At this page, users have the choice to ship nationally or internationally, and to prepare labels with or without postage added. In order to create labels with postage, the user will be required to first register on the http://www.usps.com site.
>
> Follow the links to put in the addressing information and print your labels.

4. Government Sites: Federal	
Code of Federal Regulations (C.F.R.) http://www.gpoaccess.gov/cfr/index.html	This site provides the full-text searchable, mirror image of the *Code of Federal Regulations* (C.F.R.). The C.F.R. is the codification of the rules published in the *Federal Register* by the federal executive departments and agencies.
Congressional Record Index http://www.gpoaccess.gov/cri/index.html	The *Congressional Record Index* is a publication of the Joint Committee on Printing, Congress of the United States. The database is updated daily when Congress is in session and indexes the daily issues of the *Congressional Record.* Unlike the paper editions, these databases cumulate from the beginning of the session of Congress. Each year of the *Congressional Record Index* can be searched individually; however, selecting the historical database searches for all years except the current year.
Department of Justice Homepage http://www.usdoj.gov	The homepage for the U.S. Department of Justice.

Federal Judiciary Homepage http://www.uscourts.gov	This site is a "first place to look" when there is a need for information about the federal courts. The site provides rules of practice and links to particular courts around the nation.
***Federal Register,* Daily Table of Contents** http://www.access.gpo.gov/ su_docs/aces/fr-cont.html	The U.S. Government Printing Office makes available in "pdf" and "html" formats the daily *Federal Register.* This is a boon for those wanting immediate copies of notices and rulemaking, as the paper copy of the *Federal Register* is often days behind the electronic version, which is available the day of publication.
FIRSTGov.gov[45] http://www.firstgov.gov	This site is a government Web site to provide the public with easy, one-stop access to all online U.S. Federal Government resources.
GrayLIT Network http://www.osti.gov/graylit/	This site was developed by the Department of Energy's Office of Scientific and Technical Information (OSTI), in collaboration with DOD/DTIC, NASA, and EPA. The GrayLIT Network is a portal for technical report information generated through federally funded research and development projects.
List of C.F.R. Sections Affected http://www.gpoaccess.gov/lsa/	This is the online version of the C.F.R. reference. The *List of C.F.R. Sections Affected* (L.S.A.) allows the researcher to bring a published regulation up to date—knowing whether any changes to the regulation have been proposed or adopted since its formal publication.
THOMAS Legislative Information http://thomas.loc.gov	Three major information types are covered by THOMAS: Legislation, Congressional Record, and Committee Information. In addition, under the Congressional Record heading, the days-in-session calendars for the House and Senate are available.
***United States Code* (U.S.C.)** http://www.gpoaccess.gov/ uscode/index.html	This site provides the full-text searchable *United States Code* (U.S.C.). The U.S.C. is the codification by subject matter of the general and permanent laws of the United States.

(continued)

---

[45] FIRSTGov™ is the U.S. government's official Web portal.

USAJOBS® http://jobsearch.usajobs.opm. gov/agency_search.asp	This site allows searches in the Office of Personnel Management's federal job openings database. Searches may be restricted to certain agencies and keywords used to limit results.
U.S. Government Information Locator Service http://www.access.gpo.gov/ su_docs/gils/index.html	"The *Government Information Locator Service* (GILS) is an effort to identify, locate, and describe publicly available Federal information resources, including electronic information resources. GILS records identify public information resources within the Federal Government, describe the information available in these resources, and assist in obtaining the information. GILS is a decentralized collection of agency-based information locators using network technology and international standards to direct users to relevant information resources within the Federal Government."
U.S. Postal Service http://www.usps.com	The U.S. Postal Service provides many useful tools and tips from its Web site.

5. Government Sites: State

The state site links provide resources to documents, laws, regulations, policies, forms, and other materials. Various sites provide links to all the states' home-pages for easier access to separate states across the country.

Internet Research Scenario: Employee Drug Testing

In this scenario, our client is reviewing its employee drug testing policy and wants to be sure that it does not conflict with state laws in any of the twenty-three states where the employer has employees. For this scenario, we go to Cornell Law School Legal Information Institute's state statutes links.

> Open the Internet browser software, and go to the following URL: http://www.law.cornell.edu/topics/state_ statutes.html. At this site, select the link to state "employment and labor" statutes.
> That link brings up a state-by-state list of employment and labor laws. For this scenario, we followed the link to the Georgia statutes.
> At the first screen, we were presented with a search screen. We searched for "drug test." In the list of hits, or results, was section 34-9-415. Follow the title 34 links to sections 410 through 421.

5. Government Sites: State

Center for Information Law and Policy's State Web Locator[46] http://www.infoctr.edu/swl	This is a list of links to state government Web sites. It provides an easy mechanism for finding unknown state Web sites.
Directory of Public Record Vendors Online[47] http://www.brbpub.com/pubrecsites.asp	BRB Publications, Inc., provides a links Web site to free federal and state government searchable Web sites, along with some important nongovernment sites. The links are categorized by state so that it is easy to locate related state information.
Guide to Law Online: U.S. States and Territories http://www.loc.gov/law/guide/usstates.html	This is the U.S. Library of Congress's Guide to Law Online: U.S. States and Territories, which provides comprehensive links to state and territory Web sites, reference materials, and documents.
1938-1941 Illinois Historical Aerial Photography Project http://www.isgs.uiuc.edu/nsdihome/webdocs/ilhap/index.html	This is a digital archive of Illinois historical aerial photographs from 1938 through 1941. The collection consists of more than 30,000 prints.
Illinois Register on the Internet http://www.cyberdriveillinois.com/departments/index/register	This is the Illinois Secretary of State's Web site for access to full text of the state's administrative register, retrievable in pdf format.
State Administrative Codes[48] http://www.nass.org/acr/	This is a linking index to state sites that provide Internet access to administrative rules.
State Statutes http://www.law.cornell.edu/topics/state_statutes.html	Links to state statutes on the Internet, compiled topically (by law area) by Cornell Law School.

6. Government Sites: Municipal

Municipal Internet sites are often less helpful in legal research. Generally these local sites provide tourism and business information. These sites are great for

---

[46] Copyright © 1995-2003, Center for Information Law and Policy.
[47] Copyright © 2002, BRB Publications, Inc. All rights reserved.
[48] Copyright © 2004, Administrative Codes and Registers.

finding out general information about particular places. Some Web sites, though, like those listed here, provide municipal and building codes, and compliance information and forms.

Links to cities' homepages nationwide are beyond the scope of this section, but those sites are found easily enough through Internet search engines.

Internet Research Scenario: Local Building Codes

In this scenario, our client is seeking to expand its facility located in Atlanta, Georgia. For this scenario, we go to the Municipal Code Corporation's page to see if the building code is available there. A screenshot of the Municipal Code Corporation's homepage is shown in Figure 3-2.

> Open the Internet browser software, and go to the following URL: http://www.municode.com. At this site, there is a link to "Online Codes," so we follow that.
>
> That link brings up a listing of states. We then follow the "Georgia" link. On the next page, we select a link to the Atlanta codes and are presented with an option for "frames" or "no frames." Either selection results in a page that allows keyword searching in the online code. Searching on "building" brings up many relevant code sections.

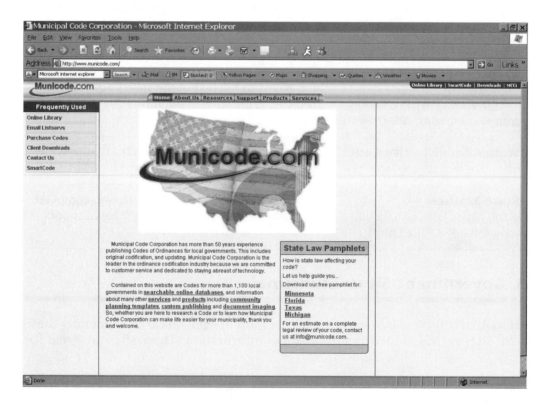

Figure 3-2 Municode.com homepage.
Reprinted with permission. Copyright © 2003, Municipal Code Corporation.

6. Government Sites: Municipal	
Municipal Code Corporation[49] http://www.municode.com	This site provides online versions of selected municipal codes from around the country.
State and Local Government on the Net by Piper Resources[50] http://www.statelocalgov.net/index.cfm	A comprehensive guide that links to numerous state and local government-sponsored Internet sites.
State and Territorial Air Pollution Program Administrators http://www.cleanairworld.org	The State and Territorial Air Pollution Program Administrators (STAPPA) and the Association of Local Air Pollution Control Officials (ALAPCO) are two national associations representing air pollution control agencies in 54 states and territories and over 150 major metropolitan areas across the United States.

7. Legal Research Database (Commercial) Sites

Searching in legal databases is discussed in detail in Chapter 6. That chapter also provides some Internet research scenarios for working with these resources. These are listed here, along with some others, simply for cross reference and completeness.

7. Legal Research Database (Commercial) Sites	
LexisNexis® Academic[51] http://www.lexisnexis.com/academic/1univ/acad/default.asp	Students can use LexisNexis® Academic to access primary source material such as case law, statutes, and regulations or dive into secondary source materials such as legal news or law reviews for background or analysis of a legal topic. They can even validate their case law research with *Shepard's*® Citations for the Supreme Court. Speak to your instructor or your school librarian for the LexisNexis® Academic URL address from your institution.

(continued)

---

[49] Copyright © 2003, Municipal Code Corporation.
[50] Copyright © 1995-2005, Piper Resources.
[51] Materials available in this Web site are protected by copyright law. Copyright © 2005, LexisNexis®, a division of Reed Elsevier Inc. All rights reserved.

LexisNexis® Services[52] http://www.lexis.com	This is one of two broad-based legal information services that provide, for a price, the text of their vast resources over the Internet.
Loislaw™[53] http://www.loislaw.com	This is one of two economical but not as comprehensive legal information providers that provide, for a price, the text of their legal resources over the Internet.
VersusLaw®[54] http://www.versuslaw.com	This is one of two economical but not as comprehensive legal information providers that provide, for a price, the text of their legal resources over the Internet.
Westlaw®[55] http://www.westlaw.com	This is one of two broad-based legal information services that provide, for a price, the text of their vast resources over the Internet.

8. Selected Legal Service Provider Sites

In today's environment of sophisticated technological machinery, systems, software, databases, and courtrooms, legal service providers, specialists, and vendors are often necessary and required. These links and vendors are listed for reference only, and the listing is not meant to be a recommendation.

Internet Research Scenario: Litigation Support Services

In this scenario, the litigation team has a trial scheduled for a federal district court in another state. The courtroom where the trial is scheduled is set up for computer interaction and display, and the judge has indicated that he expects counsel to take advantage of the courtroom's sophisticated tools. For this scenario, we will consult several Internet resources to prepare for trying the case. For one, we will review the Findlaw® Litigation Support Services links and prepare a list of suggested vendors to submit a "request for proposal" to. Secondly, we will go to the Robert Half® Legal Web site to investigate the costs associated with paralegal temporaries, which may be needed in support of the case.

> Open the Internet browser software, and go to the following URL: http://marketcenter.findlaw.com/scripts/search.pl?vendor=7&ac=110&pa=110&search=state&direction=1.

---

[52] Materials available in this Web site are protected by copyright law. Copyright © 2005, LexisNexis®, a division of Reed Elsevier Inc. All rights reserved.
[53] Loislaw™, Loislaw.com™, and LOIS LawWatch™ are trademarks of Loislaw.com, Inc. Copyright © 2005, Loislaw.com, Inc.
[54] Copyright © 2000-2005, VersusLaw, Inc. All rights reserved.
[55] Copyright © 2005, West, a Thomson business. All rights reserved.

At this site, there is a link to Legal Technology. Following that link brings up several potential vendors to contact for assistance or to make requests for proposals to.

Next we went to the Robert Half® Legal Web site at http://www.rhi.com and follow the link to Robert Half® Legal.

At this site, information can be reviewed on the temporary or permanent placement of paralegals. Also, an e-mail address is provided so that more detailed information may be requested.

8. Selected Legal Service Provider Sites	
Expert Witness Internet Resources http://www.nocall.org/experts.htm	The site, put together by the Northern California Association of Law Libraries, is a collection of links to experts and to other collections of expert witnesses lists and links.
IKON Corporation http://www.ikon.com	This is a leading national full-service document services company.
Kroll Ontrack[56] http://www.krollontrack.com	Kroll Ontrack provides large-scale electronic and paper-based discovery and computer forensics services and software to help attorneys, investigators, corporations, and legal professionals recover, review, manage, and produce information and documents.
Litigation Support Service Links http://marketcenter.findlaw.com/scripts/search.pl?vendor=7&ac=110&pa=110&search=state&direction=1	This site provides a comprehensive listing of nationwide litigation support service providers.
Merrill Corporation http://www.merrillcorporation.com	This is a leading national document services company.
Robert Half® Legal http://www.rhi.com	Robert Half® Legal specializes in project and full-time professionals for law firms and corporate legal departments throughout the United States and Canada.
TrialGraphix®[57] http://www.trialgraphix.com	This is a leading demonstrative evidence and trial consulting services company.

---

[56] Copyright © 2005, Kroll Ontrack Inc.
[57] Copyright © 1991-2005, TrialGraphix, Inc. All rights reserved.

9. Legal and Paralegal Professional Reference Sites

Legal and paralegal reference sites are useful for professional information, current literature, profession-related links, policies, salary surveys, job lists, and other materials.

Internet Research Scenario: Jobs Database

In this scenario, we have a friend who is relocating, for personal reasons, to Washington, D.C. Our friend is interested in paralegal opportunities in that area. For this scenario, we go to the National Federation of Paralegal Associations' Web site.

> Open the Internet browser software, and go to the following URL: http://www.paralegals.org. At this site, there is a link to the Career Center. Taking it brings up the option to search the jobs database. The search screen allows searches to be limited to a particular city and state.
>
> In a search for Washington, D.C., three positions were returned.

9. Legal and Paralegal Professional Reference Sites	
American Association for Paralegal Education http://www.aafpe.org	The AAfPE site provides educator resources and information on paralegal programs around the country.
American Bar Association http://www.abanet.org	The ABA's Web site provides general information and links, as well as much practice-specific and paralegal-related information.
National Association of Legal Assistants[58] http://www.nala.org	The NALA Web site provides information on continuing education and professional certification programs, as well as selected links for legal assistants.
National Federation of Paralegal Associations http://www.paralegals.org	The NFPA™ is a national organization consisting of member associations of paralegals. It provides resources and information on the paralegal profession, an online version of its professional journal, and a job bank.

---

[58] Copyright © 2004, National Association of Legal Assistants.

DISCUSSION QUESTIONS

1. Search for "Internet search engines" at several of the search engine Web sites listed in this chapter. What sorts of hits or Web sites are typically returned in answer at most of the Web sites searched?
2. Considering the large number of search engines available on the Web, how would you evaluate and select a "few" particular search engines as your standard or best ones?
3. In a job search (that is, looking for a job), what value or purpose do you think there is in searching a jobs database, such as America's Job Bank?
4. If a research project has been given to you to find a good source for Supreme Court opinions, what site would you recommend? Why?
5. Why would you use the electronic *Code of Federal Regulations* when you could just use the paper copy in the library? List three reasons the electronic format would be a better resource.

PROJECTS

1. Search for an Internet site that provides a conversion factor or table or program to convert $3.5 million from "1990 dollars" to "2004 dollars." What did you find?
2. Take a look at Microsoft®'s TerraServer images for your state/city/ neighborhood. Find and print a photo of your house.
3. Search for the *United States Code* sections that concern the naturalization of immigrants to the United States.

CHAPTER 4

Essentials of Research on the Internet: Search Engines

SUMMARY

This chapter reviews and sets out the inclusive and selective methods of searching and defines and explains keyword searching with terms and phrases, keyword connectors and search characters, the "combination" and "nesting concept," stop words, and synonyms. Also, search planning and searching methods are discussed and illustrated. The use of multiple search engines is reviewed, and suggestions are provided for maximizing search results. The student will learn how to review and search within found Web pages for sought-after keywords. Finally, searching pitfalls are discussed.

OBJECTIVES

- The student will be able to develop inclusive and selective methods of searching on the Internet.
- The student will be able to search the Internet with keyword terms and phrases, using connectors, characters, combinations and nesting, stop words, and synonyms.
- The student will be able to set out a plan for searching for particular information.
- The student will have an understanding of how the use of a mix of search engines will locate the most relevant pages.
- The student will review and use in-document searching tools.
- The student will be familiarized with searching pitfalls.

Internet Research

Internet research places the world of information (data and documents) at your (computer display) feet. With a basic understanding and knowledge of what the Internet is about, the CALR professional is now almost prepared to begin Internet research. Yet, in preparing to do Internet research, as with any other type of research, planning ahead is critical.

Computer-aided legal research professionals must necessarily spend suitable time considering keywords and phrases that will return the best-related search hits or pages. It is crucial to consider, even list, appropriate terms and synonyms that will capture documents relating to the idea or topic sought.

Inclusive Method or Selective Method

Theoretically, researchers may use the "inclusive" or the "selective" method of searching. As the terms suggest, the *inclusive* method will include everything, usually including the kitchen sink. The inclusive method of searching will retrieve all of the relevant sources, but it will also return many irrelevant ones. The *selective* method allows researchers to limit the amount of "junk" hits returned, while increasing the odds that something important may be missed.

Keyword Search Terms and Phrases: Searching Basics

A *keyword* is a word that is likely to be found in the information or documents searched for. Keywords may be combined to refine the search or may be turned into an exact phrase by putting the words in quotes. A general rule is that if too many hits or pages are returned (inclusive), it may be necessary to narrow the search (selective). This would be accomplished by adding keywords and phrases to the search. If the search keywords or phrases return too few hits (selective), then the search should be expanded (inclusive). This would be accomplished by deleting some of the keywords and phrases listed in the search.

Connectors

Keywords and phrases in queries may be refined at many of the search engines by using "Boolean"-type connectors. The connectors AND, OR, NOT (or AND NOT), and NEAR (or ADJ) tell search engines which keywords to include or exclude and whether keywords should appear close to each other. At some of the search engines, the connectors must be used in ALL CAPS in order to operate correctly. It is best to refer to each search engine's help materials if there is a question about whether the site supports connectors and if they are case-sensitive.

The following are the primary search connectors. With each connector, examples are given of how a search statement including the connector would be used.[1]

    1. The AND statement
The AND (sometimes an "&" is allowed, but check each particular Web site for its requirements) statement is used to require that all search terms be present in the documents listed in results. It can also be described as a *Match All* search. Some search engines (such as Google™) will perform an AND search by default. Researchers should read about the specifics of the search engine used to determine if the default value is AND rather than OR for search queries.
- elton AND john
- boiled & potatoes

---

[1] Thanks to Christian R. Andersen for preparing the connectors section.

2. The OR statement

The OR statement is used to allow any of the specified search terms to be present in the documents listed in results. It can also be described as a *Match Either* search. In general, many of the major search engines default to an OR or *Match Either* search, though they tend to rank pages containing all terms first (check each particular Web site for its requirements).

- illness OR sickness OR injury

On many search engines, the same OR statement may be stated this way:

- illness sickness injury

3. The NOT statement

The NOT statement is used to require that a particular search term NOT be present in documents listed in results. It can also be described as an *Exclude* command. Many search engines support the "−" symbol as a means of doing a NOT or *Exclude* search. Many of the major search engines also support the NOT or the AND NOT format (check each particular Web site for its requirements).

- illness NOT cancer
- Johnson −Lyndon

4. The NEAR (or ADJ) Statement

The NEAR (or ADJ (adjacent)) statement is used to specify that search terms should appear close to each other. Not too many of the search engines support the NEAR command.[2] It is important to check each particular Web site for its requirements.

- ergonomics NEAR program
- george ADJ washington

Truncation Characters

Researchers should use truncated words with the use of the asterisk or some similar character (such as "!") as a wildcard to pick up differing versions of the terms or where the search terms appear in other words or phrases. For example, "inspect*" would locate uses of "inspection" and "inspected" as well as "inspect." The wildcard tells the search engine to match all characters before it. In this way, any matching words with differing characters after the stem word "inspect" will be matched to the query term if the search engine supports truncation. Of course, again, it is best to refer to the search help materials if there is a question about whether the site supports truncation characters and for which characters may be used. Remember, on the Internet, every site is different and every site is unique.

For another example, the query "environ*" would return hits that contained the following terms:

- environment
- environmental
- environmentalist

---

[2] AOL® Search, AltaVista®, Lycos®, and WebCrawler® support the NEAR command.

Or, for instance, "sign!" in a query would find all occurrences of the following terms:

- signed
- signature
- signatory

The "Combination" or "Nesting Concept"

Many search engines support the use of combining or nesting in queries. To combine or nest in a search query, parentheses are used. For example, to search for movies or recordings of Shakespeare's play *The Tempest*, this search might be used:

- (shakespeare AND tempest) AND (movie OR recording)

In this example, the documents returned by the search engine must have both "shakespeare AND tempest" AND will also have either "movie OR recording."

Stop Words

The search engines often will ignore common words and characters. These are known as stop words. Terms such as "the," "where," and "how" and certain single digits and single letters are not included in searches unless the researcher indicates that they are essential. To do this, the plus sign ("+") is placed in front of the term. For instance, on Google™, to search for *Star Wars, Episode I*, the researcher would use

- Star Wars Episode +I

Remember that Google™ defaults to AND, and so it is searching for "Star AND Wars AND Episode AND +I."

Synonyms

In preparing search queries, synonyms (and perhaps antonyms) must be considered. For example, the terms "automobile," "car," and "vehicle" may be used interchangeably in an automobile accident case. The query

- automobile OR car OR vehicle

will probably find more relevant documents than may be appropriate or needed in the research. Typically, the OR connector can be omitted, but check the search engine's "search help."

The Search Professional Must Have a Good Sense of What Is Being Sought

The scope of information available on the Internet is extraordinary. Likewise, finding the jewels of information among the multitude of pebbles can be maddening and take hours if the CALR professional does not carefully plan out the search.

Many of the Internet search engines are excellent for sifting the "wheat from the chaff" in the mountains of data on the Internet. To begin a search, the researcher must have a good sense of what is being searched for. Having "sort of an idea of approximately what is wanted" will lead to millions of search hits, with few being close to what is really wanted. In addition, there is so much material on the Internet that a researcher will inevitably see a lot of junk mixed in with the diamonds.

Use a Mix of Search Engines to Locate Most Relevant Pages

Generally, the CALR professional should go first to one of the big, established search engines, such as Google™ or AltaVista®. With these sites, with a properly designed search query, chances are good that the information desired may be found in the first thirty or forty hits or page references returned. If a particular document was searched for and is found, the job is done. If the search brought up some information but nothing exactly on point, then it is recommended that the search be conducted on at least one more but preferably on several more search engines.

One especially important point is that because of the way that search engines are designed (each is unique and functions in a unique manner), each produces qualitatively and quantitatively different search results. For example, in running the query "osha inspection" on some of the popular search engines, we discovered the following results:

- Google™ found "about" 623,000 pages
- AltaVista® found 255,000 pages
- Excite™ found 97 pages.

The pages found at these different sites did include some duplication, but it is notable that much unique material was located. As a CALR professional, you must look at numerous search engine results to gain confidence that what is found on the search topic fairly represents what is actually available on the Internet.

Review and Search Within Found Pages

The relevance of many of the Internet pages or documents found in search results may not be immediately apparent on opening a found item. Often it will be necessary to find the particular keyword(s) in the context of the document to discern its applicability and utility.

For Internet pages that are in HTML or for simple text documents, fortunately, much like other Windows-type computer software (like Microsoft® Word), the Internet browser software also contains a built-in Find tool. Under the Edit menu selection, select the Find tool and type in the keyword to go very

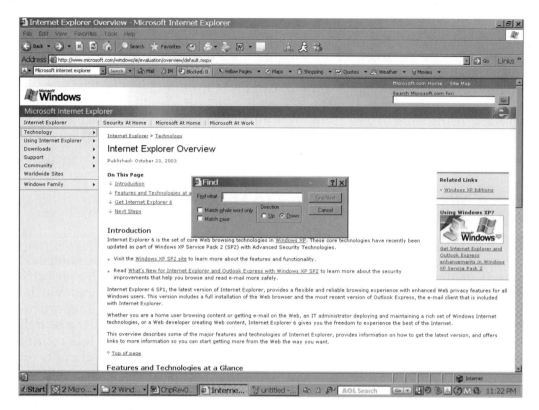

Figure 4-1 The Find tool.
Reprinted with permission. Copyright © 2004, Microsoft.com.

quickly to the word in the document. This same Find feature is also supported by Microsoft® Word and Microsoft® Excel and the Adobe Acrobat® Reader® software that enables the researcher to "find" or locate keywords within files found. A screenshot of the Find tool is shown in Figure 4-1.

Internet Search Results

An Internet search will typically find many different kinds of files. Some of the file types, such as plain text—**txt** or **ASCII**—files, will in many cases be indexed by the search engine **spiders** word for word. Other file types, such as **portable document format** or **pdf** files, will in some cases only be retrievable to the extent that they have been well indexed in the linking/html files. The following chart lists and explains most Internet file types.

File Suffix	File Types
asp	active server page, a program-enabled active page
com	an executable or program file

csv	a formatted ASCII text file
db, dbf, mdb	types of database files
exe	an executable or program file
htm or html	Hypertext Markup Language file
gif	common Web page image file format
jpg	common image file format
mid	high-quality audio file format
mim	Internet e-mail compressed file format
mov	common file format for video files
mp3	high-quality audio file format
mpg	common file format for video files
pdf	formatted file "what you see is what you get" image
tif	popular graphic image file format
txt	plain text ACSII file
wks, wk*	common spreadsheet format file
xls, xl*	common spreadsheet format file
zip	compressed file format

Other Pitfalls

In an interesting analogy, Glenn S. Bacal notes that

> [F]or the unfocused researcher, the opportunity to digress, to scurry down paths that seem interesting, if not relevant, to a particular search task will be overwhelming. The Internet is to the intellect what the circus was to entertainment. Each homepage deliberately beckons with a barker's promise: "Come right in! Welcome! Right this way!" Each site is anxious to get you intellectually enticed enough to visit, and to visit often.

[M]any sites feature and prominently display "visitor counters," often with a large number of visitors being displayed. This might convince the new visitor that this site must be worth the visit, just like a full parking lot at a restaurant might appear to be assurance of the quality of the food. But site visitors, beware. First of all, these counters are often not a measure of the number of visitors, but the number of hits on each page at the site. A single visitor to a site who clicks on ten pages might be recorded on a counter as ten rather than one, depending upon how the counter works. Furthermore, it's obvious that certain Web site counters are not accurate. Some are frozen, and some may have been manipulated. Some manipulated Web site counters are to gullible consumers in the late 1990s what some manipulated automobile odometers were to gullible consumers in the 1950s.[3]

Also on the Internet are vast resources that are hidden behind password-protected areas. Large databases like the Bureau of National Affairs, the *New York Times* and the *Wall Street Journal* are accessible through the Internet but only after registration and putting in your password. Consequently, search engines will not pick up any of these hidden resources.

The Meta Search Engines

The meta search engines search the Internet by searching and reporting back on the results generated by other search engines. There are two types of meta search engines: one type searches a number of engines and does not collate the results. This means the researcher must look through a separate list of results from each engine that was searched; duplicates may be noted over and over. Some meta search engines require you to visit each individual search site to view your results, while others will bring the results back to their sites.

When results are brought back to the site, a certain limitation is placed on what is allowed to be retrieved, either based on a maximum number of pages or a searching time limitation. With this type of meta search engine, the results may be comprehensive and sometimes overwhelming. An example of this type of meta search engine is Dogpile® (http://www.dogpile.com). Dogpile® may save time for some Internet researchers because it automatically searches numerous "favorite search engines" and then ranks and orders the results.

The other type of meta search engine returns a single list of results, often with the duplicate hits removed. This type of meta engine always brings the results back to its own site for viewing. In these cases, the engine retrieves a certain maximum number of documents from the individual engines it has searched and cuts off the list after a certain point as the search is processed. Mamma (http://www.mamma.com) is a good example of this type of search engine.

There is also a stand-alone search engine called Copernic® (http://www.copernic.com) that installs itself on your hard drive and interacts with a variety

---

[3] *See* Glenn S. Bacal, J. D., M.B.A., The Practical Litigator's 1999 Guide to Internet Research (1999).

of different search engines. The more resources you have, the better your search results will be.

Internet Research Scenario: Finding an Expert Witness

In this scenario, we have a client who wishes to retain an expert on condemnation law. The issue is that the state department of transportation is planning to take some of the client's land for a public purpose. The team attorney has been asked by the client to make recommendations as to the top three or four condemnation law experts in the nation.

The Research Project

Compile for the team attorney, from the Internet, a list and backup information (such as biographies, publications, etc.) on the top three or four condemnation law experts in the nation.

For this scenario, you may assume that the American Bar Association Web site (http://www.abanet.org) was already consulted and that a general search of the Internet is suggested by the team attorney.

Keywords

Condemnation OR (eminent domain)

Selected Search Sites

For this project, we searched the Dogpile® (http://www.dogpile.com) site and got the following results:

Web results for "Condemnation OR (eminent domain)"—70

Now limit the search by running a more selective search. Try the same search engine with the revised search phrase:

Expert AND Condemnation OR (eminent domain)

For this revised search parameter, we got the following results:

Web results for "Expert AND Condemnation OR (eminent domain)"—63

An example of one of the returned search items is: Appraisal Group One, experts in eminent domain/condemnation appraisal, electric power line easements, gas pipeline easements and stigma damages. Expert witness service nationwide.

CONCLUSION

In conclusion, CALR on the Internet involves going on line and doing research on selected topics. In preparing to do Internet research, as with any other type of research, planning ahead is critical. Legal professionals must spend suitable time considering keywords and phrases that will return the best related search hits.

The researcher must have a good sense of what is being searched for. Query design and statements should be planned out, and consideration should be given to whether the "inclusive method" or the "selective method" is appropriate for the given project. Planning the appropriate search engines to use is key to successful research. Use a mix of search engines to locate the most relevant pages.

DISCUSSION QUESTIONS

1. Have you used the Internet for research before? If so, what for?
2. Which of the major search engines do you find to be the best sources for the information in which you are interested or that you have needed?
3. Give an example of where an Internet directory would be more useful than a search engine.
4. Is the use of the Internet sufficient in itself for locating information on an identified expert witness? Why or why not?

PROJECTS

1. Search the Internet for a defense-friendly asbestos expert. Recommend three such experts to your instructor.
2. Search the Internet for a material safety data sheet (MSDS) on polychlorinated biphenyls. Did you find more than one? Was it a government or an industry document?

CHAPTER 5

Legal Research (Sources) on the Internet

Lyonette Louis-Jacques

SUMMARY

This chapter explains why the Internet is useful for legal research and describes some of the major resources available on the Internet for researching the law of the United States and other countries, comparative law, and international law. It concludes with tips for the Net-traveling researcher.

OBJECTIVES

- The student will learn about doing legal research on the Internet.
- The student will learn of the major resources available on the Internet for researching the law.
- The student will be provided with tips for the Net-traveling researcher.

Why Use the Internet for Legal Research?

In the past few years, many new resources have been put on the Internet that facilitate legal research work. The sheer number and variety of resources can sometimes make it difficult to determine where to start, how to choose among similar resources, and how to keep up to date on available resources. The present guide is intended to explain why the Internet is useful for legal research and to describe some of the major resources available on the Internet for researching the law of the United States and other countries, comparative law, and international law. It concludes with some tips for the Net-traveling researcher.

This chapter illustrates sources of legal information on the Internet. While the links are constantly updated, links cited may become outdated or not found. It is recommended that readers visit Ms. Louis-Jacques's Web site, with updated hyperlinks to cited resources, found at http://www.lib.uchicago.edu/~llou/mpoctalk.html. This chapter is based on the "Virtual Presentation" talk presented at the Midwestern Professors of Color Conference, St. Louis, Missouri (Mar. 30, 1996, updated Mar. 1, 2005), by Ms. Lyonette Louis-Jacques, Foreign and International Law, Librarian and Lecturer in Law, University of Chicago Law School. Used and adapted with permission.

The Internet is a cheap alternative to the use of commercial databases such as LEXIS® and Westlaw® for finding primary legal materials such as U.S. federal and state statutes, bills, cases, and regulations. Sometimes these materials are available more quickly on the Internet than on LEXIS® and Westlaw® (especially if they relate to the law of cyberspace, the Internet, computer law, immigration law, the First Amendment and censorship, communications law, intellectual property, major criminal trials, antitrust law, elections, or other hot topics).

Sometimes, the Internet is the only place where you will find some primary materials. Examples include legislation and case law from foreign countries, treaties involving foreign countries, e-mail addresses and other directory information for legal professionals worldwide, materials in areas of law that have been traditionally underrepresented in print and electronic legal publications (women and the law; human rights; the rights of lesbians, gay men, bisexuals, and transgendered people; law and literature—for instance, e-texts of Jane Austen's writings; Roman law; law and popular culture), and nonlegal materials that are important to law work or interdisciplinary research.

Types of Resources That Are on the Internet

The Internet can augment an average law library's resources by providing alternative copies of print materials and information that cannot be found in the law library in print or electronic format. Some examples of the types of resources that are on the Internet follow:

- Census information at http://www.census.gov
- Uniform and model acts at http://www.law.upenn.edu/library/ulc/ulc.htm
- News at http://www.lib.uchicago.edu/e/law/news
- Publishers' catalogs at http://www.lib.uchicago.edu/e/law/db/ref/publishers.html
- Worldwide library catalogs at http://www.lib.uchicago.edu/LibInfo/Law/catalogs.html
- Full text of articles from electronic law and nonlaw journals at http://www.lib.uchicago.edu/LibInfo/Law/lawrev.html
- Books (such as the classics) at http://classics.mit.edu
- Bookstores, such as Barrister Books (academic textbooks) at http://www.barristerbooks.com and Amazon at http://www.amazon.com
- Poetry at http://dir.yahoo.com/Arts/Humanities/Literature/Authors/Poets
- Shakespeare's works at http://www-tech.mit.edu/Shakespeare
- Classical music at http://www.classicaliscool.com
- *Bartlett's Quotations* at http://www.bartleby.com/bartlett
- Song lyrics at http://dir.yahoo.com/entertainment/music/lyrics
- Comic strips at http://www.unitedmedia.com/comics/dilbert
- Tax forms at http://www.irs.gov/formspubs/index.html
- Sports information at http://www.yahoo.com/Recreation/Sports, or professional baseball and basketball players' salaries at http://asp.usatoday.com/sports/basketball/nba/salaries/default.aspx
- Legal documents (including transcripts of hearings, reports, briefs, memoranda, complaints, indictments, oral arguments, etc.) at http://www.courttv.com.

The Internet is strongest for nonlegal materials and for legal materials that are usually not found or will not be available as quickly on LEXIS®, Westlaw®, and print publications in your law library.

Where to Start Your Internet Legal Research

If this is your first time on the Internet, it is good to hunt down a legal research guide. The guides are good to check before embarking on legal research on the Internet. They describe and link to legal resources generally available on the Internet or list existing Internet legal research guides.

- Jim Milles, *Law on the Web,* at http://lawlib.slu.edu/library/LawOnTheWeb. html (this is one of the best places to start, because it is a well-organized list of U.S. legal resources on the Internet—statutes, cases, etc.—with links)
- Andrew Zimmermann, *Zimmermann's Research Guide: An Online Encyclopedia for Legal Researchers,* at http://www.lexisnexis.com/infopro/ zimmerman
- Genie Tyburski, *The Virtual Chase: Legal Research Guide,* at http:// www.virtualchase.com/resources/index.shtml and *Legal and Factual Research on the Internet* at http://www.virtualchase.com/legalresearcher/ index.html
- Lyonette Louis-Jacques, Lyo's *Law Lists* (browsable text), at http://www. lib.uchicago.edu/~llou/lawlists/info.html (provides instructions and a keyword search feature for subscribing to about 1200 law-related e-mail lists and about 150 Usenet newsgroups)
- *The Social Science Information Gateway (SOSIG): Law* at http://www. sosig.ac.uk/law
- Argus Clearinghouse at http://www.clearinghouse.net (includes research guides on all sorts of topics, including law, many with hypertext links) While this has been a recommended site, it is currently posting a message that it will not be updated anymore.

Major Internet Sites for Law

Alternatively, you can browse through some of the major Internet sites for law. If you become familiar with the following sites, you can do research on the Internet for legal questions more effectively. These Web sites normally arrange information by legal subject (antitrust law, civil rights, immigration law, etc.), by type of document (constitutions, court cases, statutes, treaties, etc.), by source (governmental agency, international organization, law firm, law school, publisher), or by intended audience (law students, law librarians, etc.).

- LexisONE.com (for the full text of all U.S. Supreme Court cases, the last five years of federal and state appellate court cases, legal forms, and an Internet legal research guide; free, but must register; intended to be useful for small businesses and solo practitioners) at http:// www.lexisone.com.

- FindLaw®, http://www.findlaw.com (provides a well-organized starting point for legal research—with links to just about everything related to law on the Internet)
- Indiana University Law School World Wide Web Virtual Library for Law at http://www.law.indiana.edu/v-lib/index.html
- Cornell University Law School's Legal Information Institute (LII) at http://www.law.cornell.edu (includes links by legal subjects (Law About) and Law by Source), also, the Library's Legal Research Encyclopedia at http://www.lawschool.cornell.edu/library/encyclopedia
- Emory University Law School Electronic Reference Desk and Federal Courts Finder, at http://www.law.emory.edu/LAW/refdesk/toc.html
- University of Chicago Law School at http://www.uchicago.edu
- Library of Congress at http://www.loc.gov/ and its *Guide to Law Online* at http://www.loc.gov/law/guide; *Guide to U.S. Law: Federal* at http://www.loc.gov/law/guide/uscode.html; and *Guide to U.S. Law: States and Territories* at http://www.loc.gov/law/guide/usstates.html
- Washburn University Law School at http://www.washlaw.edu (This is a wonderful site! It includes AALS information, and much, much more law-related information.)
- Hieros Gamos (Lex Mundi) at http://www.hg.org (This site aims toward being a comprehensive law site.)
- American Bar Association *LAWlink: ABA Legal Research Starting Points* page at http://www.abanet.org/lawlink/home.html
- Internet Legal Research Group (ILRG) at http://www.ilrg.com
- American Law Sources Online (ALSO) at http://www.lawsource.com/also
- FirstGov at http://www.firstgov.gov/Topics/Reference_Shelf.shtml#Laws, with links to U.S. federal and state legal resources
- Yahoo!® Law Links at http://dir.yahoo.com/Government/laws, with subject catalog of the Internet, including many key links

Note that for the full text of recent court decisions and rulings and other documents related to cases, such as complaints, briefs, and so on, a useful Web site is CourtTV's Legal Documents at http://www.courttv.com/archive/legaldocs. Some fee-based services include:

- Westlaw by Credit Card case service at http://creditcard.westlaw.com
- VersusLaw at http://www.versuslaw.com
- Loislaw at http://www.loislaw.com

However, these sites are not as comprehensive as the legal databases, Lexis-Nexis® at http://www.lexisnexis.com and Westlaw® at http://www.westlaw.com.

Internet Keyword Search

You can do a keyword search of Internet sites by using one of the many Internet directories or indexes. Some of my favorite directories with search capabilities are (note that they are extremely useful when looking for nonlaw information also):

- Google™ at http://www.google.com. Google™ dominates the search engine market by enabling users to search the Web, Usenet, and images with features that include caching and translation of results and an option to find similar pages.
- Lycos® at http://www.lycos.com is a great robotic index to Internet Web sites (over 90%)—quick results for keyword searches.
- Yahoo!® at http://www.yahoo.com is a subject catalog and keyword index to the Internet.
- AltaVista® at http://altavista.com is a very popular Internet search engine.
- Topica: Email Lists Made Easy at http://lists.topica.com.
- Tile.net™ at http://tile.net is another "list of lists" but only of lists run by the LISTSERV® and Lyris software.

General Descriptions of and Links to the Internet

General descriptions of and links to these and other Internet search engines are available at the following sites:

- Yahoo!® at http://dir.yahoo.com/Computers_and_Internet/Internet/World_Wide_Web/Searching_the_Web/Search_Engines_and_Directories
- University of Chicago at http://www.lib.uchicago.edu/e/net

E-Mail Lists

You can browse or do a word search through the several public listserv and e-journal archives that exist to find answers to your question or to see if your topic has been discussed before. Specifically, they are:

- Yahoo!® Groups: Law at http://dir.groups.yahoo.com/dir/Government__Politics/Law
- LegalMinds at http://www.legalminds.com has archives of hundreds of law-related electronic discussion groups and also provides a free service from FindLaw® for starting your own discussion group/mailing list (at http://www.egroups.com).
- Washburn archives many lists at http://lists.washlaw.edu/mailman/listinfo.
- American Bar Association has list archives at http://mail.abanet.org/archives/index.html.

You can ask for help in finding useful Internet resources by posting a message to one of the many law-related lists that exist. You can identify a relevant list by searching Lyo's *Law Lists* at http://www.lib.uchicago.edu/cgi-bin/law-lists. Other lists of interest include the following:

- AALSMIN-L: Discussion list of the Section on Minority Groups of the Association of American Law Schools. Send the following e-mail message to *listserv@ube.ubalt.edu*: subscribe aalsmin-l Your Name Institution.
- COC-L: Clinicians of Color in Law Schools. Send the following message to *listserv@ube.ubalt.edu*: subscribe coc-l Your Name (school).

- LATINO-LAW-PROFS: Latino Law Professors Communication List. Send the following message to *listproc@ucdavis.edu*: subscribe latino-law-profs Your Name.
- MINLAW-L: Law School Experiences of Minorities. Send the following message to *listserv@listserv.uark.edu*: subscribe minlaw-l Your Name.
- TRIBALLAW: Tribal Law forum for discussion of laws and policy affecting Native Americans in North America. Send the following message to *listserv@niec.net*: subscribe triballaw Your Name.
- YLOPEARL: Asian Pacific American Law Professors Discussion Group. Send the following message to *listserv@listserv.syr.edu*: subscribe ylopearl Your Name.
- IMMPROF: Immigration Law Professors List. Send the following message to *listproc@lists.colorado.edu*: subscribe immprof Your Name.
- MIDWSTPOCCONF: Midwestern People of Color Legal Scholarship Conference (subscription is subject to approval of list owner). Send the following message to *listserv@assocdir.wuacc.edu*: subscribe midwstpocconf Your Name.
- NNALSA: National Native American Law Students Association. Send the following message to *listserv@listserv.arizona.edu*: subscribe nnalsa Your Name.
- RPOCLSC: Regional People of Color Legal Scholarship Conferences list; restricted to people of color in legal education, particularly those who attended a legal scholarship conference; subscribe by contacting Professor Vernellia Randall.
- LAWPROF: Law Professors and Lecturers. Send the following message to *listserv@chicagokent.kentlaw.edu*: subscribe lawprof Your Name.
- AFFAM-L: Affirmative Action list. Send the following message to *listserv@cmsa.berkeley.edu*: subscribe affam-l Your Name.
- AFAM-INTL: Forum for African-Americans in academia and business and law to discuss international issues. Send the following message to *listproc@u.washington.edu*: subscribe afam-intl Your Name.
- NET-LAWYERS: Lawyers and the Internet. Send the following message to *listserv@peach.ease.lsoft.com*: subscribe net-lawyers Your Name.
- CLNET: Chinese Law Net: Send the following message to *listproc@u.washington.edu*: subscribe clnet Your Name.
- ASIA-LAW: Canada-based Asian Law List. Send the following message to *majordomo@unixg.ubc.ca*: subscribe asia-law.
- AALLC: List of the Asian American Law Librarians Caucus of the American Association of Law Libraries. Send the following message to *listserv@ftplaw.wuacc.edu*: subscribe aallc Your Name.
- BLACK-LIB: List of the African American/Black Law Librarians Caucus of the American Association of Law Libraries. Send the following message to *listserv@houston.law.howard.edu*: subscribe black-lib Your Name.
- LAW-LIB: Law Librarians (mainly United States). Send the following message to *listproc@ucdavis.edu*: subscribe law-lib Your Name.
- INT-LAW: Foreign, Comparative, and International Law Librarians. Send the following message to *majordomo@listhost.ciesin.org*: subscribe int-law.

- EURO-LEX: All EUROpean Legal Information Exchange. Send the following message to *listserv@listserv.gmd.de*: subscribe euro-lex Your Name.

Electronic News Sources: Usenet Newsgroups and Internet Listservs

News, Weather, & Sports (University of Chicago) at http://www.lib.uchicago.edu/e/law/news includes extensive links to worldwide news sources on the Internet. *See also* ClariNet e-News subscription service at http://www.clarinet.com (see, for instance, clari.news.blacks, clari.news.crime.hate, clari.news.immigration, clari.news.minorities.misc, clari.news.issues.death_penalty, clari.usa.law.supreme, clari.world.*, etc.).

General Usenet Newsgroups for Current Awareness are available on the Internet at

- http://groups-beta.google.com/group/soc.culture.african.american
- http://groups-beta.google.com/group/soc.culture.asian.american
- http://groups-beta.google.com/group/soc.culture.mexican.american

Law Journals, Magazines, Newsletters

The Internet is awash in law-related journals, magazines, and newsletters. Many of the resources are in full text. For instance:

- The *African-American Law and Policy Report* (University of California – Berkeley (Boalt Hall Law School)) is at http://www.boalt.org/ALPR.
- *Asian Law Journal* (University of California – Berkeley) is at http://www.asianlawjournal.org.
- The *Michigan Journal of Race & Law* is at http://students.law.umich.edu/mjrl/index.htm.
- The *Journal of Gender, Race and Justice* (University of Iowa College of Law) is at http://www.law.uiowa.edu/journals/grj.
- The *American Indian Law Review* (AILR, The University of Oklahoma Law Center) is at http://www.law.ou.edu/lawrevs/ailr.
- The *National Black Law Journal* (University of California at Los Angeles) is at http://www.law.columbia.edu/current_student/student_service/Law_Journals/black_law.
- The *University Law Review Project* (a service of FindLaw® and the Coalition of Online Law Journals) is at http://www.lawreview.org.
- *Law Journals* (Washburn University Law School) has links to journals on the Internet, and includes a full-text index, at http://www.washlaw.edu/lawjournal.
- The *Legal and Law-Related Journals* are indexed at http://www.hg.org/journals.html (Lex Mundi's Hieros Gamos Web site).
- LexisNexis®/Anderson Publishing Co.'s *On-Line Directory of Law Reviews and Scholarly Legal Periodicals* provides a list of addresses, phone numbers, and fax numbers and is available at http://www.lexisnexis.com/lawschool/prodev/lawreview.

How to Keep Track of New Internet Legal Resources

The following sites are useful to find out about new Internet resources related to law (other than the ones listed in C. Burgess Allison's guide (previously listed) and the INT-LAW and NET-LAWYERS lists):

- The Virtual Chase electronic research news alert (TVC Alert) service, at http://www.virtualchase.com/TVCAlert/index.html
- InSITE-L: the Cornell University Law Library's electronic newsletter for announcements of key Internet resources at http://www.lawschool.cornell.edu/lawlibrary/Finding_the_Law/insite.html
- Site-tation: the American Bar Association's legal resources announcements list, archived at http://www.abanet.org/tech/ltre/site-tation/home.html
- Law Library Resource Xchange (LLRX): links to law and technology resources for legal professionals at http://www.llrx.com

Tips for the Net-Traveling Researcher

Always consult local resources first. These could be your institution's own Internet resources (Web, gopher, etc.), librarian, catalog, expert in the area you are researching, and so on. Finding answers in resources nearby can save you time and money. It can be more efficient than Internet research; sometimes what you are looking for may not be available on or from Internet resources. This tip is particularly valuable when using Internet listservs; you do not want to post to a list a request for information without first asking people locally if they have the information. It may make your institution or your colleagues look bad or not up to snuff. There may actually be a resource locally that could help.

Try to develop an approach to research using the Internet. Become familiar with a few sites and search engines. It is always good to know what Web site to use to begin your search and, if that site does not hold an answer to your question, what search engine to use to find relevant sites. If you do not know how to approach getting an answer to your research question, ask your librarian for help. Never rely completely on Internet resources. They are useful complements to print and electronic resources and can sometimes be the only place to find a needed document, but the Internet does not have all needed law resources. There are still some gaps in what is available on the Internet for legal research, and there may continue to be gaps. Have alternative plans for finding the information you need, just in case, especially if you are in urgent need of the information.

Other Guides to Legal Research Using the Internet

The following Web pages contain useful information on researching the law using Internet resources:

- *Finding Law-Related Internet Resources,* by Cindy Chick, is at the Law Library Resource Xchange at http://www.llrx.com/sources.html.
- *Legal Research FAQ* is Mark Eckenwiler's guide to print sources for American legal research at http://www.faqs.org/faqs/law/research.

- *Factbooks About the American Legal System* (American Bar Association Division for Media Relations and Public Affairs), including factbooks in pdf format on the American Judicial System, Women and the Law, Law and the Elderly, Children and the Law, and the American Criminal Justice System, are available at http://www.abanet.org/media/factbooks/home.html.
- *Legal Research: On Paper and Online* (Nolo Press guide) is at http://www.nolo.com/ChunkLR/LR.index.html.
- *The Practicing Attorney's Home Page* (Peter Krakaur) is at http://www.legalethics.com/index.law.
- *The Internet Lawyer* (Josh Blackman), which has links to *How to Find Anything on the Net, Fact-Finding Research, Cool Sites for Lawyers,* and *Legal Research* on the Internet generally, is at http://www.mddailyrecord.com/newsletters/internetlawyer/pub.

Special Topics

Special topical resources and sites follow:

- Race, Health Care and the Law at http://academic.udayton.edu/health
- Race, Racism and the Law at http://academic.udayton.edu/race
- Gender and the Law at http://academic.udayton.edu/gender

Organizations and Universities

Organizations and universities are on the Internet as well. For example:

- MWPOC: Midwestern People of Color Legal Scholarship Conference is at http://www.unl.edu/ashavers/mwpoc.htm.
- NBLSA: National Black Law Students Association is at http://www.nblsa.org.
- NAPABA: National Asian Pacific American Bar Association is at http://www.napaba.org.
- NAPALC: National Asian Pacific American Legal Consortium is at http://www.napalc.org.
- NAPALSA: National Asian Pacific American Law Students Association is at http://www.napalsa.org.
- AALDEF: Asian American Legal Defense & Education Fund is at http://www.aaldef.org.

Faculty Homepages

Finally, faculty pages are more and more available over the Internet. These are a few exemplary sites:

- Vernellia R. Randall is at http://law.udayton.edu/NR/exeres/34A198E3–086D-4F85-B251-E28D13C206FD.htm.
- Anna Shavers is at http://www.unl.edu/lawcoll/fac-shavers.html.
- JURIST: Legal News & Research is at http://jurist.law.pitt.edu.

CONCLUSION

It is possible to be overwhelmed by the myriad of resources available on the Internet (and in print and electronic formats generally). It is amazing how much law-related information is published! A good approach is to have a research plan. If you are uncertain where to begin, ask your librarian, a colleague, or someone else who might be familiar with your legal research topic. Remember that sometimes the fun stuff on the Internet not only is useful for taking a break in work, but also can help you become more efficient, familiar, and comfortable with using resources on the Internet for legal research. So explore anything you are interested in. And have fun!

DISCUSSION QUESTIONS

1. Given the immense number of law-related Internet sites, how do you decide which resources to visit and where to search?
2. Which particular sites, out of all these cited by Lyonette Louis-Jacques, would you recommend to your associates and/or employer?
3. You are assigned to the legal team on the new multimillion-dollar lawsuit that concerns a contract that went bad with a Chinese (People's Republic of China) commercial entity. The attorneys are wanting to receive regularly updated information on developments in China. Which of Ms. Louis-Jacques's cited resources would you suggest to them for this purpose?

PROJECTS

1. Sign up to the Net-Lawyers: Lawyers and the Internet e-mail list.
2. Sign up to Site-tation, the American Bar Association's legal resources announcements list.

CHAPTER 6

Searching in Legal Databases on the Internet

Linda M. Furlet

Craig B. Simonsen

SUMMARY

This chapter reviews the use of legal research databases, including preliminary planning for a CALR session; searching for legal documents; entry and modification of the search statement; retrieval and use of search results; determining which CALR database is the best to use; and using LEXIS®, Westlaw®, and Loislaw™.

OBJECTIVES

- The student will learn about legal research databases.
- The student will learn how to plan for a CALR session.
- The student will learn how to search for legal documents, including entry and modification of the search statement and retrieval and use of search results.
- The student will learn about which CALR database is the best to use.
- The student will be introduced to LEXIS®, Westlaw®, and/or Loislaw™, and will get to have some hands-on practice with those systems (to the extent that they are available at the student's school).

Searching in Legal Databases

These days, without leaving the office, a CALR researcher can search through what seems like an infinite volume of documents and information contained in Internet-accessible legal databases. A search in an Internet legal database can save countless hours of manual research time in the law library. The Internet legal database is in essence an electronic law library.

Even as little as five years ago, legal researchers were required to manually search through sometimes wholly inadequate law libraries or were required to sign up for costly monthly and access fees to search through proprietary computer databases for needed legal documents and treaties. Now, through the Internet, CALR researchers have point-and-click access to vast sources of information, including legal databases. While access fees are still charged, users now have choices for payments and may select one-time charges to credit cards. Even attorneys in solo practices and smaller firms can find information needed to enhance arguments and build great cases without the expenditure of significant time or money that may have, in the past, otherwise been required in the collection of support information. In this chapter, several of the legal databases are discussed, while free Web sites are reviewed in other chapters.

With the publication of so much searchable material on the Internet, one may be strongly tempted to forego the cost of searching on legal databases. Indeed, the Internet has already had the happy effect of lowering the cost of legal research. Most court documentation cannot, by law, bear a copyright, so anyone can upload it to the Internet without fear of copyright violation.

Legal databases, however, bring to the table their timeliness. Because they are, primarily, subscription-based, their revenues support staff that keep their information up to date. A free service, such as many of the legal resource sites now found on the Internet, depends on the goodwill of the site's Web master to keep it fresh and timely. This is why many of the best sites are government, university, and school affiliated. Remember, though, that when it is free, it is a labor of love, and updating is performed when the Web master has time.

Legal Databases

Legal databases provide researchers with extensive libraries of case law, statutes, journals, annotations, and other legal source material. All of this information is stored in full-text format, allowing for comprehensive search queries.

In addition to factual and law-related research, the online legal databases provide a great resource for working with case law. For instance, legal briefs and motions prepared during the term of a proceeding often cite too many, if not tens and hundreds of cases. Computer-aided legal research professionals are well tooled to assist with this massive citing to case law in two ways. First, the legal databases make the retrieval of multiple, full-text cases an easy process. Second, the cites to case law and case law quotations are also easily checked for correctness and for case status (such as "overruled") automatically. These tools are reviewed in more detail subsequently.

There are numerous legal databases available over the Internet, although these are primarily fee-based services. The two primary legal database services are LEXIS® and Westlaw®. Also, Loislaw™ is a competing service available at many law and paralegal schools.

Preliminary Planning for a CALR Session

To get the most out of a CALR session and to minimize online fees, prepare and formulate a query before signing onto a legal database. The preliminary steps for preparing a CALR session follow:

- Understand the nature of the case that is being researched, and formulate its issues. Define each issue as narrowly as possible. For this to be possible, it is imperative that the researcher have a concise understanding of the case facts and issues, as well as an understanding of the legal issues that have been identified by the attorneys on the legal team.
- Determine the form of the results wanted from the search (i.e., a quick answer to a question; a printout of all found documents, regardless of their relation to the case; etc.). This simplifies the retrieval of the proper information. For instance, if the legal team just needs a summary of a legal point of law, then a legal memorandum may have to be prepared. Or perhaps the attorneys wish to evaluate the legal documents (such as statutes, regulations, agency polices, and case law) themselves, and so the researcher just needs to find applicable documents and print them.
- Identify all keywords to search for, including synonyms and antonyms. The keywords may be taken directly from the facts and/or issues to be searched. These words often exist in many forms, including plurals, possessives, and derivatives of a common root. Word form is very important. If certain forms of a keyword or certain synonyms or antonyms are overlooked, a significant document may be missed in the query.
- Often, keywords chosen are used in relation to other words. Necessarily, an effective query must identify the relation between words and their variations. The context of words should be thoroughly examined.

After the preceding steps have been performed, a preliminary query can be formulated. The query should be double-checked for accuracy and written out before signing on to the legal database.

Searching for Legal Documents

To search for materials in a legal database on the Internet, start by identifying the keywords and framing your search. A detailed discussion of keywords and their usage in queries is found in Chapter 6.

In searching for legal documents, as a rule, single keywords do not make for effective queries, with the exception of searches for truly unique names or words. So, unless the word is extremely specialized, a single keyword query will usually be too broad and return too many documents. For instance, in a false arrest case, the single keyword "arrest" does not constitute an effective query. On the other hand, by searching for both "false AND arrest," the query will be more productive. Unlike the Internet search engines, generally, the legal databases also search for words within a certain proximity to each other. The "/n" connector performs this function. The "n" element stands for the number of words between the two keywords. "/6" searches for keywords within six words of one another, regardless of their order. For example, *environ! /3 protect!* will search for phrases that contain "environmental" within three words of "protection." Running queries will generate a list that contains all the documents meeting the requirements of the query.

Many additional search variations are available on the legal databases. It is, generally, possible to query by

- case name,
- reporter number of the case,

- presiding judge,
- attorneys of record, or
- party.

Whether LEXIS® and Westlaw® or Loislaw™, check the particular legal database help search specifications for each service used.

A legal database researcher can query for all cases in which a particular federal judge cited a particular federal case. This type of research is virtually impossible using manual research techniques, but it can be crucial to a case, because it gives the litigator information on how best to construct a legal argument that may receive the judge's favorable review. Such strategic research techniques are limited only by the imagination of the researcher.

The legal database researcher can also modify a query if it has yielded too many cases, through the addition of a modifying conjunction. For instance, the query: *search and seizure w/20 "probable cause"* may yield several hundred cases, but the query can be modified by adding "and automobile w/10 passenger." The resulting modified query would look like this: *search and seizure w/20 "probable cause" and automobile w/10 passenger*.

The researcher may freely make modifications as necessary but must keep in mind that "the meter is running" and that these are for-fee services. In the middle of a modified search, the researcher can alter the parameters of the search.

While researching a constitutional case involving both federal and state law, a researcher may wish to change from a federal library to a state library to inquire whether a state law gives greater protection than federal law. File changes within libraries are permitted in the middle of a search.

Entry and Modification of the Search

Once the query is prepared, sign onto the legal database and enter the query. For example, go to http://www.westlaw.com, sign on to the service, and then select the appropriate database(s) to search in. The database used for running the search will depend wholly on the information required. For only federal cases, select "Directory," then "U.S. Federal Materials," then "Cases & Judicial Materials," then "All Federal Cases After 1944 (ALLFEDS)." Once the database is selected, the query can be typed into the "Terms and Connectors [[mid]] Natural Language" box.

Be sure to check query syntax against the provider's search help if there is any doubt. When the search is completed, a list of documents or other materials that satisfy the search query is displayed. This list can be printed out for future reference.

If the search results contain too large a number of found documents, the query should be narrowed (selective); or, if the search reaps too few results, the query should be broadened (inclusive). A query can be modified with the addition or deletion of keywords or other elements of the query.

Retrieval and Use of Search Results

The results of a search may be displayed on the screen, printed, or downloaded for later use. Probably the most useful function of legal databases is the retrieval of the full text of legal source materials, as opposed to bibliographic or abstract materials. Full text allows the researcher to determine immediately whether the materials found by the search query are appropriate for the legal problem at hand. This eliminates the further step of looking up text manually.

Due to the increased speed of full-text review, a researcher may stay on line and modify the search query until the most useful materials are found. Computer-aided legal research is similar to manual research in many ways. Manually, a researcher uses a descriptive word index to look up materials in books. However, CALR is much more efficient and flexible than manual research could ever be.

Other Legal Database Tools

As already noted, CALR professionals are able to deal with the often massive citing to case law in briefs and motions in two ways. First, the legal databases make the retrieval of multiple, full-text cases an easy process. Second, the citations to case law and case law quotations are also easily checked for correctness and for case status (such as "overruled") automatically.

WestFind & Print®

WestFind & Print® is found at http://findprint.westlaw.com/Desktop/default.aspx. Use this site to automatically "find" and print (to the printer or to your e-mail as an attachment or to download to Microsoft® Word or to pdf or other options) cited documents very quickly. Of course, the key to the use of this tool is that the case citations must be known for this service to work.

Internet Research Scenario

For this scenario, we are assisting an attorney who is preparing a response to a memorandum in support of a motion for summary judgment. The attorney has provided us with a copy of his draft memorandum and is requesting that all of the cited case law be copied for the senior attorney's review. Here are the case citations we will use:

521 U.S. 203.

523 U.S. 666.

436 P.2d 189.

299 F.3d 748.

Go to http://findprint.westlaw.com/Desktop/default.aspx. On this page, at the "1. Enter Citations" textbox window, type in the preceding citations. In typing the citations, in this instance and also on LEXIS® or Westlaw®, it is not necessary to type in the "." or other spaces in the numerical citation. After each case citation, insert a semicolon and a hard return ("Enter" key).

At the "2. Select Results Options" window, select "Text" and "Full Text Documents."

At the "3. Select Delivery Options" window, select "E-mail" and select "Choose Format: Word." Then type in your e-mail address where the documents will be attached.

Finally, at the "Sign-On Window," type in your Westlaw® password and your "Client I.D." Then hit the "GO" button and watch for your results.

WestCheck Brief Citation Checking Software

While an Internet tool is not available, Westlaw®'s WestCheck® software allows you to automatically check the citations to case law and case law quotations embedded in a brief or memorandum. It also provides indications as to the correctness of the citations and checks on the case status (such as "overruled") with *Shepard's*® Citations when run.

To run the WestCheck® software, the CALR professional must obtain the proprietary software from Westlaw®. Once installed and opened on your computer, the software prompts for a document name or number, which it then reads and extracts all of the cited case law and case quotations. Otherwise, it also allows the user to type in the citation list when the underlying document is not available.

Be sure to review and set up the report display and other options before running WestCheck® so that all of the information that is required is captured on the first run. Options include whether or not to run *Shepard's*®, whether or not to run Auto-Cite®, whether or not to run QuoteCheck™, and whether or not to print the full text of the cases.

Which CALR Database Is the Best?

LEXIS®, Westlaw®, and Loislaw™ each has its own advantages and disadvantages. The choice of one over the other is usually personal preference rather than clear superiority, or it may involve a cost decision. Generally, there is no consensus in the legal profession that one legal database is "better" than another.

That said, however, every once in a while, the authors find themselves finding one document on one legal database service—such as LEXIS®—that is not found on any of the others. So, suffice it to say, if something is not found on LEXIS®, look on Westlaw®, and vice versa.

Several other factors may also sway a choice of legal database. For instance,

- the kind of legal research that is usually performed,
- the need for specific libraries,
- the billing method of the database service, and
- even the smile on the customer representative's face (or voice).

In one admittedly biased analysis, Figure 6-1 provides an illustrative comparison between LEXIS® and Westlaw®, the two primary CALR databases.

Comparing Westlaw®
and LexisNexis® Features

Moving from lexis.com to westlaw.com® doesn't mean that you have to relearn research skills. You'll find similar features and services in westlaw.com, along with powerful new resources. The following list includes commonly used Westlaw® tools and their LexisNexis® equivalents, where available.

Signing on

westlaw.com	lexis.com
My Sign On	Custom ID
My Westlaw®	Add/Edit tabs
Change Client ID	Enter Client
Westlaw® Options	Options

Retrieving a Document

westlaw.com	lexis.com
Find a Document	Get a Document
Find by Title	Get by Party Name

Searching for Information

westlaw.com	lexis.com
Customizable Tabbed Pages	*no equivalent*
Find a Person Wizard	*no equivalent*
Find a Company Wizard	*no equivalent*
Find a Database Wizard	*no equivalent*
Westlaw® Directory	Sources
Scope (detailed information about a database)	Source Information
Recent Databases list	Last 20 Sources
Favorite Databases list	*no equivalent*
Terms and Connectors search method	Terms and Connectors search method
Natural Language search method	Natural Language search method
Control Concepts (for Natural Language searching)	Mandatory Terms
KeySearch®	Search Advisor
Custom Digest	*no equivalent*
Table of Contents service	*no equivalent*
Research Trail	History

Viewing Results

westlaw.com	lexis.com
Result List	Cite
ResultsPlus™	*no equivalent*
Full-text document display	Full

Figure 6-1 "Comparing Westlaw® and LexisNexis® Features.
Thanks to Susan Hyser, attorney and Westlaw® account manager, for this analysis. Information current as of Mar.1, 2004. Reprinted with permission of Thomson/West.

Viewing Results, continued

westlaw.com	lexis.com
Split-Page view and Full-Page view	*no equivalent*
West Key Number System®	*no equivalent*
West synopsis	Case summaries
West headnotes	LexisNexis® headnotes (Core Concepts)
Term arrows	Term arrows
Best arrows (available from Natural Language search result)	Term arrows
Locate in Result	FOCUS
Edit Search	Edit Search
Documents in Sequence	Book Browse
Link Viewer	*no equivalent*

Checking Citations

westlaw.com	lexis.com
KeyCite®	*Shepard's®* Citations Service
KeyCite status flags	*Shepard's* Signals
KeyCite depth of treatment stars	*no equivalent*
KeyCite quotation marks	*no equivalent*
KeyCite Notes®	*no equivalent*
Table of Authorities	*Shepard's* Table of Authorities

Staying Current

westlaw.com	lexis.com
KeyCite Alert	*no equivalent*
WestDocket Alert	*no equivalent*
Profiler Alert	*no equivalent*
WestClip®	ECLIPSE

Delivering Information

westlaw.com	lexis.com
Print Doc	*FAST* Print
Print/Deliver Manager	Delivery Manager
Copy with Reference	Copy with Cite

This document is current through March 1, 2004. There may be recent changes to the interface and functionality of Westlaw or LexisNexis that are not reflected in this documentation.

Figure 6-1 "Comparing Westlaw® and LexisNexis® Features—*Continued.*
Thanks to Susan Hyser, attorney and Westlaw® account manager, for this analysis. Information current as of Mar.1, 2004. Reprinted with permission of Thomson/West.

These features and services may change, but the key aspect to consider is that each legal database service provides different information and documents presented in different ways. In the end, for the legal researcher, it is important to try each service and then, for each research project, choose the resource that best fits the needs of the project and the researcher's preferences.

LEXIS®

LEXIS® was the first widely available legal database. It is very large and allows users to search for information by specifying keywords. The Web site for LEXIS® is located at http://www.lexis.com.

LEXIS® has developed numerous libraries in specialized areas of law, including:

- A *federal library* that contains federal case law, the *Code of Federal Regulations* (C.F.R.), Supreme Court briefs, the *Federal Register*, and the *United States Code* (U.S.C.)
- A *state library* containing case, statutory, and administrative law from all U.S. territories and the fifty states
- Specialized libraries on subjects such as tax, bankruptcy, intellectual property, foreign law, trade regulations, and so on
- A *general library*, called NEXIS, containing supplementary information such as magazines, newspapers, wire services, and newsletters

LEXIS® also allows the researcher to check the validity of case law in several ways. *Shepardizing* is available to follow the citation of a case through later opinions. The Auto-Cite® function allows a researcher to check whether a case has been overruled. Document lists provided by Auto-Cite® will provide references from the ALR library and all cases in which the case citation appears.

Using Lexis.com

LEXIS® provides several options for selecting a particular database or law source to search

- by choosing from a database that you recently used,
- by typing in the database identifier, or
- by exploring sources through browsing the directory and particular topics listings.

After selecting a source, a search box appears on the screen. One advantage of LEXIS® is its "Natural Language" query. That allows a phrase or a "natural" sentence to be typed and queried rather than using the old-fashioned terms and connectors. For instance, with a "Natural Language" search, the query might look like this:

> I'm looking for CERCLA case law where there is a question as to the generator's liability because of a statute of limitation argument

Whereas, with terms and connectors, the query statement might look like this:

> CERCLA AND generator! /5 liability /30 "statute of limitation"

LEXIS® also offers the Search Advisor for finding legal materials based on a classification system of substantive law areas. The researcher may choose a legal topic from the last twenty selected, find a topic, or explore legal topics and subtopics arranged in a hierarchical manner. The researcher may also narrow the range of the Search Advisor by selecting a jurisdiction, selecting Terms and Connectors or Natural Language search techniques, narrowing the search to specified types of legal materials, or narrowing the date by date range.

On LEXIS®, a query returns results in one of three ways:

1. A citation list
2. The search terms surrounded by twenty-five words of content (term mode)
3. Full text

After the researcher completes the search, it can be saved to be rerun at a later time. Or, the searcher may narrow the query to refine the search result or to find documents with similar citation or language patterns. You may print or download the found document(s) to disk, fax, e-mail, or printer.

Internet Research Scenario

In this instance, there was an April 5, 2001, U.S. District Court (N.D. Ala.) opinion (*United States v. Mountain Metal;* and *Exide Corp. v. Aaron Scrap Metal*) that was not available on the Court's Web site. Was it obtainable anywhere else? This time, we will look for it on LEXIS®.

Go to http://www.lexis.com. Select the link for "Log In Now." Fill in the sign-on I.D. and password for online access.

From the main research page, first select "Federal Legal - U.S.," then "U.S. District Court Cases." Then, an "Enter Search Terms" screen opens. Search for the case title keywords and restrict the date to April of 2001.

In this case we searched for: (mountain /3 metal or excide /6 aaron) and Date(is 04/2001)

The query located the wanted opinion at *United States v. Mountain Metal Co.*, 2001 U.S. Dist. LEXIS 4610 (April 5, 2001).

Westlaw®

West published legal volumes before it developed its legal database and, accordingly, uses the same key number system that its legal books use. Westlaw® is a very large, comprehensive legal database that allows users to search for information by specifying keywords. The Web site for Westlaw® is located at http://www.westlaw.com.

Westlaw®'s Web site is a fully functional and comprehensive legal resource that harnesses the research power, quality, accuracy, and depth and breadth of content found in the traditional Westlaw® database research through its proprietary software. Users can navigate the Web site content using their browsers and can print documents in a two-column format for easier reading.

The Westlaw® Directory is an online index of Westlaw® databases and services. The directory is organized into categories, including source (state and federal), topical (practice area), and the type of material (treatises, law reviews, etc.). On the Database Directory page, select a folder in the right frame to view its subdirectories. Continue selecting subdirectories until the database wanted is displayed.

Select the database, such as ALLFEDS (the database identifier), to search that database. Researchers may also search a database or multiple databases recently used by selecting the "Recent Databases" folder. Researchers may also browse popular databases by selecting the Popular Databases folder. If a document's citation is known, the researcher may select "Find a Document" from the drop-down list at the top of the page. Type the citation in the "Enter Citation" text box, and select GO. For questions about the correct citation format, simply type the database abbreviation or publication abbreviation (*i.e.*, F. Supp.) to display a fill-in-the-blank template.

Internet Research Scenario

As an illustration[1] of the fill-in-the-blank template, we will retrieve Section 203 of the California Family Code.

First, go to http://www.westlaw.com, and sign on to the service.

From the main research page, select "Find a Document" from the drop-down list at the top of the page and select GO.

Then, type *ca st* in the "Enter Citation" text box, and select GO.

The citation formats for California Statutes are displayed in the right frame.

In the text box following "CA FAM s" type *203* and click GO.

The documents retrieved are listed in the left frame of the browser. Click the number in front of a citation to view the document.

Westlaw® Data Enhancements

Westlaw® provides editorial enhancements to its data, such as case synopses, headnotes, and codenotes. Westlaw® attorney-editors supplement facts, issues, procedural history, courts, judges, major holdings, and disposition of the case in a concise synopsis. In headnotes, Westlaw® attorney-editors summarize points of law contained in cases along with relevant supporting facts and statutes. Westlaw®'s new codenotes section, which appears just below the headnotes, summarizes the judicial treatment of statutes within a case. The terms listed in Westlaw®'s case synopses, headnotes, and codenotes increase the researcher's ability to find relevant cases.

Every point of law contained in every case in Westlaw®'s National Reporter System is classified under one of the 400+ digest topics in the West Key Number

---

[1] This illustration is from the Westlaw® Web site search help FAQs. Used with permission. Copyright © 2000, West Group. All rights reserved.

System®. Within each digest topic, every point of law is assigned one of approximately 100,000 key numbers. The key number system enables beginners to a field to very quickly review and digest the leading case law related to a topic.

Westlaw® integrates all cases and statutes, as well as selected administrative materials, into its KeyCite®, a citation research service.

Loislaw™

In January 2001, Loislaw.com™ became a wholly owned subsidiary of Aspen Publishers of Gaithersburg, Maryland. Aspen Publishers is a provider of legal, business, and health care information.

Loislaw™ publishes case law, statutory law, constitutions, administrative law, court rules, and other authority for all fifty states and the District of Columbia plus an "18 federal law libraries" database. All Loislaw™ law libraries are exact duplications of the official law.

Collectively, these libraries contain more than 10 million documents. Unlimited access to this entire collection is available on the Internet in the LOIS Professional Library® National Collection. Loislaw™ also contains a citation research service that is available as part of the regular subscription price. No more additional charges for citation checking! This is a definite plus over LEXIS® and Westlaw®. While not as striking or glamorous to use as LEXIS® or Westlaw®, Loislaw™ is less pricey. If case law is what is needed, then Loislaw™ may fit the bill.

CONCLUSION

These days, without leaving the office, a researcher can search through millions of legal documents contained in legal databases. A search in a legal database can save countless hours of manual research time in the law library because the legal database is, in essence, an electronic law library. Through the Internet, researchers have point-and-click access to vast sources of information, including legal databases. Even attorneys in smaller practices can find information needed to enhance arguments and build great cases without the expenditure of significant time or money that may have, in the past, otherwise been required in the collection of support information.

Numerous legal databases are available over the Internet, although these are primarily fee-based services. The two primary legal database services are LEXIS® and Westlaw®. Loislaw™ is a competing service that is available at many law and paralegal schools. Use of one or the other legal databases depends on what the researcher is looking for and the goals of the project. Each of the services has unique benefits that may be sought at some point.

DISCUSSION QUESTIONS

1. If you have access to the legal databases, try the research assignments we have discussed on each of the legal databases. What differences and similarities did you notice? Which legal database service did you like the best or find the easiest to use?

2. When, if ever, would you recommend the use of a free legal resource, such as Findlaw.com, over a legal database for a research assignment?

3. Are the legal databases only good for the "law," or do they contain sources of factual materials too? If so, illustrate your answer with several examples.

PROJECTS

1. Prepare a keyword search for the following facts/issues to be researched:

   > Our client, Smither's Grocery Store in Springfield, Missouri, employed Joe Johnson on a full-time basis to be Santa Claus for children visiting the store during the Christmas season. It was an employment-at-will. On December 4, 1998, while on a lunch break off the premises of the store, while still in his Santa Claus costume, Johnson accosted and battered an eight-year-old child who was bothering Johnson. The question is, then, Is Smither's Grocery Store going to have any (perceived or real) liability for Johnson's behavior during working hours and while wearing his working clothes?

2. Check the citations for a brief or memorandum provided by your instructor using the WestCheck® software.

CHAPTER 7

General Sources of Topical Internet Resources

SUMMARY

This chapter reviews general resources that provide directories and links to various topical materials.

OBJECTIVES

- The student will learn about general sources of topical materials.
- The student will learn how to use general sources of topical materials.

General Sources of Topical Materials

Computer-aided legal research in the topical law areas is getting easier all the time. Following are general resources that provide directories and links to various topical materials. Beginning with Chapter 9, there is a focus on particular topical and practice area Internet sites, such as alternative dispute resolution, criminal, immigration, and so on. Many of these sites provide ready access to practice area documents and information.

In this chapter, Web sites listed are those materials that are general and applicable to all or many of the practice areas. For example, federal regulations are critical to knowing and understanding the topical areas, such as environmental, immigration, labor and employment, tax, and so on. The Web sites that follow are links to those types of materials or links that are constant or similar across the practice areas, and some also critical to them.

Internet Research Scenario

One of our health-care clients called the team attorney and asked about a *Wall Street Journal* article about a Health and Human Services (HHS) Department federal rule—published just today—concerning "pregnant women and human fetuses as research subjects and pertaining to human in-vitro fertilization." The attorney told our client that we would find a copy of the rule and forward it ASAP. In the "old days," this meant, in many cases, waiting days or weeks until the firm received the day's *Federal Register* in the mail. Today, though, the

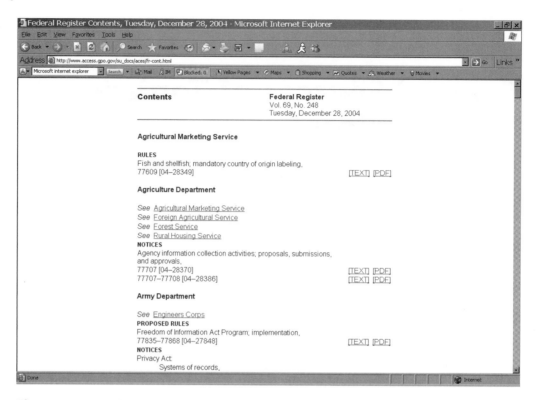

Figure 7-1 *Federal Register's* Daily Table of Contents.

attorney e-mails the team paralegal and asks that a "pdf" copy of the rule be sent to him (the attorney) right away.

To find today's *Federal Register* documents, we would use the "Daily Table of Contents." A screenshot of the "Daily Table of Contents" homepage is shown in Figure 7-1.

> Go to the *Federal Register's* Daily Table of Contents at http://www.access.gpo.gov/su_docs/aces/fr-cont.html. Scroll down the page until the rule is found, or use "Find" (in Microsoft® Internet Explorer®: <Ctrl>-<F>) to go directly to the reference.
>
> Select the "pdf" format and save it to a local disk drive or to your "Desktop." Then attach the saved file to an e-mail to the team attorney.

General Resources for Topical and Practice Area Materials

In the following table of general resources for topical and practice areas, links are sorted in alphabetical order, except that "key" federal sites are listed first and then other sites are listed. After selecting a site, type the Internet address (the URL), shown in the left column of the listing, into the browser software to get to the Internet site.

General Resources for Topical and Practice Area Materials

Code of Federal Regulations (C.F.R.) http//www.gpoaccess.gov/cfr/index.html	This site provides an online, keyword-searchable version of the C.F.R.
Federal Register (F.R. or Fed. Reg.) http://www.gpoaccess.gov/fr/index.html	This site provides an online, keyword-searchable version of the F.R.
Federal Register, Daily Table of Contents http://www.access.gpo.gov/su_docs/aces/fr-cont.html	The U.S. Government Printing Office makes available the daily *Federal Register* on line. This is a boon for those needing immediate copies of notices and rulemaking, as the paper copy of the *Federal Register* is often days behind the electronic version, which is available the day of publication.
FirstGov.gov™[1] http://www.firstgov.gov	This site is "the first-ever government Web site to provide the public with easy, one-stop access to all online U.S. Federal Government resources." "FirstGov allows users to browse a wealth of information—everything from researching at the Library of Congress to tracking a NASA mission. . . ."
U.S. Government Information Locator Service http://www.access.gpo.gov/su_docs/gils/gils.html	"The Government Information Locator Service (GILS) is essentially a card catalog. It identifies public information resources throughout the U.S. Federal Government, describes the information available in those resources, and provides assistance in obtaining the information. . . ."

Other Sites

FindLaw®[2] http://www.findlaw.com	This is "the leading Web portal focused on law and government." It provides access to a comprehensive and fast-growing online library of legal resources.

(continued)

---

[1] FirstGov.gov™ is the U.S. government's official Web portal.
[2] Copyright © 1994–2005, FindLaw, a Thomson business.

Internet Legal Research Group™³ http://www.ilrg.com	This site provides categorized indexes of thousands of select Web sites, in addition to more than 850 locally stored Web pages and downloadable files.
LexisNexis®⁴ Legal Web Site Directory http://www.lexisone.com/ legalresearch/legalguide/practice_ areas/practice_areas_index.htm	The LexisNexis® Group has done a nice job collecting topical Internet sites. Links include practice area Web sites.
Meta-Index for U.S. Legal Research http://gsulaw.gsu.edu/metaindex	This site provides a good starting place for legal research with links to other helpful sites.
State Administrative Codes⁵ http://www.nass.org/acr	This is a linking index to state sites that provide Internet access to administrative rules.
Topical Law Lists Directory http://www.lib.uchicago.edu/ cgi-bin/law-lists	This is a keyword-searchable form for finding lists and newsgroups in law topics.

CONCLUSION

The Web sites presented in the preceding table provide directories and links to various general sources of topical materials. The Web sites are applicable to all or many of the topical practice areas.

DISCUSSION QUESTIONS

1. Use several of these resources to find information in the health-care practice area. What sorts of information and documents were found in the research?
2. What about the same sort of information at the state government level?
3. How important are these materials (e.g., laws, regulations) to the topical practices?

PROJECTS

1. Locate and print out a copy of an agency notice from today's *Federal Register.*
2. Find and print a chapter list/index to the *Florida Administrative Code.*

---

³ Copyright © 1995–2005, Internet Legal Research Group. A product of Maximilian Ventures LLC.
⁴ Copyright © 2005, LexisNexis, a division of Reed Elsevier Inc. All rights reserved.
⁵ Copyright © 2004, Administrative Codes and Registers.

CHAPTER 8

Evaluating Internet Resources and Information*

Elizabeth E. Kirk

SUMMARY

This chapter discusses the evaluation of materials found on the Internet. It provides an outline of the things that should be evaluated and suggests weights that can be given to different types of materials.

OBJECTIVE

- The student will learn to examine Internet materials based on a review of: authorship, publishing body, point of view or bias, referral to other sources and/or knowledge of the literature, verifiability, and currency of the information.

"Let the Reader Beware"

The World Wide Web offers students, teachers, and researchers the opportunity to find information and data from all over the world. The Web is deceptively attractive, both for finding information and for publishing it electronically. Because so much information is available, and because that information can appear to be fairly "anonymous," it is necessary to develop skills to evaluate what you find. When you use a research or academic library, scholars, publishers, and librarians have already evaluated the books, journals, and other resources. Every resource you find has been evaluated in one way or another before you ever see it. When you are using the World Wide Web, none of this applies. There are no filters. Because anyone can write a Web page, documents of the widest range of quality, written by authors of the widest range of authority, are available on an "even playing field." Excellent resources reside alongside the most dubious. The Internet epitomizes the concept of *Caveat lector: Let the reader beware*. This document discusses the criteria by which scholars in most

---

*Chapter 8 is based on *Evaluating Information Found on the Internet* and *Practical Steps in Evaluating Internet Resources*, both written by and copyright © of Elizabeth E. Kirk, Electronic and Distance Education Librarian, Milton S. Eisenhower Library, at the Johns Hopkins University in Baltimore, Maryland (1996). Used with permission.

fields evaluate print information and shows how the same criteria can be used to assess information found on the Internet. Numerous other such papers and discussions about "how to" and "why to" evaluate Internet information may also be found on the Internet.[1]

Before You Use or Copy Any Type of Information . . .

Information is intellectual property, and intellectual property is protected by the law. Do you know and understand the meaning of "copyright"? Chapter 19 provides explanations of fair use (educational and scholarly use of copyrighted information), safe use of Web-based information, protecting your rights and those of authors you quote in your dissertation, and other related questions.

Basic criteria for evaluating all forms of information include being able to identify and verify the value of the following: authorship, publishing body, point of view or bias, referral to other sources, verifiability, and currency. Here is how each of those criteria may be analyzed in an online environment.

Authorship is perhaps the major criterion used in evaluating information: *Who wrote this?* When we look for information with some type of critical value, we want to know the basis of the authority with which the author speaks.

Identifying the *publishing body* also helps evaluate any kind of document you may be reading. In the print universe, this generally means that the author's manuscript has undergone a screening process to verify that it meets the standards or aims of the organization that serves as publisher. This may include peer review.

Point of view or bias is the concept that information is rarely neutral. Because data are used in selective ways to form information, they generally represent a point of view. Every writer wants to prove a point and will use the data and information that assist in doing so. When evaluating information found on the Internet, it is important to examine who is providing the "information" you are viewing and what might be the point of view or bias. The popularity of the Internet makes it the perfect venue for commercial and sociopolitical publishing. These areas in particular are open to highly "interpretative" uses of data.

Steps for evaluating point of view are based on authorship or affiliation:

- First, note the URL of the document. Does this document reside on the Web server of an organization that has a clear stake in the issue at hand?
- If you are looking at a corporate Web site, assume that the information on the corporation will present it in the most positive light.
- If you are looking at products produced and sold by that corporation, remember: you are looking at an advertisement.
- If you are reading about a political figure at the Web site of another political party, you are reading the opposition.

---

[1] *See,* for instance:

- Alastair Smith, *Evaluation of Information Sources, at* http://www.vuw.ac.nz/~agsmith/evaln/evaln.htm.
- The Virtual Chase, *Evaluating the Quality of Information on the Internet, at* http://www.virtualchase.com/quality. Copyright © 1996–2005, Ballard Spahr Andrews & Ingersoll, LLP. All rights reserved.
- John R. Henderson, *ICYouSee: T is for Thinking— The ICYouSee Guide to Critical Thinking About What You See on the Web, at* http://www.ithaca.edu/library/training/think.html.
- Robert Harris, *Evaluating Internet Research Sources, at* http://www.virtualsalt.com/evalu8it.htm. Copyright © 1997, Robert Harris.

- Does this document reside on the Web server of an organization that has a political or philosophical agenda?
- If you were looking for material such as scientific information on human genetics, would you trust a political organization to provide it?

Never assume that extremist points of view are always easy to detect. Some sites promoting these views may look educational. To learn more, read "Rising Tide: Sites Born of Hate" by Michel Marriott (*New York Times,* Mar. 18, 1999, at G1; available on line at http://www.nytimes.com/library/tech/99/02/circuits/articles/18hate.html).

Referral to and knowledge of the literature identify the context in which the author situates his or her work. This reveals what the author knows about his or her discipline and its practices. This allows you to evaluate the author's scholarship or knowledge of trends in the area under discussion. The following criteria serve as a filter for all formats of information:

- The document includes a bibliography.
- The author alludes to or displays knowledge of related sources, with proper attribution.
- The author displays knowledge of theories, schools of thought, or techniques usually considered appropriate in the treatment of his or her subject.
- If the author is using a new theory or technique as a basis for research, he or she discusses the value of or limitations of this new approach.
- If the author's treatment of the subject is controversial, he or she knows and acknowledges this.

Determining *accuracy or verifiability of details* is an important part of the evaluation process, especially when you are reading the work of an unfamiliar author presented by an unfamiliar organization or presented in a nontraditional way. Criteria for evaluating accuracy include the following:

- For a research document, the data that was gathered and an explanation of the research method(s) used to gather and interpret it are included.
- The methodology outlined in the document is appropriate to the topic and allows the study to be duplicated for purposes of verification.
- The document relies on other sources that are listed in a bibliography or includes links to the documents themselves.
- The document names individuals or sources that provided nonpublished data used in the preparation of the study.
- The background information that was used can be verified for accuracy.

Currency refers to the timeliness of information. In printed documents, the date of publication is the first indicator of currency. For some types of information, currency is not an issue: authorship or place in the historical record is more important (e.g., T.S. Eliot's essays on tradition in literature). For many other types of data, however, currency is extremely important, as is the regularity with which the data are updated. Apply the following criteria to ascertain currency:

- The document includes the date(s) at which the information was gathered (e.g., U.S. Census data).
- The document refers to clearly dated information (e.g., "Based on 1990 U.S. Census data").

- Where there is a need to add data or update them on an ongoing basis, the document includes information on the regularity of updates.
- The document includes a publication date or a "last updated" date.
- The document includes a date of copyright.
- If no date is given in an electronic document, you can view the directory in which it resides and read the date of latest modification.

Practical Steps in Evaluating Internet Resources

Of the evaluative criteria just discussed, three can be investigated by electronic means: authorship, publishing body, and currency. *Always remember that there are other, nonelectronic, methods of finding much of the information discussed in this document.* Visit your school's library and ask a librarian for help.

Authorship

What do we need to know about the author? When the author is someone unknown to you, ask the following questions:

- Is the document signed?
- Can I get more information on the author by linking from this page to other documents?
- Was there information about the author on the page from which I linked to this one?

If you can answer "yes" to the second or third questions, it is possible that you will have enough information for evaluative purposes, or at least enough information to help you find the author's telephone number or e-mail address so that you may contact him or her with questions.

If you can answer "yes" only to the first question, you may need to find further information on the author. There are a number of ways in which you might do this:

- Go to the homepage of the Web site where the document lives and search for the author's name using any available internal search engine or directory (works best for academic Web sites). This may help establish affiliation.
- Try searching the author's name by using a search engine. This may lead to other information on or pages by the same author.
- Try using an e-mail address finder. A compendium of finding aids and their comparative value may be found at *FAQ: How to Find People's E-Mail Addresses* by David Alex Lamb, of Queen's University, Ontario, Canada (available on line at http://www.cs.queensu.ca/FAQs/email/finding.html). This is what football fans refer to as a "Hail Mary": you are tossing a search into the unknown in the hope that it finds someone.

These are not ideal means for finding someone's credentials, even though they may help reveal someone's identity. Evaluating information usually consists of weighing a number of criteria together, so you will need to assess how important authorship is on a case-by-case basis. If no information on the author can be found, or there is no signature or attribution on the page itself, think next about the publishing body.

Publishing Body

Where are we in the geography of cyberspace? Look at the Web page you are trying to evaluate. Does it include any of the following?

- A header or footer that shows its affiliation as part of a larger Web site
- A watermark or wallpaper that fulfills the same function
- A link at the bottom or top of the page that allows you to go to the homepage of the Web site where the document lives
- A link that allows you to send a message to the site Web master.

These features help you judge the official character of a Web page. They act as an assurance that the page you are evaluating functions within some type of institutional setting. If the page is not signed, judging the official nature of a Web page is extremely important. Some Web sites do not include attributions to individual authors, so you will have to rely on your ability to evaluate the institution, or domain, where the page lives. *Caveat:* While the Web is looking better, especially official sites maintained at educational institutions or by scholarly societies, not everyone has caught up with the importance of consistent graphics or "return" links. So you may be looking at a perfectly good page that has no visual clues to its affiliation. If this is the case, move on to the next step. If your page gives no clues as to its identity, you will need to focus on the URL or address.

- Can you find the Web site's homepage by deleting all the information in the URL after the server name?
- Can you tell if the page is actually part of someone's personal account, as opposed to being part of an official site?
- If all else fails, can you find information on the server or domain? Try using BetterWhois (http//www.betterwhois.com[2]) to get the name of the owner. BetterWhois should find the identity of a server, as well as contact names and telephone numbers.

Once you find the name of the organization owning the server, you may have enough information to judge its reputation as an information source. Remember, this is only of value for official pages from a Web site. If the page you are evaluating comes from someone's personal account, you really have no idea what his or her place is within the organization or if the person is in a position to represent the organization. If you are not familiar with the organization, try one of the following:

- If it is an association of some kind, look for it at the Scholarly Societies Project (http://www.lib.uwaterloo.ca/society/overview.html[3]). Is it represented?
- For all others, search for the name of the organization using a search engine. Does anyone else have information on it? There are a number of

---

[2] Copyright © 2005, BetterWhois. com, Inc.
[3] Copyright © 2003, University of Waterloo.

very reliable printed directories to organizations, associations, and companies that may be found in your library's reference department. Drop in and talk with your librarian for help using these materials.

If you cannot ascertain either the author or publisher of the page you are trying to evaluate, you are looking at information that is as anonymous as a page torn out of a book. You cannot evaluate what you cannot verify. It is unwise to use information of this nature. Look for another source.

Currency (of the Document Itself)

Even when you can find information on the author and/or publisher of a Web page, you should still consider how "fresh" or "dusty" the document is. This is especially critical if the document discusses time-sensitive information, such as census information or other statistics. Look for internal confirmation of the information:

- Does it use a caption such as "Based on 1990 U.S. Census data"?
- Does it include information within the document such as "Closing stock prices, September 30, 1996"?
- Is the statistical source listed in a bibliography to the page?

If you cannot ascertain where the statistical information comes from or what its age is, you are once again looking at anonymous information.

It is also valuable to know when a page was last updated. Has it been "pruned" or "dusted" lately, or has it been sitting on the shelf?

- Look at the bottom of the page. Does it have a "last updated" date?
- Use the "Document info" feature in the "View" menu on Netscape®. Does it tell you the date?
- Change the URL by backing up to the last slash (/) in the address. This may allow you to see the details of the directory or subdirectory of the server including your page. Usually the last modification date is included.
- Search the title of the page using a search engine that provides the dates of documents archiving within the search engine's database (such as AltaVista®). There should be a date in italics included in the information on the page; this may demonstrate how old the page is, but it will not indicate whether the page has been revised since the search engine initially picked it up.

It is valuable to know the age and "updatedness" of your page, because you may be looking at an orphaned or superseded document that has been replaced by other information.

Search Engines

If you found information using one of the search engines available on the Internet, such as AltaVista®, a directory of the Internet such as Yahoo!®, or any of the services that rate World Wide Web pages, you need to know:

- How the search engine decides the order in which it returns requested information. Some Internet search engines sell top space to advertisers who pay them to do so. Read *"Caveat emptor* on the Web: Ad and Editorial Lines Blur" by Saul Hansell and Amy Harmon (*New York Times,* Feb. 26, 1999, at A1; not available on line).
- That Internet search engines are not like the databases found in libraries.
- How that search engine looks for information and how often its information is updated. This information should be available at the search engine's site.
- How that rating service evaluates Web pages. This, too, should be available at the rating service's site.

CONCLUSION

All information, whether in print or by byte, needs to be evaluated by readers for authority, appropriateness, and other personal criteria for value. If you find information that is "too good to be true," it probably is. *Never use information that you cannot verify.* Establishing and learning criteria to filter information you find on the Internet is a good beginning for becoming a critical consumer of information in *all* forms. "Cast a cold eye," as Yeats wrote, on everything you read. Question it. Look for other sources that can authenticate or corroborate what you find. Learn to be skeptical, and then learn to trust your instincts.

DISCUSSION QUESTIONS

1. After this review, do you think that you can now determine the credibility of information or documents obtained from any particular Web site? Why or why not?
2. Review the suggested supplemental articles available on the Internet for assessing Internet sources. Compare these articles to this chapter. Are there any substantive differences?

PROJECTS

1. In regard to Discussion Question 1, give an example of your evaluation of documents from three types of Internet sources: government documents, company or business documents, and other documents for which the source is not clear.
2. For a final U.S. Environmental Protection Agency rule, published yesterday in the *Federal Register,* prepare a summary for class presentation that reviews:
   1. Who is the author?
   2. Who is the publisher?
   3. What is its currency?

CHAPTER 9

Administrative Law Internet Sources and Sites

SUMMARY

This chapter provides a brief introduction to the administrative law practice area and provides descriptions of and links to related Internet Web sites with documents and useful resources.

OBJECTIVES

- The student will learn about the administrative law practice area.
- The student will be introduced to practice area related Internet Web sites.

Administrative Law

This chapter lists Internet sites in the administrative law practice area. For background and information about what administrative law is, users are encouraged to visit the University of Memphis' Internet essay on the topic (at http://exlibris.memphis.edu/resource/unclesam/admin.html), with useful links to related materials. Essentially, administrative law is the basis on which federal and state agencies under the executive branch draw their authority to act and through which their actions are reviewed.

Many federal laws enacted by Congress require executive agencies to issue binding regulations to promote the purposes of the law. That usually means a complex rulemaking process, with publication in the *Federal Register* of a "Notice of Proposed Rulemaking" (NPRM), a proposed rule, and then a final rule. After publication in the *Federal Register* as a final rule, the regulations are then codified in the annual *Code of Federal Regulations* (C.F.R.).

Similarly, state laws enacted by state assemblies also often require state agencies to issue binding regulations to promote the purposes of the state law. That may also mean a complex rulemaking process, with publication in a state register of an NPRM, a proposed rule, and then a final rule. After final publication of a final rule, the state regulations may also be codified in a state compilation of administrative rules.

Federal and state agencies also engage in adjudicative (or quasi-judicial) activities. Typically the agency will adjudicate issues between itself and a regulated party. These proceedings may end up in a published order or opinion, which may set precedents and have a future impact on the law. Many agencies publish official reports of their final decisions. An example of such agency is the Illinois Pollution Control Board.

Federal and state agencies also promulgate and publish a host of policy, guidance, and directive documents that are meant to explain agency rules and to promote compliance with those rules. Policy, guidance, and directive documents do not have the same force of law as rules, because the documents are not put through the rigorous public notice and comment procedures that rules are; but often they can detail agency expectations and assumptions relating to areas of law and compliance.

Internet Research Scenario

In this scenario, one of the firm's largest clients has called. The client has been informed by the federal Occupational Safety and Health Administration (OSHA) that it will be conducting an ergonomics inspection at several of the client's facilities. While the client is vaguely aware that there had been OSHA rules adopted by the outgoing Clinton presidency and then suddenly withdrawn under the then new Bush administration, the client has no ergonomics policy or program in place and no understanding of what the current requirements are.

The research that we have been asked to do is to identify key federal ergonomics documents and Web sites. To do so, we would start by reviewing the list of key OSHA links (in OSHA Chapter 23). There, we see that a few reference sites should be reviewed.

First, go to http://www.osha.gov. At the OSHA homepage, use the Site Index at the top of the page and take the link to "E" words. Select the "ergonomics" link listed as one of the "E" words. That brings up OSHA's current materials related to ergonomics.

Then back up, using the "go back" button in the browser, to the http://www.osha.gov homepage. There, select OSHA's Search tool, and in the search box run a search for "ergonomics." That search brings up a long list of related pages and documents.

Next, go to the related National Institute for Occupational Safety and Health (NIOSH) Web site at http://www.cdc.gov/niosh/homepage.htm/ site. A screenshot of the NIOSH homepage is shown in Figure 9-1. NIOSH is a sister agency to OSHA and is responsible for substantive research. It holds and makes available a host of information and documents relating to occupational health. At the NIOSH homepage, select its search tool, and run a search for "ergonomics" materials. That search brings up another list of related pages and documents.

This scenario illustrates that when government information and documents are needed, it is best to go directly to that source for the information. When dealing with administrative agencies, keep in mind that numerous

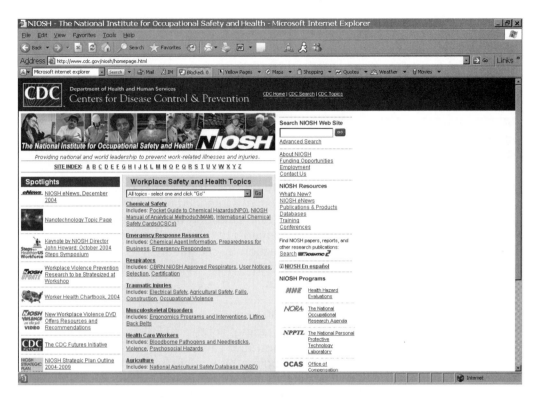

Figure 9-1   The NIOSH homepage.

agencies at the federal and state levels may have applicable and overlapping responsibilities.

Another example of such overlapping responsibilities is the U.S. Environmental Protection Agency (EPA) and the Agency for Toxic Substances and Disease Registry (ATSDR). The mission of the Agency for Toxic Substances and Disease Registry, as an agency of the U.S. Department of Health and Human Services, "is to prevent exposure and adverse human health effects and diminished quality of life associated with exposure to hazardous substances from waste sites, unplanned releases, and other sources of pollution present in the environment." See http://www.atsdr.cdc.gov/about.html. For many, the EPA's mission and the ATSDR's mission would seem indistinguishable.

Administrative Law Sites

The following topical links are sorted in alphabetical order, except that "key" federal sites are listed first and then other sites are listed. After selecting a site, type the Internet address (the URL), shown in the left column of the listing, into the browser software to get to the Internet site.

Administrative Law Sites	
See Chapter 7 for general resources of administrative law materials, including the *Federal Register* and the *Code of Federal Regulations*.	
Administrative Procedure Act and Selected Provisions of Title 5 of the U.S.C. http://www.oalj.dol.gov/ libapa.htm	This site provides the full text of the Administrative Procedure Act and other selected provisions of Title 5 of the U.S.C.
Attorney General's Manual on the Administrative Procedure Act http://www.oalj.dol.gov/public/ apa/refrnc/agtc.htm	This site provides the full text of the *Manual.* The *Manual* is intended primarily as a guide to the agencies in adjusting their procedures to the requirements of the Act. The *Manual* is arranged on a section-by-section analysis of the Act, with each of the major sections treated in a separate chapter.
***Manual for Administrative Law Judges* (2001 Interim Internet Edition), by Morell E. Mullins** http://www.oalj.dol.gov/public/ apa/refrnc/malj.pdf	The 2001 Interim Edition is a "modest updating, or upgrading," of the 3d Edition. The Office of Administrative Law Judges (OALJ) Law Library is including this work in its Internet library because of its obvious relevance to the work of its office. The OALJ, however, did not create the work, and its publication is not intended as an official endorsement of the Manual.
OALJ Rules of Practice and Procedure http://www.oalj.dol.gov/ librules.htm	This site provides the Rules of Practice and Procedure for Administrative Hearings Before the Office of Administrative Law Judges, 29 C.F.R. Part 18.
Other Sites	
ABA Administrative Procedure Database[1] http://www.law.fsu.edu/library/ admin	This site was developed with the cooperation and support of the American Bar Association's Section of Administrative Law and Regulatory Practice and the Florida State University College of Law. The site is designed to facilitate the exchange of information about federal and state administrative law among legislators, lawyers, hearing officers, judges, and citizens. It also provides links to federal and state Administrative Procedure Acts, reform proposals, and organizational and other resources.

---

[1] Copyright © 2001, Florida State University College of Law and other copyrights. All rights reserved.

Administrative Law Guide[2] http://www.jurist.law.pitt.edu/ sg_ad.htm	The Administrative Law Guide Web links, edited by Jim Rossi, Florida State University College of Law, provide a good resource and reference.
Administrative Law Research[3] http://lib.law.washington.edu/ ref/admin.htm	This site provides a how-to reference, along with links to federal and Washington State resources on administrative law research, including the laws, regulations, directories, and guides.
Administrative Procedure Act[4] http://assembler.law.cornell.edu/ uscode/html/uscode05/usc_sup_ 01_5_10_I.html	The U.S.C. sections provided by Cornell Law School.
CataLaw Administrative Law[5] http://www.catalaw.com/topics/ Administrative.shtml	This site provides links to national and international administrative law materials.
Selected Administrative Law Decisions of the U.S. Supreme Court[6] http://supct.law.cornell.edu/ supct/cases/adlaw.htm	Selected administrative law decisions of the U.S. Supreme Court compiled by Cornell Law School. A good resource for case law in this area.
State Administrative Codes[7] http://www.nass.org/acr/acr.html	This is a linking index to state sites that provide Internet access to administrative rules.
State and Local Government on the Net[8] http://www.statelocalgov.net/ index.cfm	A comprehensive guide that links to numerous state and local government-sponsored Internet sites.
Texas Administrative Code http://info.sos.state.tx.us/pls/ pub/readtac$ext.viewtac	Full text of the online *Texas Administrative Code.*
What Is Administrative Law?[9] http://exlibris.memphis.edu/ resource/unclesam/admin.html	The University of Memphis has compiled this essay, providing links to useful related materials.

[2] Copyright © 2004, Bernard J. Hibbitts. All rights reserved.
[3] Copyright © 1996–2005, M.G. Gallagher Law Library.
[4] Copyright © 2005, Cornell University.
[5] Copyright © 1996–2001, CataLaw Inc.
[6] Copyright © 2005, Cornell University.
[7] Copyright © 2004, Administrative Codes and Registers.
[8] Copyright © 1995–2005, HelloMetro.
[9] Copyright © 2005, University of Memphis.

DISCUSSION QUESTION

1. Where would you go to find policy, guidance, and support documents related to a federal rulemaking proceeding? What about a state rulemaking proceeding?

PROJECT

1. Go to the Internet site for the daily table of contents page for the *Federal Register*. Select a "notice" from today's issue and print it out in the "pdf" format. Now, visit or contact the school or community library, and ask for the published, paper copy of today's *Federal Register*. What did you find in your research?

CHAPTER 10

Alternative Dispute Resolution Internet Sources and Sites

SUMMARY

This chapter provides a brief introduction to the alternative dispute resolution (ADR) practice area and provides descriptions of and links to related Internet Web sites with documents and useful resources.

OBJECTIVES

- The student will learn about the alternative dispute resolution practice area.
- The student will be introduced to practice area related Internet Web sites.

Alternative Dispute Resolution

Alternative dispute resolution information and resources of all kinds are available on the Internet. Alternative dispute resolution is a procedure used by participants (or parties) in a dispute when a neutral third party is requested to assist the disputing parties in reaching an agreement to avoid litigation. Types of ADR include arbitration, mediation, negotiated rulemaking, and neutral fact finding.

Alternative dispute resolution provides a forum for the parties to work toward and achieve a voluntary, consensual agreement, rather than having a judge decide the case. Alternative dispute resolution can be, then, a tool for avoiding or lessening the expense, delay, and uncertainties associated with traditional litigation. It may improve communication between the participants, and it provides a forum for creative solutions to disputes.

In 1990, Congress enacted the Administrative Dispute Resolution Act of 1990 (ADR Act). The ADR Act encourages federal agencies to use ADR techniques to reduce litigation and the expenses associated with it. The ADR Act requires federal agencies to develop an ADR policy for possible uses of ADR in formal and informal adjudication, rulemakings, enforcement actions, in the issuance and revocation of licenses or permits, in contract administration, for litigation brought by or against the agency, and in other agency action.[1] Through CALR and Internet sites, ADR materials such as statutes, regulations, policies, and manuals are available, usually in full text, and often keyword searchable.

---

[1] *See* U.S. Department of Labor, *Overview of Alternative Dispute Resolution,* at http://www.dol.gov/asp/programs/adr/adrbrief.htm (September 1995).

Internet Research Scenario: Identifying Proposed Mediators

In this scenario, the firm's ADR team has just received a fax from the U.S. Department of Labor consisting of a list of potential mediators for an employment dispute. On the list of ten names, neither our client nor the team members recognize anybody.

The research that we have been asked to do is to collect bibliographical information about each of the proposed mediators to assist the ADR team in making its selection of an acceptable mediator. In this research, we would start by searching each of the names on two or more of the primary Internet search engines.

> First, go to http://www.google.com. At the Google™ homepage, use the search box at the top of the page to run a search for each named mediator. First, run the search in quotes to limit the results to the particular individual, like this: "kelly r. jones."

> If this search by itself produces sufficient documents to readily identify and make a decision as to this mediator's qualification, then go on to the next. If, however, few or no hits were found, then expand the search to include more documents, like this: "kelly jones." After running each of the names on Google™, then do the same on AltaVista® (http://www.altavista.com). If information is still brief or nonexistent for one or more names, then continue running the trouble names on a few other search engines and directory Web sites. Try Excite™ (http://www.excite.com), Lycos® (http://www.lycos.com), and Yahoo!® (http://www.yahoo.com).

> Then, with permission from the ADR team, also search for the names on one of the pay service legal databases, such as Westlaw® or LEXIS®. Permission is important because these databases can be expensive. Once this portion of the research is approved, then, for instance, go to the Westlaw® site at http://www.westlaw.com and run each of the names in the combined federal and state caselaw databases. Next, also run the names in the current literature (newspapers and journals) combined databases.

This scenario illustrates the use of both free Internet resources and the pay-as-you-go Internet legal database services. The pay sites can be important in obtaining complete research results.

Alternative Dispute Resolution Sites

The following topical links are sorted in alphabetical order, except that key federal sites are listed first, then other sites are listed. After selecting a site, type the Internet address (the URL), shown in the left column of the listing, into the browser software to get to the Internet site.

Alternative Dispute Resolution Sites	
Office of Dispute Resolution http://www.usdoj.gov/odr/ index.html	The Office of Dispute Resolution (ODR) coordinates the use of ADR for the U.S. Department of Justice. The ODR is responsible

	for ADR policy matters, ADR training, assisting lawyers in selecting the right cases for dispute resolution, and finding appropriate neutrals to serve as mediators, arbitrators, and neutral evaluators. The ODR also coordinates the Interagency ADR Working Group, an organization that promotes the use of ADR throughout federal executive branch agencies, which was created by the President and is chaired by the Attorney General.
U.S. Department of Labor's Program on Alternative Dispute Resolution http://www.dol.gov/asp/ programs/adr/main.htm	This is the Department of Labor's (DOL's) site for its ADR program. The DOL "has experimented with ADR in a number of areas." The DOL site provides full text of its ADR policies and links to other documents.

Other Sites

American Arbitration Association[2] http://www.adr.org	This site provides "the most comprehensive up-to-the-minute information about mediation, arbitration, and other forms of alternative dispute resolution (ADR)." With links to federal and state dispute resolution and mediation laws and documents.
Arbitration, U.S. Code, Title 9[3] http://www4.law.cornell.edu/ uscode/9	This site by the Legal Information Institute at Cornell University provides the keyword-searchable full text of the federal arbitration law.
Center for Information Technology and Dispute Resolution http://www.odr.info/index.php	The Center's mission is to support and sustain the development of knowledge bases, systems, and processes for resolving conflict in cyberspace, as well as to further general understanding of disputes and dispute resolution. Its links page provides many substantive articles and pages on the topic.
Code of Ethics for Arbitrators[4] http://www.lectlaw.com/files/ adr12.htm	This 'Lectric Law Library site provides the *Code of Ethics for Arbitrators in Commercial Disputes,* which was prepared in 1977 by a joint committee consisting of a special committee of the American Arbitration Association and a special committee of the American Bar Association. It has been approved and recommended by both organizations.

(continued)

---

[2] Copyright © 2004, American Arbitration Association. All rights reserved.
[3] Copyright © 2005, Cornell University.
[4] Copyright © 2000, American Arbitration Association.

Guide to Alternate Dispute Resolution[5] http://hg.org/adr.html	This site provides a "comprehensive law and government portal" to alternative dispute resolution materials.
Lawsuits & Mediation[6] http://www.nolo.com/lawcenter/index.cfm/catID/FCE46694–6BEB-4A80–89B9048DA9877F61	This site is a "self-help law center" for conflicts, mediation, suing, and court proceedings. It admonishes, "Think hard before you rush off to the court clerk's office to file a lawsuit. The idea of victory may tempt you, but as you probably know, lawsuits can be expensive, time-consuming and emotionally draining. It's far better to resolve your disputes out of court. One way to do this is through mediation."
Mediate.com[7] http://www.mediate.com	Mediate.com is dedicated to educating and encouraging the public to use mediation and other forms of ADR. The site also provides more than 1200 articles and resources available for free, arranged by topic and full-text searchable.

DISCUSSION QUESTION

1. Why would a party decide to use alternative dispute resolution rather than traditional litigation?

PROJECT

1. As an experiment, attempt to identify and research the background of ten potential arbitrators, but do the research in hardcopy books and current literature at the university or local library. Be sure to consult with the reference librarian. What were your results? How long did the research project take?

CHAPTER 11

Bankruptcy Law Internet Sources and Sites

SUMMARY

This chapter provides a brief introduction to the bankruptcy law practice area and provides descriptions of and links to related Internet Web sites with documents and useful resources.

OBJECTIVES

* The student will learn about the bankruptcy law practice area.
* The student will be introduced to practice area related Internet Web sites.

Bankruptcy Law

Generally, the federal law under Title 11 of the *United States Code* governs bankruptcy matters. The Bankruptcy Code supersedes any conflicting state law by reason of the Supremacy Clause[1] of the U.S. Constitution. With some exceptions, it is basically the same from state to state.

Bankruptcy law allows overspent debtors to develop a plan that allows the debtor to resolve debts through the division of his assets among creditors. The plan also allows the interests of all creditors to be treated with some measure of equality. Another bankruptcy provision allows a debtor to stay in business and use revenue generated to resolve debts. Bankruptcy law also allows certain debtors to be discharged of their financial obligations after their assets are distributed—even if their debts have not been paid in full.

Bankruptcy Internet sites provide the CALR researcher with the bankruptcy code, regulations, policy and directives, forms, statistics, cases, news, and court links.

---

[1] Article VI (relevant part): This Constitution, and the laws of the United States which shall be made in pursuance thereof; and all treaties made, or which shall be made, under the authority of the United States, shall be the supreme law of the land; and the judges in every state shall be bound thereby, anything in the Constitution or laws of any state to the contrary notwithstanding.

Internet Research Scenario: PACER List of Creditors

In this scenario, one of the firm's bankruptcy matters in the Arizona federal court is progressing, so the case management team needs a listing of the creditors in the case. This sort of information is maintained on the PACER system, which requires users to have registered accounts. Each time PACER is accessed a fee is charged. A screenshot of the PACER homepage is shown in Figure 11-1.

First, go to http://pacer.psc.uscourts.gov. At the PACER homepage, select "Links to PACER Websites." Then select "U.S. Bankruptcy Court - Arizona Bankruptcy Court." There, select "Click Here to Login to PACER."

Complete the "NIBS PACER Login Form" screen, by typing in the firm I.D. and password.

That brings up a "Case Information" screen that may be used to search for cases by case number, individual name, SSN, or tax identification number (TIN). Also available at this screen is a "Report Options" where case information, new cases, and creditor lists may be obtained.

This scenario illustrates the use of a pay-as-you-go fee-based CALR Internet database system. Web sites like these can be important in obtaining needed information.

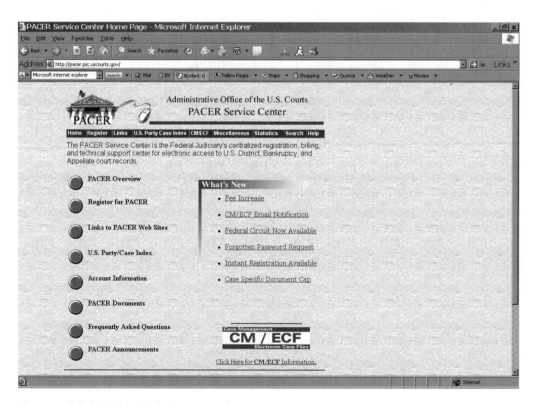

Figure 11-1 The PACER system homepage.

Bankruptcy Law Sites

The following topical links are sorted in alphabetical order, except that key federal sites are listed first, then other sites are listed. After selecting a site, type the Internet address (the URL), shown in the left column of the listing, into the browser software to get to the Internet site.

Bankruptcy Law Sites	
Federal Bankruptcy Court Links http://www.uscourts.gov/allinks.html	This is the federal judiciary page for links to all courts, including the bankruptcy courts.
U.S. Trustee Program http://www.usdoj.gov/ust	This site contains information about the U.S. Trustee Program and the federal bankruptcy system. "The U.S. Trustee Program is a component of the Department of Justice responsible for overseeing the administration of bankruptcy cases and private trustees under 28 U.S.C. §§ 586 and 11 U.S.C. §§ 101, *et seq.* It consists of 21 regional U.S. Trustee Offices nationwide and an Executive Office for U.S. Trustees (EOUST) in Washington, D.C."
Other Sites	
American Bankruptcy Institute (ABI)[2] http://www.abiworld.org	This site provides laws, statistics, cases, news, and court links. It "is the largest multidisciplinary, nonpartisan organization dedicated to research and education on matters related to insolvency."
Debt & Bankruptcy[3] http://www.nolo.com/lawcenter/index.cfm/catID/734BECB6-ADDE-4041-AEC595AF30EA15CE	This site provides a comprehensive collection of information and links relating to debt and bankruptcy.
Federal Rules of Bankruptcy Procedure[4] http://www2.law.cornell.edu/cgi-bin/foliocgi.exe/frb?	This site by the Legal Information Institute at Cornell University provides the keyword-searchable full text of the rules.
FindLaw® Bankruptcy Links[5] http://www.findlaw.com/01topics/03bankruptcy/index.html	This site provides useful links to bankruptcy forms, documents, and agencies.

(continued)

---

[2] Copyright © 2005, American Bankruptcy Institute. All rights reserved.
[3] Copyright © 2005, Nolo, Inc.
[4] Copyright © 2005, Cornell University.
[5] Copyright © 1994–2005, FindLaw.

U.S. Bankruptcy Code[6] http://www4.law.cornell.edu/ uscode/11	This site by the Legal Information Institute at Cornell University provides the keyword-searchable full text of the *United States Code.*

DISCUSSION QUESTIONS

1. Given that the bankruptcy law is governed by the Supremacy Clause and so supersedes conflicting state law, why should a practitioner review state laws?
2. What sort of Internet information or documents do you think would be useful in preparing a bankruptcy case?

PROJECT

1. If your school has access to PACER, log on to the system and experiment with finding complaints and opinions in some cases that have been filed locally. Search by party names or by case numbers if you have them. Download and print an exemplary bankruptcy petition under the Chapter 13 authority, and be prepared to discuss in class.

[6] Copyright © 2005, Cornell University.

CHAPTER 12

Business, Contract, Corporate, and Securities Internet Sources and Sites*

SUMMARY

This chapter provides a brief introduction to the business law practice area and provides descriptions of and links to related Internet Web sites with documents and useful resources.

OBJECTIVES

- The student will learn about the business law practice area.
- The student will be introduced to practice area related Internet Web sites.

Business Law

Computer-aided legal research on the Internet makes corporate information and documents for public companies easy to find. These days, though, it is not even too difficult to find Internet information on privately owned companies. In fact, many companies themselves are creating comprehensive Internet pages that detail company history, corporate documents, annual reports, and news releases.

Technically, a corporation is a legal entity created through incorporation laws. A corporation will usually begin to exist after articles of incorporation are filed with a state. This documents the corporation's creation and provides information regarding the management of its internal affairs. Many state corporation statutes also assume that each corporation will adopt bylaws to define the rights and obligations of officers, persons, and groups within the corporation's structure. States also have registration laws requiring corporations that incorporate in other states to request permission to do in-state business. The many secretaries of state offices all compile corporate information, and many now make at least summaries of the public records available over the Internet.

---

*The author acknowledges and thanks paralegal Adrienne Henry for her supplement to the links in this chapter.

Also, since Congress passed the Securities Act of 1933, there has been a significant federal component to corporations law. Federal securities law regulates how corporate securities are issued and sold. It also governs requirements of fiduciary conduct, such as requiring corporations to make full disclosures to shareholders and investors. Securities and Exchange Commission documents that are filed by companies represent a significant source of information about public companies that is available over the Internet.

Internet Research Scenario: Finding Corporate Securities and Exchange Commission Filings

In this case, our client's corporate counsel is in the initial stages of a corporate merger and acquisition, and the team attorney needs the "10K" report filed by "Sears Roebuck and Company." For this Internet research scenario:

Go to the U.S. Security and Exchange Commission's Web site at http://www.sec.gov, and run a search on the Web site's search tool ("Search for Company Filings") for corporate filings. A screenshot of the SEC homepage is shown in Figure 12-1.

Try searching various ways until you locate responsive documents. Make a note of the latest documents that are available for this entity.

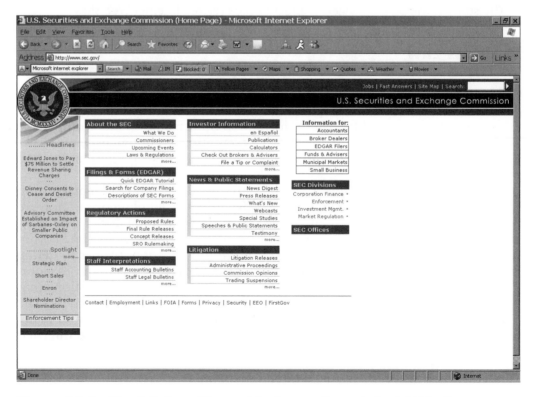

Figure 12-1 The U.S. Securities and Exchange Commission's Web site.

Business, Contract, Corporate, and Securities Law Sites

The following topical links are sorted in alphabetical order, except that key federal sites are listed first, and then other sites are listed. After selecting a site, type the Internet address (the URL), shown in the left column of the listing, into the browser software to get to the Internet site.

Business, Contract, Corporate, and Securities Law Sites	
Business Advisor http://www.business.gov	This site promotes itself as a one-stop electronic link to information and services that the government provides for the business community. The Business Advisor provides businesses the opportunity to research federal government information, services, and transactions such as assistance with starting, managing, or marketing a business; sources or types of government-guaranteed capital and credit; plus a list of lenders and private sector sources of financial assistance. This site also provides links to laws and regulations affecting businesses.
Department of Commerce http://www.commerce.gov	This site provides both international and national information on trade relations, e-commerce, and other resources.
Federal Trade Commission http://www.ftc.gov	The Federal Trade Commission enforces a variety of federal antitrust and consumer protection laws.
Securities and Exchange Commission (SEC) Homepage http://www.sec.gov	This site provides policy and guidance, as well as the Electronic Data Gathering, Analysis, and Retrieval (EDGAR) database for corporate filings.
Other Sites	
10k Wizard[1] http://www.10kwizard.com	This site provides free, real-time, online access and full-text search of the EDGAR system. You can also search historical filings from the start date of each company's existence.
CataLaw Contract and Remedy Law[2] http://www.catalaw.com/topics/Contract.shtml	This site provides links to national and international contract law materials.

(continued)

---

[1] Copyright © 2005, 10-K Wizard Technology, LLC. All Rights Reserved. 10-K Wizard® is a registered trademark of 10-K Wizard Technology, LLC.
[2] Copyright © 1996–2001, CataLaw Inc.

CEOExpress®[3] http://www.ceoexpress.com	This site was developed to organize the best resources on the Web for busy executives. It provides "easy" access to corporate and industrial information and services related to FORTUNE 500 companies.
Contract Law at Legal Information Institute[4] http://fatty.law.cornell.edu/topics/contracts.html	This site gives an overview of contract law and provides a useful directory of sources relating to this topic, including links to the federal statute affecting public contracts, the *Code of Federal Regulations,* U.S. Supreme Court decisions, and various state materials.
Corporate Watch http://www.corpwatch.org	This site provides "news, analysis, research tools and action resources to respond to corporate activity around the globe. . . . [That] also talk[s] with people who are directly affected by corporate abuses as well as with others fighting for corporate accountability, human rights, social and environmental justice. As part of the independent media, Corporate Watch is free of corporate sponsorship."
FindLaw® Contracts Links[5] http://www.findlaw.com/01topics/07contracts/index.html	This site provides useful links to contract forms, documents, and resources.
Foundation Center[6] http://www.fdncenter.org	This site presents an "independent nonprofit information clearinghouse" to provide information on foundations, corporate giving, and related subjects. Its purpose is to foster public understanding of the foundation field by collecting, organizing, analyzing, and disseminating the information.
Freeadvice.com[7] http://www.freeadvice.com/law/518us.htm	This site provides an easy-to-understand description of contract law.
GuideStar[8] http://www.guidestar.org	This site is "the Donor's Guide to the Charitable Universe." It is a searchable database of nonprofit organizations in the United States.

---

[3] Copyright © 1999–2000, CEOExpress Company.
[4] Copyright © 2005, Cornell University.
[5] Copyright © 1994–2005, FindLaw.
[6] Copyright © 2005, The Foundation Center.
[7] Copyright © 1995–2005, FreeAdvice®. All rights reserved.
[8] Copyright © 2005, Philanthropic Research, Inc. All rights reserved.

Hoover's Online— The Business Network[9] http://www.hoovers.com	This site provides proprietary company and industry information, in addition to a business-oriented perspective on money management, career development, news, and business travel.
Institute of International Commercial Law[10] http://cisgw3.law.pace.edu	This site provides access to the United Nations Convention on Contracts for the International Sale of Goods (CISG) Database and to international commercial law, including the uniform international sales law of countries that account for two-thirds of all world trade.
Internet Law Library: Business, Finance, Economic, and Consumer Protection Laws http://www.lectlaw.com/ inll/92.htm	This site provides links to an impressive collection of state, federal, and international business, finance, economic, and consumer protection laws.
IOMA's Business Management Supersite[11] http://www.ioma.com	This site provides the Institute of Management and Administration's (IOMA) collection of free documents and information products for business professionals.
Law About Corporations[12] http://www.law.cornell.edu/ topics/corporations.html	This site provides information on corporations, including their formation, decisions regarding and related tax codes, useful links to state laws on corporations, the UCC, and the relevant CFR.
Legal Forms for Lawyers[13] http://www.alppublishing.com/	This site is useful to obtain copies of samples of legal forms for corporate and securities lawyers.
Lex Mercatoria http://www.jus.uio.no/lm/	This site monitors international trade and commercial law and includes a number of other international law areas.
NASD Regulation, Inc. (NASD)[14] http://www.nasdr.com	This site provides information pertaining to NASD registered brokers, arbitrations, enforcement actions, investor resources, and other security industry links.

(continued)

North American Securities Administrators Association, Inc.[15] http://www.nasaa.org	This site is valuable to any individual or organization seeking protection from securities fraud. The NASAA is a voluntary association with a membership consisting of the sixty-six state, provincial, and territorial securities administrators in the fifty states, the District of Columbia, Canada, Mexico, and Puerto Rico. In the United States, the NASAA is the voice of the fifty state securities agencies responsible for grassroots investor protection. Also on the site are information on franchising and raising capital, small investment advisers, "blue sky" securities laws, and various UCC forms.
SEDAR—Canada[16] http://www.sedar.com	This is the site for SEDAR, the System for Electronic Document Analysis and Retrieval, which is used to file securities-related information electronically with the Canadian Securities Administration. Documents may also be retrieved from SEDAR, including public securities filings and company/mutual fund profiles.

DISCUSSION QUESTIONS

1. Name two or three Internet sources of corporate information and documents.
2. What value is there in reviewing Internet examples of forms and form "boiler-plate" contract language?
3. In a corporate transaction, such as a merger or acquisition, what types of sites and kinds of information would the CALR researcher look for in performing a "due diligence" review?

PROJECTS

1. Do some Internet research on GE Credit. Is that entity related to General Electric Company? If so, in what way? If not, how do you know?
2. Telephone your state Secretary of State's Office and inquire about the process involved in requesting corporate documents in person or by U.S. mail. How does that process compare to the documents that the state Secretary of State's Office makes available on the Internet, if any?

---

[15] Copyright © 2004, North American Securities Administrators Association, Inc.
[16] Copyright © 1998, 1999, CDS INC. All rights reserved.

CHAPTER 13

Criminal Law Internet Sources and Sites

SUMMARY

This chapter provides a brief introduction to the criminal law practice area and provides descriptions of and links to related Internet Web sites with documents and useful resources.

OBJECTIVES

- The student will learn about the criminal law practice area.
- The student will be introduced to practice area related Internet Web sites.

Criminal Law

Computer-aided legal research will provide a fair amount of criminal law information that is available on the Internet. Documents such as statistical analyses and reports on trends in criminal offenses and criminality are abundant. There are also the fifty states' and the cities' and counties' sex offender lists, which are, in many cases, now publicly available on the Internet. These lists enable community, school, church, and other public administrators to take steps to ensure that the people they employ in children's programs are not known sex offenders. Inmate databases are also published on the Internet in some states.

One expert concludes, "[E]ven in this age of instant access to digitized information, old fashioned 'gumshoe' techniques usually must be relied upon for the research of criminal records."[1] Lynn Peterson indicates that "there is no such thing as a national criminal records check. There is one 'nationwide' criminal database, the FBI database, which is known as the NCIC (National Crime Information Center). The FBI database is NOT public record and cannot be legally accessed by anyone other than criminal justice agencies."

Ms. Peterson concludes that "checking criminal court records at the county level is the method used in most parts of the country. In some counties, felony and misdemeanor records are maintained in a combined index; in others, felonies and misdemeanor records must be checked separately. [The] *Sourcebook to Public*

---

[1] Lynn Peterson, *Navigating the Maze of Criminal Records Retrieval—Updated*, at http://www.llrx.com/features/criminal2.htm. Copyright © 1996–2001, Law Library Resource Xchange, LLC. All rights reserved.

Records Information (http://www.publicrecordsources.com/PRRS.asp) provides detailed descriptions of each jurisdiction, which can be extremely helpful in determining which court or courts should be checked for felonies and misdemeanors." The *Sourcebook* is available on line for an annual subscription fee.

Internet Research Scenario: Finding Local Criminal Procedural Rules

In this scenario, we have a corporate client whose managerial employee has been indicted for "environmental crimes." The employer has an interest in defending its employee, because any activities for which the employee is found guilty may be attributed to the employer.

To assist its employee and in its own interest, the employer hires the firm to defend the employee in the federal criminal environmental law case. It is pending in the Southern District Court of Indiana. The lead attorney has requested a set of the local rules of criminal procedure.

In this case, the researcher realizes that there is a link to the federal courts Web site, with supplemental links to its nationwide district courts listed in Chapter 3 in the section on "Government Sites—Federal."

> Go to the federal judiciary's Web site, at http://www.uscourts.gov. A screenshot of the U.S. Courts homepage is shown in Figure 13-1. Follow the link to "Court Links."

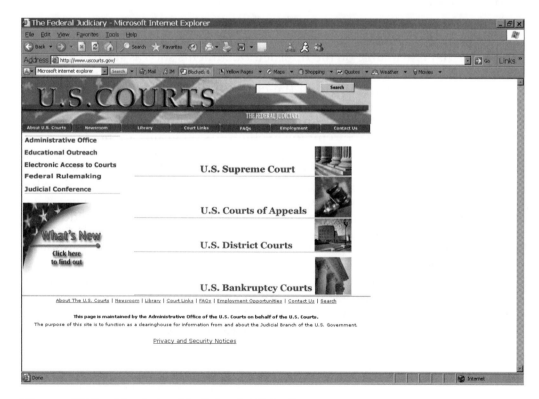

Figure 13-1 The federal judiciary's Web site.

Then, follow the link to Indiana courts, by selecting the Seventh Circuit on the map image, or by selecting it off the courts list. Then go specifically to the Indiana Southern District Court. There, follow the link to "Court Information," then "Forms/Publications," and then "View Court Publications (including Local Rules)."

At this screen there is a link to "Local Rules." Select that link to open a pdf file of the local rules, including the local criminal procedural rules.

Save the rules to the disk or print them out.

Criminal Law Sites

The following topical links are sorted in alphabetical order, except that key federal sites are listed first, followed by other sites. After selecting a site, type the Internet address (URL), shown in the left column of the listing, into the browser software to get to the Internet site.

Criminal Law Sites	
Bureau of Alcohol, Tobacco, Firearms and Explosives http://www.atf.treas.gov	The homepage for the Bureau of Alcohol, Tobacco, Firearms and Explosives.
Bureau of Justice Statistics http://www.ojp.usdoj.gov/bjs	This federal government site provides information, data, and statistics on crimes, victims, and justice.
Bureau of Prisons http://www.bop.gov	This federal government site provides statistics on inmate demographics, sentences, and offenses.
Computer Crime and Intellectual Property Section http://www.cybercrime.gov	This site, sponsored by the Computer Crime and Intellectual Property Section (CCIPS) of the Criminal Division of the U.S. Department of Justice, is frequently updated. Resources include documents on computer crime, intellectual property crime, and cybercrime. The site is organized by: policy and programs, cases, laws and statutes, manuals, press releases, congressional testimony, letters, and reports.
Internet Fraud Complaint Center http://www.ifccfbi.gov/index.asp	This is a federal site devoted to addressing fraud committed over the Internet. The site represents a partnership between the Federal Bureau of Investigation (FBI) and the National White Collar Crime Center (NW3C). The IFCC site includes complaint forms for electronic submission and statistics regarding alleged categories of fraud as well as victim and perpetrator information.

(continued)

U.S. Sentencing Commission http://www.ussc.gov	This site provides the full text, keyword searchable, of the U.S. Sentencing Guidelines.

Other Sites

ABA Criminal Justice Section[2] http://www.abanet.org/crimjust/home.html	The site provides comprehensive criminal justice resources for individuals interested in the criminal justice system.
Buffalo Criminal Law Center—Criminal Law Resources on the Internet[3] http://wings.buffalo.edu/law/bclc/resource.htm	This site provides access to criminal law materials from the United States and throughout the world, including criminal codes, criminal procedure codes, and enforcement codes.
CyberTipline[4] http://www.cybertipline.com	The National Center for Missing and Exploited Children established the CyberTipline to serve as a national online clearinghouse for tips and leads about child sexual exploitation.
Florida Corrections Offender Information Network http://www.dc.state.fl.us/activeinmates/search.asp	This system provides research on individual inmates and on categories of inmates within the state.
Kentucky Offender Online Lookup System http://www.corrections.ky.gov/kool/	This system provides research on individual inmates and on categories of inmates within the state.
MegaLaw.com® Criminal Law Page[5] http://www.megalaw.com/top/criminal.php	This site provides links to the criminal laws in the fifty states, and to the State's Attorney General Web sites for the fifty states.
National Criminal Justice Reference Service (NCJRS) http://www.ncjrs.org	This site is one of the most extensive sources of information on criminal and juvenile justice in the world, providing services to an international community of policymakers and professionals. The NCJRS site is a collection of clearinghouses supporting all bureaus of the U.S. Department of Justice, Office of Justice Programs (OJP): the National Institute of Justice, the Office of Juvenile Justice and Delinquency Prevention, the

---

[2] Copyright © 2005, American Bar Association. All rights reserved.
[3] Copyright © 2005, University of Buffalo Law School.
[4] Copyright © 2005, National Center for Missing & Exploited Children. All rights reserved.
[5] MegaLaw.com® is a registered trademark of MegaLaw.com, LLC. Copyright © 2000–2004, MegaLaw.com, LLC. All rights reserved.

	Bureau of Justice Statistics, the Bureau of Justice Assistance, the Office for Victims of Crime, and the OJP Program Offices. It also supports the Office of National Drug Control Policy.
Proceedings of the Old Bailey, London 1674 to 1834[6] http://www.oldbaileyonline.org	This site is described as "a fully searchable online edition of the largest body of texts detailing the lives of non-elite people ever published, containing accounts of over 100,000 criminal trials held at London's central criminal court."
Prosecuting Attorneys, District Attorneys, Attorneys General, and U.S. Attorneys[7] http://www.eatoncounty.org/ prosecutor/proslist.htm	This site, compiled by the state of Michigan's Eaton County Prosecuting Attorney, provides links to government attorneys across the nation.
Public Records Research System http://www.publicrecordsources. com/PRRS.asp	The Public Records Research System (PRRS) provides information on how to access public records direct from the source. This site appears extensive, with up-to-date resources that contain in-depth profiles of county courts, including detailed information on over 6900 civil, criminal, and probate courts at the county and municipal level.
State Sex Offender Registries[8] http://www.prevent-abuse-now. com/register.htm	This site links to the fifty states' Internet registries of sex offenders.

DISCUSSION QUESTIONS

1. If your client was suddenly and unexpectedly facing a federal criminal indictment, where might you acquire information as to the possible penalties?
2. Why would a school system, a church, or other business that works with children wish to search the various lists of sexual offenders now widely published on the Internet?

---

[6] Copyright © 2003, The Old Bailey Proceedings Online.
[7] Copyright © 1997–2005, Eaton County Prosecuting Attorney Jeffrey L. Sauter; and Copyright © 1997–2005, Eaton County Information Systems.
[8] Copyright © 1996–2003, N. Faulkner.

PROJECT

1. Pretend that you are a concerned parent and that you wish to review the local sex offenders list. You are just looking for names that you might recognize. Can you find a local list? Was it difficult to review? Did any names jump out at you?

CHAPTER 14

Elder and Aging Law Internet Sources and Sites

SUMMARY

This chapter provides a brief introduction to the elder and aging law practice area and provides descriptions of and links to related Internet Web sites with documents and useful resources.

OBJECTIVES

- The student will learn about the elder and aging law practice area.
- The student will be introduced to practice area related Internet Web sites.

Elder Law

Sources of materials relating to elder and aging law on the Internet are constantly increasing. These include the laws, rules, policies, program requirements, and the agencies that administer them and many others.

Josefina G. Carbonell, the U.S. Assistant Secretary for Aging, defined in a recent speech what elder and aging law are all about. She said that

> [f]or the United States, the continued improvement in the lives of older people and their families is a priority. We are committed to strengthening and modernizing our health insurance program for the elderly, improving access to health care, expanding prescription drug benefits, and preventing disease. We are reshaping our current system of long-term care so people may stay in their own homes and communities as long as possible. We are also committed to supporting high quality research to address all aspects of aging—health and disability trends, conditions and diseases that primarily affect older people, and physical, and behavioral characteristics of the aging process.[1]

---

[1] Remarks by Josefina G. Carbonell, Assistant Secretary for Aging, U.S. Department of Health and Human Services, UNECLAC Regional Intergovernmental Conference on Aging, Santiago, Chile (Nov. 19, 2003) (at http://www.aoa.dhhs.gov/press/speeches/2003/11_Nov/speeches_archive_11_20.asp).

Figure 14-1   The Social Security Administration's Web site.

Elder and aging law deals with a large number of different laws and various implementing agencies. For instance, there are the Administration on Aging, the National Institute on Aging, and the Social Security Administration, just to name a few.

Internet Research Scenario: Social Security Forms

In this scenario, we need to draft for a client a Modified Benefits Formula Questionnaire (SSA–150).

Go to the SSA's Web site, at http://www.ssa.gov. A screenshot of the SSA.gov homepage is shown in Figure 14-1. Follow the link to "Resources—Forms." At this screen there is another link to "Benefit Claims Supporting Forms." Follow that link to download the needed form in "pdf" format, which can then be filled in by hand or with an "old-fashioned" typewriter.

Elder and Aging Law Sites

The following topical links are sorted in alphabetical order, except that key federal sites are listed first, then other sites are listed. After selecting a site, type the Internet address (the URL), shown in the left column of the listing, into the browser software to get to the Internet site.

Elder and Aging Law Sites

Administration on Aging: Elders Rights & Resources http://www.aoa.gov/eldfam/ Elder_Rights/Elder_Rights.asp	The "AoA has a strong commitment to protecting the rights of seniors. Our community-based long-term care programs allow millions of seniors to age in place with dignity. AoA also supports a range of activities at the state and local level designed to prevent elder fraud and abuse, inform seniors of their rights, and help them to make end-of-life decisions." The Web site provides links to legal hotlines and legal services, health insurance assistance and counseling programs, long-term care ombudsmen, and information and documents on preventing fraud and abuse.
FirstGov for Seniors[2] http://www.firstgov.gov/Topics/ Seniors.shtml	This is the federal government's portal to government elder and aging-related Web sites.
National Institute on Aging http://www.nia.nih.gov	The National Institute on Aging leads a broad scientific effort to understand the nature of aging and to extend the healthy, active years of life. The site provides news and information on aging issues.
Office for Victims of Crime: Elder Abuse http://www.ojp.usdoj.gov/ovc/ publications/infores/elder/ welcome.html	This site provides information resources that offer victim assistance information, research findings, educational materials, and strategies for program and policy development specific to elder abuse.
Social Security Administration http://www.ssa.gov	This site provides 17 separate services which include applying for retirement benefits on line and requesting a Medicare card on line.
State and Area Agencies on Aging http://www.aoa.gov/eldfam/ How_To_Find/Agencies/ Agencies.asp	This site provides links to state elder and aging government agency Web sites.

Other Sites

American Association of Retired People[3] http://www.aarp.org	The AARP is a nonprofit membership organization dedicated to addressing the needs and interests of persons fifty and older. Through

(continued)

---

[2] FirstGov.gov™ is the U.S. government's official Web portal.
[3] Copyright © 1995–2005, AARP. All rights reserved.

	information and education, advocacy and service, it seeks to enhance the quality of life by promoting independence, dignity, and purpose.
MegaLaw.com® Elder Law Page[4] http://www.megalaw.com/top/elder.php	This site provides links to the elder laws in the fifty states and to the state Attorney General Web sites for the fifty states.
National Council on the Aging[5] http://www.ncoa.org	"The National Council on the Aging is a national network of organizations and individuals dedicated to improving the health and independence of older persons; increasing their continuing contributions to communities, society and future generations; and building caring communities." The Web site provides news and information about aging, along with information about aging research and conferences.
National Senior Citizens Law Center[6] http://www.nsclc.org	"The National Senior Citizens Law Center advocates nationwide to promote the independence and well-being of low-income elderly individuals and persons with disabilities." This site provides links to current news and to issue papers on important topical areas.

DISCUSSION QUESTION

1. Do you think that the accessibility of elder and aging related agencies on the Internet has made it easier for the elderly to find and locate information and resources that they require? Why or why not?

PROJECT

1. Research the Internet for a Work History Report (SSA-3369) form, and complete this form in draft for a senior citizen whom you know. If possible, request the senior's assistance to get the form completed as correctly as possible.

---

[4] MegaLaw.com® is a registered trademark of MegaLaw.com, LLC. Copyright © 2000–2004, MegaLaw.com, LLC. All rights reserved.
[5] Copyright © 2005, National Council on the Aging.
[6] Copyright © 2000, National Senior Citizens Law Center.

CHAPTER 15

Environmental Law Internet Sources and Sites

SUMMARY

This chapter provides a brief introduction to the environmental law practice area and provides descriptions of and links to related Internet Web sites with documents and useful resources.

OBJECTIVES

- The student will learn about the environmental law practice area.
- The student will be introduced to practice area related Internet Web sites.

Environmental Law

The Environmental Protection Agency (EPA) and many states should be applauded for efforts to make useful and relevant information not only available on the Internet but graphically dynamic as well. This chapter provides a glimpse of some of the environmental information that is available through CALR on the Internet.

For instance, the EPA's award-winning Envirofacts Data Warehouse provides users with comprehensive information on the environmental permit and compliance of thousands of regulated facilities across the country. The EPA's Sector Facility Initiative Project (SFIP) provides even more compliance-related, facility-specific information for various business sectors selected by the EPA as pilot projects.

The EPA's Region V Office of Regional Counsel's page provides environmental research links and compliance information for regional cases. The Environmental Defense Fund's "Scorecard" site provides the community with information about what sort of chemicals and wastes are being used and generated by your neighbors. The EPA's Office of Enforcement and Compliance Assurance Page has made hundreds of policy and guidance documents available over the Internet.

Internet Research Scenario: The CERCLA 106 Order

In this case, the EPA has served our client with a unilateral administrative order (UAO). The UAO requires our client to undertake the immediate removal and cleanup of a waste recycling facility that the EPA claims our client used for waste recycling. The case team, in its review of the matter, has determined that a review of applicable EPA policy and guidance documents would be helpful. In this scenario, for locating applicable EPA policy and guidance documents, we would start by doing simple keyword searches on the EPA's main search page. A screenshot of the EPA.gov homepage is shown in Figure 15-1.

Go to http://www.epa.gov, and select the "Advanced Search" button. At the search screen, note that it states right at the top: "Enter words or phrases SEPARATED BY COMMAS." Then there is an option to select searching for "ALL" keywords or "ANY" keywords. In this case, select "ANY" keywords, and type in the following: unilateral administrative order, UAO. This search brought up numerous on-point pages and documents, including one titled: "Cleanup Enforcement–Superfund—Orders. This Web page describes how Administrative and/or Unilateral Orders are used in the superfund enforcement process."

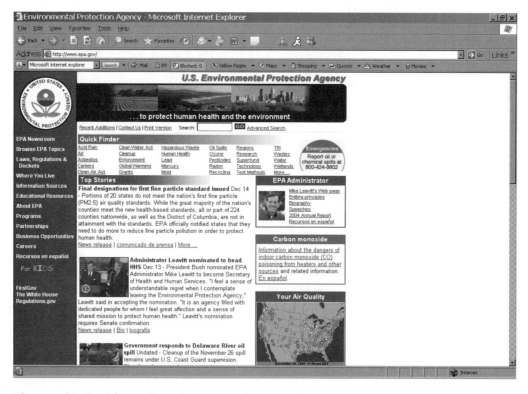

Figure 15-1   The U.S. Environmental Protection Agency's Web site.

Environmental Law Sites

The following topical links are sorted in alphabetical order, except that key federal sites are listed first, then other sites are listed. After selecting a site, type the Internet address (the URL), shown in the left column of the listing, into the browser software to get to the Internet site.

Environmental Law Sites	
Agency for Toxic Substances and Disease Registry http://www.atsdr.cdc.gov	The ATSDR homepage provides information and documents on preventing exposure and adverse human health effects and diminished quality of life associated with hazardous substances from waste sites, unplanned releases, and other sources of pollution present in the environment.
Air and Radiation http://www.epa.gov/air/ index.html	This site provides access to rules, policy, and guidance documents produced by the Office of Air and Radiation since the Clean Air Act Amendments of 1990.
Chemicals Information http://yosemite.epa.gov/oswer/ ceppoweb.nsf/content/ chemicalinfo.htm	This site provides access to substantial chemical-related information. Visit this site for quick links to the *Title III Consolidated List of Lists,* the Toxics Release Inventory, the EHS Chemical Profiles, Envirofacts, Chemical Health and Safety Data Web Sites, and MSDS Web Sites.
Enforcement and Compliance Docket and Information Center (ECDIC) http://www.epa.gov/compliance/ resources/policies/index.html	This site provides Internet access to regulatory, case settlement, and other policy-related information supporting the agency's enforcement and compliance activities.
Enforcement and Compliance History Online (ECHO) http://www.epa.gov/echo	This site takes the EPA's EnviroFacts data (see below) and mixes in enforcement data to report better site compliance information for certain properties. The ECHO site currently provides integrated compliance and enforcement information for approximately 800,000 regulated facilities nationwide.
EnviroFacts Data Warehouse http://www.epa.gov/enviro	This EPA site is a remarkable resource for regulators, the regulated community, and the public at large. For example, federal and state regulators can immediately find out the historical compliance record for any facility. The

(continued)

	regulated community can find out what everyone else knows about its business! So-called "bounty hunters" and citizen's groups can determine whether a local facility is a good corporate citizen or whether its compliance record shows numerous problem areas.
FOIA Page http://www.epa.gov/foia	This is EPA's Freedom of Information Act page, where it provides contact persons and addresses and downloadable copies of frequently requested materials.
Personnel Locator Page http://www.epa.gov/epahome/ locator.htm	This site provides an easy search tool for locating EPA personnel, with their addresses, telephone numbers, and e-mail addresses. Searches may be limited to an individual name or location.
U.S. Environmental Protection Agency http://www.epa.gov	The main page into EPA's Internet domain. Check here first for all environmental issues.
Other Sites	
clay.net® Government Agency, State-Main Links[1] http://www.clay.net/statag.html	This site provides updated links to state EPA-like agencies.
Cornell Law School's Legal Information Institute Page on Environmental Law[2] http://www.law.cornell.edu/ topics/environmental.html	This site provides the full text of environmental laws, regulations, and cases.
ECOLEX[3] http://www.ecolex.org	This site is the "world's largest environmental law database." For instance, ECOLEX provides online access to over 100,000 legal references including treaties, national legislation, soft law and other nonbinding policy and technical guidance documents, judicial decisions, and law and policy literature. In addition, since the 1972 Stockholm Conference on the Human

---

[1] Copyright © 1995–2005, John N. Clay. All rights reserved. Clay.net® Reg. U.S. Pat. & Tm. Off.
[2] Copyright © 2005, Cornell University.
[3] Copyright © 2005, ECOLEX, Food and Agriculture Organization of the United Nations (FAO), The World Conservation Union (IUCN), and the United Nations Environment Programme (UNEP) and their licensors.

	Environment, there has been a growth in the number of Multilateral Environmental Agreements (MEAs) negotiated by governments. Users of ECOLEX can now examine any one of approximately 450 MEAs and see which governments have signed or ratified that MEA. Conversely, it is also possible to see all the MEAs signed or ratified by any one government.
Environmental Law Reporter® Cases[4] http://www.elr.info/litigation	This site provides free Internet access to the full text of hundreds of environmental law cases. Researchers, though, will need the "_____ ELR _____" citation in order to find the sought-after cases.
FindLaw® Environmental Law News[5] http://news.findlaw.com/legalnews/environment	This site provides daily updates on environmental law news.
Policy and Guidance Documents: A Chronological, Historical Index[6] http://www.seyfarth.com/firm/news/newsletter_sample.asp?pubid=124654422001&from=practice&group=environ&groupid=4&area=	This site provides a chronological, historical (policy and guidance before 1998) listing of selected EPA policy and guidance documents.
Scorecard.org (Scorecard) by the Environmental Defense Fund (EDF)[7] http://www.scorecard.org	The Scorecard site, operated by the Environmental Defense Fund, provides detailed analyses of environmental and related information that is available through numerous federal agencies. These analyses are then made available to users simply by entering a U.S.P.S. ZIP Code.
Seyfarth Shaw EPA Links[8] http://www.seyfarth.com/practice/links.asp?groupid=4	This is an especially good resource of links to EPA and EPA-related sites, including federal agency sites, sources of cases, laws, and regulations.

---

[4] Copyright © 2005, Environmental Law Institute®.
[5] Copyright © 1994–2005, FindLaw.
[6] Copyright © 1993, Clark Boardman and Callaghan, a division of Thomson Information Services, Inc. Used at this site with permission.
[7] Copyright © 2005, Environmental Defense and LocusPocus.
[8] Copyright © 2005, Seyfarth Shaw LLP.

DISCUSSION QUESTION

1. What Internet sources should be reviewed in a literature search for the health effects of a specific chemical substance? Take polychlorinated biphenyls (PCBs), for instance.

PROJECT

1. In a comparative review for data content and quality, find and print the same record (let's say, for a "Waste Management" facility in Emelle, Alabama) from the EPA's RCRIS database: once from the Internet EnviroFacts database, and once from the LEXIS® database. Do they differ in any significant ways? Is there any reason to ever consult both resources? Explain.

CHAPTER 16

Family Law Internet Sources and Sites

SUMMARY

This chapter provides a brief introduction to the family law practice area and provides descriptions of and links to related Internet Web sites with documents and useful resources.

OBJECTIVES

- The student will learn about the family law practice area.
- The student will be introduced to practice area related Internet Web sites.

Family Law

Computer-aided legal research resources on the Internet for family law include federal enforcement sites that assist in locating noncustodial (the parent who does not have child custody after a divorce or separation) parents, establishing paternity, establishing child support obligations, and enforcing child support orders. Internet family-related sites provide laws, rules, reports, research papers, policy, and links to state family programs.

Internet Research Scenario: Child Support Enforcement Program

In this scenario, the state has contacted the firm and is requesting a proposal (RFP) for legal assistance in the development and establishment of a statewide Child Support Enforcement Program. While the firm has some experience in the subject matter, the RFP team has requested that all relevant information be compiled. To do so:

> Go to the Federal Office of Child Support Enforcement Program's (CSEP) Web site at http://www.acf.dhhs.gov/programs/cse/index.html. A screenshot of the CSEP homepage is shown in Figure 16-1. Begin reviewing and printing just about all of the items available at the site.

Judgment certainly is important, but in research scenarios such as this, it is usually better to overcollect information than to be too selective. Unnecessary materials can be easily put aside, but something that was not provided and

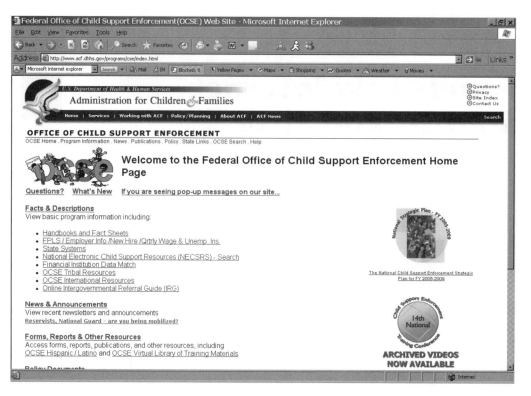

Figure 16-1 The Federal Office of Child Support Enforcement Program's Web site.

should have been can be a problem. In reviewing the materials listed on the CSEP Web site, it is easy to see how a site such as this may provide hundreds and thousands of pages of useful, on-point materials.

Family Law Sites

The following links are sorted in alphabetical order, except that key federal sites are listed first, then other sites are listed. After selecting a site, type the Internet address (the URL), shown in the left column of the listing, into the browser software to get to the Internet site.

Family Law Sites

Administration for Children and Families, U.S. Department of Health and Human Services http://www.acf.dhhs.gov	This is the homepage for the Administration for Children and Families (ACF) within the Department of Health and Human Services (HHS), which is responsible for federal programs that promote the economic and social well-being of families, children, individuals, and communities.

Federal Office of Child Support Enforcement http://www.acf.dhhs.gov/ programs/cse/index.html	This site presents the Child Support Enforcement Program, which provides four major services: locating noncustodial parents, establishing paternity, establishing child support obligations, and enforcing child support orders. Reports, policy, and links to state programs are available on the site.
National Adoption Information Clearinghouse http://naic.acf.hhs.gov	The National Adoption Information Clearinghouse was established by Congress in 1987 to provide free information on all aspects of adoption. This site provides many links, including those to adoption directories, publications, parent networks, and related federal and state legislation (legal Issues).
U.S. Consumer Product Safety Commission http://www.cpsc.gov	This is the official site of the CPSC, an independent federal regulatory agency, whose purpose is to help keep American families safe by reducing the risk of injury or death from consumer products. It includes its prompt to consumers to "report unsafe products."

Other Sites

DivorceNet[1] http://www.divorcenet.com	This site claims to be "the Net's largest divorce resource since May 1995." It includes links to a "state-by-state resource" area, divorce lawyers nationally, many topical chat rooms, and family-based articles.
FindLaw's Family Law Resources[2] http://www.findlaw.com/ 01topics/15family/index.html	This site provides links to responsible state and federal government agencies, the full text of laws and regulations, and other government documents.
Focus on the Family[3] http://www.family.org	This site, though Christian-oriented, provides resources in helping to preserve traditional values and the institution of the family. Its resources are considerable and may be helpful in finding materials and experts on traditional family-related issues. For instance, it provides online, full-text research papers on the following topics: abortion, bioethics, education, euthanasia, and gambling.

(continued)

---

[1] Copyright © 2000, LawTek Media Group, LLC. All rights reserved.
[2] Copyright © 1994–2005, FindLaw.
[3] Copyright © 2005, Focus on the Family. All rights reserved. International copyright secured.

Legal Information Institute's Law About Divorce: An Overview[4] http://www.law.cornell.edu/ topics/divorce.html	This site provides federal cases and state laws and cases concerning divorce law. It features state uniform laws adopted by various states, such as the Uniform Marital Property Act, the Uniform Marriage and Divorce Act, the Uniform Premarital Agreement Act, and the Uniform Interstate Family Support Act.
State Family Law Statutes[5] http://www.law.cornell.edu/ topics/state_statutes2.html# family	This site by the Legal Information Institute at Cornell University, provides links to state family law statutes.

DISCUSSION QUESTION

1. Consider that you have a client whose former spouse has stopped paying alimony and child support. Which Internet sites, if any, would you suggest for information and resources that might assist your client?

PROJECT

1. Visit the National Adoption Information Clearinghouse Web site and review its links to legal issues for your state. Were you able to find a citation to the applicable state statute? Was there an Internet link provided to the statute?

---

[4] Copyright © 2005, Cornell University.
[5] Copyright © 2005, Cornell University.

CHAPTER 17

Health-Care Law Internet Sources and Sites*

SUMMARY

This chapter provides a brief introduction to the health-care law practice area and provides descriptions of and links to related Internet Web sites with documents and useful resources.

OBJECTIVES

- The student will learn about the health-care law practice area.
- The student will be introduced to practice area related Internet Web sites.

Health-Care Law

Computer-aided legal research on the Internet provides abundant information about health care and related resources. For instance, one site "offers specialists, primary care physicians, and other health professionals, the Web's most robust and integrated multispecialty medical information and education tool." Besides primary sources of laws and regulations, health-care terminology may be found on the Web, including "classical and contemporary medical terms, including pertinent scientific items, abbreviations, acronyms, jargon, institutions, projects, symptoms, syndromes, eponyms, and medical history." Another site provides the Web's "best collection of health-care policy and regulatory materials."

Internet Research Scenario: Anthrax Scare

In this scenario, the question being posed is: Can anthrax be spread from person to person? To answer this question, we would go to the Centers for Disease

*The author acknowledges and thanks Marilyn Mason, Legal Nurse Consultant, for her supplement to the links in this chapter.

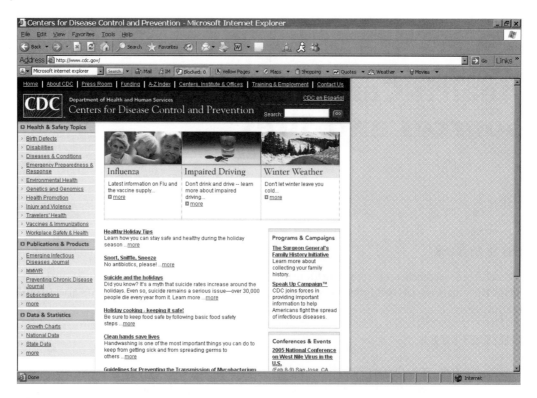

Figure 17-1   The Centers for Disease Control and Prevention's Web site.

Control and Prevention Web site and do a general search of its site with the site-specific search engine.

> Go to the Centers for Disease Control and Prevention's Web site at http://www.cdc.gov. A screenshot of the CDC.gov homepage is shown in Figure 17-1. In the search box provided on the homepage, type in the keyword "anthrax." This site-specific search brings up a wealth of information on the topic and a specific answer to the question being posed.

Health-Care Law Internet Sources and Sites

The following links are sorted in alphabetical order, except that key federal sites are listed first, then other sites are listed. After selecting a site, type the Internet address (the URL), shown in the left column of the listing, into the browser software to get to the Internet site.

Health-Care Law Internet Sources and Sites

Agency for Healthcare Research and Quality http://www.ahcpr.gov	This is the homepage for the Agency for Healthcare Research and Quality (AHRQ), whose research provides evidence-based information

	on health-care outcomes, quality, and cost, use, and access. The AHRQ was formerly known as the Agency for Health Care Policy and Research.
Centers for Disease Control and Prevention (CDC) http://www.cdc.gov	This is the Centers for Disease Control and Prevention (CDC) site. The CDC is an agency of the Department of Health and Human Services. It performs many of the administrative functions of the Agency for Toxic Substances and Disease Registry (ATSDR), a sister agency, and is one of eight federal public health agencies within the Department of Health and Human Services. The Director of CDC also serves as the Administrator of ATSDR.
Centers for Medicare & Medicaid Services (CMS) http://cms.hhs.gov/default.asp? fromhcfadotgov=true	This is the site for the Centers for Medicare & Medicaid Services. Programs that the CMS is responsible for include Medicare, Medicaid, State Children's Health Insurance Program (SCHIP), Health Insurance Portability and Accountability Act of 1996 (HIPAA), and Clinical Laboratory Improvement Amendments (CLIA).
Food and Drug Administration http://www.fda.gov	This is the homepage for the FDA. The "FDA ensures that the food we eat is safe and wholesome, that the cosmetics we use won't harm us, and that medicines, medical devices, and radiation-emitting consumer products such as microwave ovens are safe and effective. [The] FDA also oversees feed and drugs for pets and farm animals. Authorized by Congress to enforce the Federal Food, Drug, and Cosmetic Act and several other public health laws, the agency monitors the manufacture, import, transport, storage, and sale of $1 trillion worth of goods annually, at a cost to taxpayers of about $3 a person."
healthfinder® http://www.healthfinder.gov	This site provides a free gateway to reliable consumer health and human services information developed by the U.S. Department of Health and Human Services. Find online publications, clearinghouses, databases, Web sites, and support and self-help groups, as well as the government agencies and not-for-profit organizations that produce reliable information for the public.

(continued)

National Center for Complementary and Alternative Medicine (NCCAM) at the National Institutes of Health (NIH) http://nccam.nih.gov	The NCCAM conducts and supports basic and applied research and training and disseminates information (through this site, and other media) on complementary and alternative medicine to practitioners and the public.
National Institutes of Health (NIH) http://www.nih.gov	This is the homepage for the NIH. "Founded in 1887, the National Institutes of Health today is one of the world's foremost medical research centers, and the Federal focal point for medical research in the U.S. The NIH, comprised of 25 separate Institutes and Centers, is one of eight health agencies of the Public Health Service which, in turn, is part of the U.S. Department of Health and Human Services."
National Women's Health Information Center http://www.4woman.gov	This site provides a gateway to the vast array of federal and other women's health information resources. Users can link to, read, and download a wide variety of women's health-related material developed by the Department of Health and Human Services, the Department of Defense, other federal agencies, and private sector resources.
Other Sites	
Health Law Hippo[1] http://hippo.findlaw.com/ hippohome.html	This site provides the Web's "best collection of health-care policy and regulatory materials."
Hospitals and Asylums, Title 24, USC[2] http://assembler.law.cornell.edu/ uscode/html/uscode24/usc_sup_ 01_24.html	This site provides the *United States Code* sections for the hospitals and asylums law.
Medscape®: The Online Resource for Better Patient Care®[3] http://www.medscape.com	This site "offers specialists, primary care physicians, and other health professionals the Web's most robust and integrated multispecialty medical information and education tool."

---

[1] Copyright ©1996–2000, Health Hippo.
[2] Copyright © 2005, Cornell University.
[3] Copyright © 1994–2005, Medscape.

MedTerms.com Medical Dictionary[4] http://www.medterms.com	This site contains classical and contemporary medical terms, including pertinent scientific items, abbreviations, acronyms, jargon, institutions, projects, symptoms, syndromes, eponyms, and medical history.
State Health Facts Online[5] http://www.statehealthfacts.kff. org/cgi-bin/healthfacts.cgi?	The Kaiser Family Foundation's State Health Facts Online resource "contains the latest state-level data on demographics, health, and health policy, including health coverage, access, financing, and state legislation."

DISCUSSION QUESTIONS

1. If asked for health reports on AIDS or some other national health issue, how and where would you search for this information on the Internet?
2. How would you use Internet information in the evaluation of medical experts?

PROJECT

1. Assume that you have a minor daughter who is intent on getting a tattoo. What can you learn from the Food and Drug Administration as to the agency's position with regard to tattoos generally?

---

[4] Copyright © 1996–2005, MedicineNet, Inc. All rights reserved.
[5] Copyright © 2005, Kaiser Family Foundation.

CHAPTER 18

Immigration Law Internet Sources and Sites

SUMMARY

This chapter provides a brief introduction to the immigration law practice area and provides descriptions of and links to related Internet Web sites with documents and useful resources.

OBJECTIVES

- The student will learn about the immigration law practice area.
- The student will be introduced to practice area related Internet Web sites.

Immigration Law

These days immigration issues seem to be often in the news. The Elián Gonzalez case was a curiosity to the nation and highlighted how immigration issues can divide families and friends. Business immigration is also often in the news. It seems that the press is expounding weekly the need for more "H-1B" professionals. It is true, though, for those seeking permanent residency in the United States, that there are many more applicants than there are visas available.

To assist CALR professionals, this chapter lists Internet sites in the immigration law practice area. It is increasingly important that the visa application and supporting materials be well researched and prepared. Computer-aided legal research professionals can provide human resource and legal professionals with the information that is required to support visa applications.

For instance, in family immigration, the U.S. Citizenship and Immigration Services' (USCIS) Internet site provides the full scope of applicable forms required and provides helpful guides and directions to assist even novices through the difficult application process. The National Visa Center's site provides regular updates on the status of visa availability.

In business immigration, the H-1B visa application process requires detailed job descriptions, which, regrettably, are not always forthcoming from the petitioners (the proposed employer). An Internet savvy CALR professional, though, can go to the U.S. Department of Labor (U.S. DOL) job descriptions databases and make short work of the process. In addition, by using U.S. DOL job descriptions, applicants may be sure in the process to state the proper keywords, which will (hopefully) be convincing to USCIS officials as the application materials are reviewed. Or, for instance, when the USCIS is not convinced and challenges the employer's statement that the position requires the minimum of a bachelor's degree in a field related to the proposed position, the Internet can make it fairly easy to collect advertisements from employers around the country that also require a bachelor's degree for the same or similar position. Bureau of Labor Statistics statements concerning the occupation are another helpful Internet resource for making that argument.

Internet Research Scenario: The H-1B Petition "Kickback"

In this case, the USCIS has issued a Request for Evidence (RFE) that requests evidence showing that the position of graphic designer is one that requires a bachelor's degree. In this scenario, to collect such evidence, we can do a simple keyword search at the Web site for the U.S. Bureau of Labor Statistics in its *Occupational Outlook Handbook* (*OOH*), 2004–2005 edition. A screenshot of the *OOH* homepage is shown in Figure 18-1.

Go to http://www.bls.gov/oco, and follow the "OOH Search/A-Z Index" link. Then, at the "OOH Search" textbox, type in the following: Designer. This search brings up the *OOH* section on Designers (http://www.bls.gov/oco/ocos090.htm), with specific references to graphic designers. This document indicates that "visual artists usually develop their skills through a

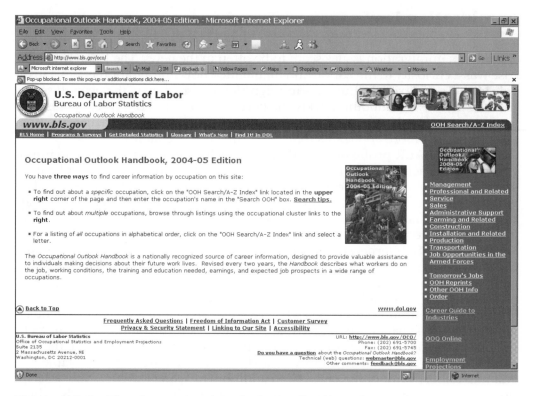

Figure 18-1 The *Occupational Outlook Handbook*'s Web site.

bachelor's degree program or other postsecondary training in art or design." Also, "graphic designers must demonstrate artistic ability and creative thinking. Academic training leading to a bachelor's degree in art or design has almost become a necessity."

This sort of evidence, that is, evidence coming from a sister agency of the USCIS, adds significant weight in responding to USCIS RFEs. Having the required evidence virtually a few clicks away and right on your desktop makes doing these kinds of research projects, not easy, but quickly done.

The online copy of the *OOH* is another example of the federal government making available, in user-friendly format, information and documents that really are an asset and an aid to the public at large. The U.S. Bureau of Labor Statistics should be commended.

Immigration Law Sites

The following topical links are sorted in alphabetical order, except that key federal sites are listed first, then other sites are listed. After selecting a site, type the Internet address (the URL), shown in the left column of the listing, into the browser software to get to the Internet site.

Immigration Law Sites	
Immigration Forms and Fees http://uscis.gov/graphics/ formsfee/forms/index.htm	This is the source for INS forms and fees information. Many of the forms are pdf "fill-able" forms.
Law Enforcement and Border Management http://uscis.gov/graphics/shared/ lawenfor/index.htm	This site links to the relevant sections of the USCIS, the U.S. Immigration and Customs Enforcement (ICE), and the U.S. Customs and Border Protection (CBP) Web sites.
Laws, Regulations, and Guides http://uscis.gov/graphics/ lawsregs/index.htm	This site provides information on laws, regulations, and interpretations controlling immigration and the work of the immigration-related bureaus of the Department of Homeland Security.
LCA Online Application System http://www.lca.doleta.gov	This site provides a system that allows the completion, submission, and immediate receipt of the certified Labor Condition Application ETA Form 9035E. Wow! This process used to take weeks!
National Customer Service Center http://uscis.gov/graphics/ services/NCSC.htm	This site provides links to an automated messages system on a variety of topics. Eventually, the USCIS intends to publish the complete text of the automated messages here.

(continued)

National Visa Center, U.S. Department of State http://travel.state.gov/visa/ visa_1750.html	The National Visa Center (NVC) processes all approved immigrant visa petitions after the Immigration and Naturalization Service approves them.
Occupational Outlook Handbook http://www.bls.gov/oco	This is the Web site for the U.S. Bureau of Labor Statistics *Occupational Outlook Handbook* (*OOH*), 2004–2005 edition. This is an excellent resource for immigration professionals, especially in analyzing and explaining occupations and job duties.
O*NET™ OnLine http://online.onetcenter.org	This site provides the U.S. Department of Labor's "occupational network" (O*NET™ OnLine). It is based largely on data supplied by occupational analysts using sources such as the *Dictionary of Occupational Titles* (DOT).
Student and Exchange Visitor Information System (SEVIS) http://www.ice.gov/graphics/ sevis/index.htm	This is the homepage for SEVIS, a government, computerized system that maintains and manages data about foreign students and exchange visitors during their stay in the United States.
U.S. Citizenship and Immigration Services http://uscis.gov/graphics	This is the homepage to USCIS. Here forms and guidance documents can be found and downloaded.
U.S. Department of State's Page for Consular Links http://usembassy.state.gov	This site provides links to the U.S. missions and embassies that process the immigration visas sought by friends and clients. Visiting these sites when visas are needed may provide useful information for the visitors.
UnitedStatesVisas.gov http://www.unitedstatesvisas.gov	This site is the "official source of information about U.S. visa policy and procedures. Use this site to learn about the visa application process, understand current requirements, and get updates on recent developments. This site serves as a single point of access to U.S. visa information. It will connect you to additional, in-depth information found on Web sites managed by the U.S. State Department and the U.S. Department of Homeland Security."
Visa Appointment Reservation System http://www.nvars.com	This site provides a system for booking nonimmigrant visa interviews. Interviews may be booked at the U.S Embassy in Ottawa, Canada, and at other selected Consulates General in Canada and Mexico.

Other Sites	
American Immigration Law Resources on the Internet[1] http://www.wave.net/upg/immigration/resource.html	This site provides considerable immigration links. It's worth a look.
American Immigration Lawyers Association[2] http://www.aila.org	This site, for its members, provides useful information and documents after entering the right password.
Center for Immigration Studies http://www.cis.org	The Center for Immigration Studies contains new articles, brief topical background reports, and a selection of links.
County and City Databooks http://fisher.lib.virginia.edu/collections/stats/ccdb	This resource provides WWW access to the electronic versions of the 1988 and 1994 County and City Data Books.
Immigration Portal[3] http://www.ilw.com	This is a useful reference site, with links to key immigration information.
National Immigration Law Center[4] http://www.nilc.org	The National Immigration Law Center (NILC) is a national support center whose mission is to protect and promote the rights and opportunities of low-income immigrants and their family members. The Center conducts policy analysis and impact litigation and provides publications, technical advice, and trainings to a broad constituency of legal aid agencies, community groups, and pro bono attorneys.
U.S. Immigration Code On Line[5] http://www.fourmilab.to/uscode/8usc/8usc.html	This site provides access to the complete text of the United States Immigration and Nationality Act at Title 8 of the *United States Code.* Hyperlinks have been embedded in the *Code* to permit following cross-references between sections with a simple mouse click. A WAIS-based full-text search engine allows the quick location of *Code* sections by content.

---

[1] Copyright © 1995–1999, Information Technology Associates. All rights reserved.
[2] Copyright © 1993–2005, American Immigration Lawyers Association.
[3] Copyright © 1999–2004, American Immigration LLC.
[4] Copyright © 2005, National Immigration Law Center.
[5] This site, at the *Index Librorum Liberorum* at Fourmilab in Switzerland, is compiled by John Walker.

DISCUSSION QUESTIONS

1. In business immigration, since the immigration forms are typically in a proprietary automated software package, what value do you see in having access to Internet forms from the INS?
2. Under the NAFTA treaty with Canada and Mexico, which categories of professions are eligible for U.S. "TN" work visas? Where would you look for that information? What is the source document? In how many Internet locations did you find this, if at all?

PROJECT

1. The new associate for immigration wants to know what the USCIS's position or policy is concerning the use of computer- and Internet-generated forms for immigration applications. See if you can find an answer to this on the Internet.

CHAPTER 19

Intellectual Property Law Internet Sources and Sites*

Christian R. Andersen

SUMMARY

This chapter provides a brief introduction to the intellectual property law practice area and provides descriptions of and links to related Internet Web sites with documents and useful resources.

OBJECTIVES

- The student will learn about the intellectual property law practice area.
- The student will be introduced to practice area related Internet Web sites.

Intellectual Property Law

Intellectual property is rapidly proving to be the lifeblood of the Internet. As a result, a wide variety of Web sites are available on the subject, so much so that it proves difficult to sort through them. Often users and developers of Web sites believe that the Internet is a type of "free zone." There is a perception that the rules and laws of intellectual property do not exist on the Web. Not only do they still apply, but several are actually intensified by the ease of the use of the Web and the dissemination of information.

At a quick glance, it may seem that the concepts of "intellectual property" and the "Internet" do not have much in common. However, this could not be farther from the truth. Although the Web does not appear to have recognizable boundaries, it actually is built on the foundation of intellectual property rights.

The three basic areas of intellectual property are patents, trademarks, and copyright. Patent law relates to the protection of inventions and the methods for using ("practicing") inventions. Trademark law is concerned with words, symbols, or devices that identify the products and services of a company or

---

*The original summary of intellectual law, in the first edition of this manuscript, had been a stand-alone chapter, separate from the intellectual law links listed in this chapter. Commenters on drafts of this edition suggested the narrative belonged here, and so it is.

enterprise. Copyright law protects original works of authorship from being copied without permission. Finally, copyright law extends to the protection of an idea rather than the actual idea itself.

Patent Law: What Is Protected

Patent law protects inventions and processes (utility patents) and ornamental designs (design patents). Inventions and processes protected by utility patents can be electrical, mechanical, or chemical in nature. Examples of works protected by utility patents are a computer chip, genetically engineered bacteria for cleaning up oil spills, a computerized method of running cash management accounts, and a method for curing rubber. Examples of works protected by design patents are a design for the sole of running shoes, a design for sterling silver tableware, and a design for a water fountain.

Obtaining Patent Protection

There are strict requirements for the grant of utility patents and design patents. To qualify for a utility patent, an invention must be novel (new), useful, and "nonobvious." To meet the novelty requirement, the invention must not have been known or used by others in this country before the applicant invented it, and it also must not have been patented or described in a printed publication in the United States or a foreign country before the applicant invented it. This includes publication of the idea on the Internet. The novelty requirement guarantees that a patent is issued in exchange for the inventor's disclosure to the public of the details of his or her invention. If the inventor's work is not novel, the inventor is not adding to the public knowledge, so the inventor should not be granted a patent.

To meet the nonobviousness requirement, the invention must be sufficiently different from existing technology and knowledge so that at the time the invention was made the invention as a whole would not have been obvious to a person having ordinary skill in that field. An inventor needs to keep his or her eye on the clock. Even if the invention or process meets the requirements of novelty, utility, and nonobviousness, a patent will not be granted if the invention was patented or described in a printed publication in the United States or a foreign country or on the Internet more than one year before the application date or if the invention was in public use or on sale to the public in the United States for more than one year before the application date. This limitation is known as the one-year bar date.

Scope of Protection

A patent owner has the right to exclude others from making, using, or selling the patented invention or design in the United States during the term of the patent. Anyone who makes, uses, or sells a patented invention or design within the United States during the term of the patent without permission from the patent owner is an infringer—even if he or she did not copy the patented invention or design or even know about it.

Before June 8, 1995, utility patents were granted for a period of seventeen years. After that date, patents are issued for twenty years after filing, with certain extensions available. Design patents are granted for a period of fourteen years. Once the patent on an invention or design has expired, anyone is free to make, use, or sell the invention.

Trademark Law: What Is Protected

Trademarks and service marks are words, names, symbols, shapes, colors, sounds, scents, or any combination of different devices used by manufacturers of goods and providers of services to identify their goods and services and to distinguish their goods and services from goods manufactured and sold by others. Trademarks identify the source of the goods or services being offered. A label on a pair of jeans or the name on the "For Sale" sign in front of a house can either bring in customers or send them away, depending on the reputation that name has with the public.

For trademarks used in commerce, federal trademark protection is available under the federal trademark statute, the Lanham Act.[1] Many states have trademark registration statutes. It is important to remember that trademark rights derive from the use of the trademark and not the registration of the trademark with the federal or any state government. For example, the McDonald's Corporation would have strong trademark rights in the "McDonald's" brand even if it had never registered the mark, due to the extensive use of the name in connection with its restaurants. This is particularly important to remember in relation to the growth of the Internet. Users of trademarks on the Internet may not take the time to register their marks, but they are establishing their rights through their sites.

Availability of Protection

Trademark protection is available for words, names, symbols, or devices that are capable of distinguishing the owner's goods or services from the goods or services of others. A trademark that so resembles a trademark already in use in the United States as to be likely to cause confusion or mistake is not only not protectable but is an infringement of the mark it resembles. In addition, trademarks that are "descriptive" of the functions, quality, or character of the goods or services must meet special requirements before they will be protected.

Obtaining Protection

The most effective trademark protection is obtained by filing a federal trademark registration application in the Patent and Trademark Office. Federal law also protects unregistered trademarks, but such protection is limited to

---

[1] 15 U.S.C.S. § 1051.

the geographic area in which the mark is actually being used. State trademark protection under common law is obtained by adopting a trademark and using it in connection with goods or services. This protection is limited to the geographic area in which the trademark is actually being used. State statutory protection is obtained by filing an application with the state trademark office.

Scope of Protection

Trademark law in general, whether federal or state, protects a trademark owner's commercial identity. This concept is also known as the trademark owner's goodwill and reputation. Goodwill is built through the customer's recognition of the trademark as a name that represents a certain level of quality. A trademark owner's use and investment in such expenses as advertising give the trademark owner the exclusive right to use the trademark on the type of goods or services for which the owner is using the trademark.

Any person who uses a trademark in connection with goods or services in a way that is likely to cause confusion is an infringer. Trademark owners can obtain injunctions against the confusing use of their trademarks by others, and they can collect damages for infringement.

Specific Trademark Concerns on the Internet

As already discussed, a trademark is a word, image, slogan, or other device designed to identify the goods or services of a particular party. Trademark infringement occurs when one party utilizes the mark of another in such a way as to create a likelihood of confusion, mistake, or deception with the consuming public. The confusion created can be that the defendant's products or services are the same as that of the trademark owner or that the defendant is somehow associated, affiliated, connected, approved, authorized, or sponsored by the trademark owner. Since most Web sites will contain discussions of products or services, Web site developers should be aware of the potential trademark issues.

There is nothing inherently wrong with the identification of other parties' products on a Web page by using their trademarks. Nonetheless, some parties have made inappropriate claims of trademark infringement every time they see one of their marks on another party's page. Sometimes, however, a Web site does violate the trademarks of another. Web page designers should avoid trademark usage that might cause confusion among viewers as to the source or sponsorship of the Web page.

It is common to find a link to another Web page made through a company's name, trademark, or logo. In most cases, this type of link will not cause trademark concerns unless the use causes the type of confusion that has been discussed. However, the use of another party's logo without its permission may be more likely to raise the type of confusion that creates trademark infringement, since a graphical logo arguably creates a stronger impression of affiliation than mere text in other countries.

Domain Names as Trademarks

A **domain name** is an alphabetic representation of underlying Internet address. Domain names consist of two parts: (1) a nomenclature, followed by (2) a generic abbreviation identifying the type of organization (or country, outside the United States). Consider, for example, gte.com. The generic abbreviation (.com) is known as the **top-level domain (TLD),** and the preceding nomenclature (gte) is known as the *second-level domain.*

The following seven designations are the traditional global TLDs managed by various domain-name registries:

1. .edu: for educational organizations
2. .com: for commercial entities
3. .net: for computers of network providers such as InterNIC
4. .int: for international databases and organizations established by international treaties
5. .org: for other organizations
6. .gov: for federal government offices and agencies
7. .mil: for the U.S. military

In November 2000, the Internet Corporation for Assigned Names and Numbers (ICANN) announced that it had selected seven new generic top-level domains that would be created in addition to the existing ones. This was the first addition of generic global top-level domains since 1989. Many of these new top-level names are now being used. They include the following:

- .aero: for airlines, airports, computer reservation systems and related industries.
- .biz: for businesses. However, it is unclear how the company would handle requests from individuals and nonbusiness groups.
- .coop: for business cooperatives such as credit unions and rural electric coops.
- .info: for general information sites.
- .museum: for accredited museums worldwide. The name will be restricted, and registration would not be available to those organizations that could not meet the criteria as an accredited museum.
- .name: for individuals. It would reserve second-level names such as andersen.name and let individuals register christian.andersen.name or betty.andersen.name.
- .pro: for professionals. Physician John Doe, for example, could register as johndoe.med.pro. If John Doe were a lawyer, he could register as johndoe.law.pro. As with .museum, this will be a restricted name. Individuals will have to prove their professional status.

For trademark owners, the use of domain names by other parties causes trademark confusion and infringement for the trademark owner. The public can be confused and misled by the misappropriation of trademarks if used as domain names by other third parties. Domain names also can cause dilution of trademarks. In addition, where a bookseller and a television producer may never have had a problem before, if they both wish to use "amazon" as a domain name, they could see each other in court.

The Internet has also opened up a wealth of new problems for trademark owners in cyberspace. Cybersquatters and brokers both create obstacles for trademark owners. Cybersquatters are individuals who take domain names that are common mistakes in typing addresses (such as housse.com or house.org instead of house.com) and use them to misdirect traffic on the Internet. One of the most famous individuals to do so was Daniel Khoshnood, who took thousands of names and used them to link to adult entertainment sites. The National Aeronautics and Space Administration (NASA) felt so strongly that it sought and won court action against Khoshnood's use of nasa.com. The spirit of entrepreneurship is alive and well on the Web in the form of domain-name brokers. These individuals register domain-names for the sole purpose of selling them to other individuals and companies.

Reclaiming a Domain Name Registered by Another

Occasionally, upon searching for a domain name, a party may discover that someone else has already taken its corporate name or trademark as a domain name. It is often difficult to decide what steps to take once you discover a troubling domain name. You should first determine if the domain is live and active with a Web site. If this is the case, you can take immediate action through the courts or by directly contacting the owner of the domain name. There is also the option of contacting the host service directly to shut down the offending site. Agreements with most host services contain provisions that allow the disruption of service if a violation of federal law occurs on a site.

The Anticybersquatting Consumer Protection Act

The Anticybersquatting Consumer Protection Act (ACPA) was signed on November 29, 1999, as part of the Intellectual Property and Communications Omnibus Reform Act of 1999. It prohibits the unauthorized registration of trademarks as Internet domain names by creating civil liability for anyone who "registers, traffics in, or uses" a domain name that is identical to, confusingly similar, or dilutes a trademark.[2]

The registrant must, however, have a "bad-faith intent to profit," which the ACPA specifies is to be determined by reference to a nonexhaustive list of factors that "may" be considered, including

- the intellectual property rights involved,
- whether the domain name is a person's legal or commonly used name,
- whether any prior use of the domain name was made in connection with the offering of goods and services,
- whether there was a bona fide noncommercial or fair use of the mark in a site accessible under the domain name,

---

[2] 15 U.S.C.S § 1125(d)(1)(A).

- the registrant's intent to divert or confuse the trademark holders' customers or to tarnish or disparage the mark by creating a likelihood of confusion concerning the site sponsorship,
- offers by the registrant to sell the domain name to the mark holder prior to use,
- the presence of materially false or misleading contact information for the site,
- the registrant's warehousing of other domain names, or
- whether the mark is distinctive or famous.[3]

The ACPA similarly prohibits nonconsensual registration of a domain-name that "consists of the name of another living person, or a name substantially and confusingly similar thereto . . . with the specific intention to profit from such name by selling the domain name for financial gain."

The ACPA affords somewhat limited remedies, including domain-name cancellation and other injunctive relief. Actual damages as well as statutory damages of between $1,000 and $100,000 per domain name are also available for trademark violations. Only injunctive relief and prevailing party attorneys' fees are available to redress the registration under personal name provisions.

An example of an action now possible under the ACPA is *Harrods Ltd. v. Sixty Internet Domain Names,* 110 F. Supp. 2d 240 (E.D. Va. 2000). In this case, the plaintiff, owner of the Harrods Department Store in London, England, brought an action known as an *in rem*[4] proceeding under the ACPA against sixty Harrods-formative domain names owned by an Argentine business.

In addition to relying on the *in rem* provision of the ACPA, the plaintiff also asserted claims for trademark infringement, trademark dilution, and federal unfair competition. Initially, the court dismissed the plaintiff's *in rem* claim for failure to plead the element of bad-faith intent to profit. You must show that the registrations were done to cause an economic impact on the plaintiff. Often, cybersquatters will offer to sell the domain name to another individual who would have rights in the name. This can be used as evidence of bad-faith intent to profit. Another such case was *Yahoo! Inc. v. Wu,* Civ. A. No. 00–178-A (E.D. Va. Feb. 3, 2000). In this action, the defendants registered the domain name "21yahoo.com," operated a Web site bearing the mark 21YAHOO at that name, and offered free stock in a company called 21Yahoo.com, Inc. Defendants also registered numerous other domain names containing variations of the Yahoo!® mark. Plaintiff Yahoo! Inc. began receiving complaints from consumers inquiring about a barrage of chain e-mail messages claiming that "Yahoo" had begun a new Web site in China entitled 21Yahoo and was offering ten shares of free stock in the new company for anyone who registered at the 21Yahoo.com site.

Yahoo! Inc. sued defendants alleging trademark infringement, dilution, and violation of the ACPA. Addressing only the trademark infringement and false designation of origin claims, the court found plaintiff likely to succeed on the merits, noting that Yahoo!® was a famous mark and that the balance of

---

[3] 15 U.S.C.S § 1125(d)(1)(B)(i).

[4] An *in rem* proceeding is one in which the defendant is a piece of property rather than an individual. In this case, the property is the domain name itself. Prior to the passage of the ACPA, *in rem* cases were most often used in real estate matters such as absentee landlords who could not be found. Often, domain-name registrants cannot be found.

harms weighed significantly in its favor. The court granted a temporary restraining order, enjoining defendants from using the disputed marks and domain names and requiring Network Solutions Inc. (the Registrar) to put the domain names on hold pending the outcome of the proceedings. The court subsequently granted the plaintiff's motion for preliminary injunction on February 11, 2000.

Another clear violation of the ACPA occurred when a domain name incorporating the trademark of another was used for adult entertainment purposes. In *Mattel, Inc. v. Internet Dimensions Inc.*, 55 U.S.P.Q.2d 1620 (S.D.N.Y. 2000), plaintiff Mattel, maker of BARBIE® dolls, brought this action against Internet Dimensions Inc. and its owner, Benjamin Schiff, operators of a pornographic Web site at the domain name barbiesplaypen.com. The court held that defendants' use and registration of barbiesplaypen.com violated the ACPA because (1) the BARBIE mark was distinctive and famous, (2) barbiesplaypen.com was confusingly similar to plaintiff's BARBIE mark, and (3) defendants registered and used barbiesplaypen.com with a bad-faith intent to profit. In finding a bad-faith intent to profit, the court took into account, among other factors, defendants' registering of multiple domain names containing third-party trademarks and supplying false contact information when registering those names. The court ordered defendants to transfer the domain name to Mattel and entered a permanent injunction barring defendants from the commercial use and infringement of any of Mattel's BARBIE marks. However, in order to prove damage, you must show that the public would confuse the third-party site as a site offered by another company. This plays into the question of what has loosely come to be known as First Amendment rights. Names that incorporate such colorful phrases as "sucks" or "blows chunks" are held not to be in violation of the ACPA, because the public would not believe that a company would post a "sucks" site about itself.

For example, in *Lucent Technologies, Inc. v. Lucentsucks.com*, 95 F. Supp. 2d 528 (E.D. Va. 2000); *Lucent Technologies v. Johnson*, 56 U.S.P.Q.2d 1637 (C.D. Cal. 2000), the plaintiff filed an *in rem* action under the ACPA against the domain name lucentsucks.com. The court noted dicta that "[d]efendant argues persuasively that the average consumer would not confuse lucentsucks.com with a website sponsored by plaintiff." In short, "[a] successful showing that lucentsucks.com is effective parody and/or a site for critical commentary would seriously undermine the requisite elements for the causes of action at issue in this case." However, Lucent did eventually prevail in a finding of bad faith under the ACPA because the defendant's Web site sold pornography and the defendant offered to sell the domain name to the plaintiff for $10,000, both of which are evidence of bad faith. The court rejected the defendant's argument for a per se rule that "yourcompanynamesucks" domain names constitute a "safe harbor" under the First Amendment, because it did not challenge the sufficiency of the plaintiff's claim and was therefore inappropriate on a motion to dismiss. Similarly, despite the defendant's claim that he reasonably believed his domain-name registration was a fair use, the court held that this "particularistic, context-sensitive analysis" should be conducted at the summary judgment stage, not during a motion to dismiss.

You can also take advantage of the ICANN Uniform Domain-Name Dispute-Resolution Policy (UDRP) found at http://www.icann.org/udrp/udrp.htm. The Policy, approved by ICANN, provides for out-of-court arbitration if a domain-name dispute arises. It creates a form of mandatory arbitration that constitutes a substantial change to the way domain-name disputes were previously treated, making it easier, in particular, for trademark owners to claim domain names held by other parties (the cybersquatters).

Prior to the UDRP, the domain-name landscape resembled the American West in the 1880s. Network Solutions, Inc. (NSI), the former sole domain-name registrar, had maintained a laissez-faire, "hear no evil, see no evil" approach to domain disputes, refusing to act unless a party that objected to a registered domain could produce a certified trademark identical to another party's name.

The UDRP changed all that by allowing a trademark owner or anyone with common law rights to a trademark to file an administrative complaint in the case that a domain name is held to satisfy all (or some, depending on whom you believe) of the following conditions:

- The domain name is identical or "confusingly similar" to a trademark or service mark in which the complainant has rights.
- The domain-name registrant is held to have "no rights or legitimate interests" in the domain name.
- The domain name was registered "in bad faith."

The ICANN appointed three bodies to act as the arbiters for the UDRP: the World Intellectual Property Organization (WIPO), the National Arbitration Forum (NAF), and eResolution. As of July 2001, there have been 4039 actions instituted involving 7011 domain names, 394 of which are still pending. The actions have resulted in the transfer of 4491 names from the original registrant to the party that brought the UDRP action. It is important to note that a decision under the UDRP can be challenged in court.

If you are in a dispute with another legitimate owner of a name, in resolving the conflict, you can consider jointly sharing a domain name in which the Web page would have links to both companies' sites. Finally, there is the strategy of waiting it out. Unlike any other trademark disputes, problematic domain names may literally go away. Many people who register domain names do not pay the required fees. These people do get an initial registration. The domain name is eventually removed by the registry if the fees are not paid. Continued diligence is warranted, however, as these individuals may re-register.

Copyright Law: What Is Protected

Copyright protection is available for "works of authorship." The Copyright Act[5] states that works of authorship include the following types of works that are of interest to the multimedia or Web developer or anyone who accesses the Web:

- Literary works
- Musical works
- Dramatic works
- Pantomimes and choreographic works

---

[5] 17 U.S.C.S §§ 101-1010.

- Pictorial, graphic, and sculptural works
- Motion pictures and other audiovisual works
- Sound recordings

Any incorporation of these types of works into Web sites and other electronic media has copyright implications. It is important to remember that copyright protects the expression of an idea and not the idea itself.

Obtaining Copyright Protection

Copyright protection arises automatically when an "original" work of authorship is "fixed" in a tangible medium of expression. Registration with the Copyright Office is optional, but you must register before or immediately after you file an infringement suit. Unlike patent and trademark rights, which are validated over time, the copyright in an item exists from the moment of creation.[6] The copyright in the work immediately becomes the property of the author who created the work.

In copyright law, the terms "original" and "fixed" have specific legal meanings. A work is considered to be "original" if it was originated by the author and was not copied from some preexisting work. That is, no part of the finished work was taken from any other work. A work is considered to be "fixed" when it is made "sufficiently permanent or stable to permit it to be perceived, reproduced, or otherwise communicated for a period of more than transitory duration." Even copying a computer program into the Random-Access Memory (RAM) has been found to be of sufficient duration for it to be "fixed."

Neither the "originality" requirement nor the "fixation" requirement is stringent. An author can "fix" words, for example, by writing them down, typing them on an old-fashioned typewriter, dictating them into a tape recorder, or entering them into a computer. A work can be original without being novel or unique. For example, there are many original books about murder mysteries with similar plots. Although the butler may always be the culprit, each book can be original to the different authors.

Interestingly enough, only minimal creativity is required to meet the originality requirement. A work can incorporate preexisting material and still be original. When preexisting material is incorporated into a new work, the copyright on the new work covers only the original material contributed by the author. The use of the preexisting work should only be after the author has obtained the permission of the prior author or the preexisting work has become part of the public domain (discussed subsequently).

Scope of Protection

Copyright protects against copying the "expression" in a work, not against copying the work's ideas. The difference between "idea" and "expression" is one of the most difficult concepts in copyright law. The most important point to un-

---

[6] 17 U.S.C.S. § 302.

derstand is that one can copy the protected expression in a work without copying the literal words (or the exact shape of a sculpture, or the exact "look" of a stuffed animal). When a new work is created by copying an existing copyrighted work, copyright infringement exists if the new work is "substantially similar" to the work that was copied. The new work need not be identical to the copied work. A copyright owner has five exclusive rights in the copyrighted work:

1. *Reproduction Right.* The reproduction right is the right to copy, duplicate, transcribe, or imitate the work in fixed form.
2. *Modification Right.* The modification right (also known as the derivative works right) is the right to modify the work to create a new work. A new work that is based on a preexisting work is known as a "derivative work."
3. *Distribution Right.* The distribution right is the right to distribute copies of the work to the public by sale, rental, lease, or lending.
4. *Public Performance Right.* The public performance right is the right to recite, play, dance, act, or show the work at a public place or to transmit it to the public. In the case of a motion picture or other audiovisual work, showing the work's images in sequence is considered "performance." Sound recordings—recorded versions of music or other sounds—do not have a public performance right.
5. *Public Display Right.* The public display right is the right to show a copy of the work directly or by means of a film, slide, or television image at a public place or to transmit it to the public. In the case of a motion picture or other audiovisual work, showing the work's images out of sequence is considered "display."

In addition, certain types of works of "visual art" also have "moral rights"[7] that limit the modification of the work and the use of the author's name without permission from the original author. As a recent example, on November 20, 2000, it was reported that veteran English rock star Ozzy Osbourne filed a $20 million copyright infringement suit in Los Angeles against DirectTV and other entertainment companies over rights in a pay-per-view telecast of a concert he claims was taped for Internet play only. As the artist, he has the right to control the use of his copyrighted performance, in this case the broadcast of the concert.

Anyone who violates any of the exclusive rights of a copyright owner is an infringer of the author's copyright rights. A copyright owner can recover actual or, in some cases, statutory damages (which can be as high as $100,000 in some cases) from an infringer. In addition, courts have the power to issue injunctions (orders) to prevent or restrain copyright infringement and to order the impoundment and destruction of infringing copies.

The term of copyright protection depends on three factors: who created the work, when the work was created, and when it was first distributed commercially. For copyrightable works created on and after January 1, 1978, the copyright term

---

[7] The Visual Artists Rights Act of 1990, Pub. L. No. 101-650, 601-610, 104 Stat. 5089, 5128 (1990) (codified at 17 U.S.C.S. § 106A (1988)).

for those created by individuals is the life of the author plus fifty years. The copyright term for "works made for hire" (discussed in the next paragraph) is seventy-five years from the date of first "publication" (distribution of copies to the general public) or 100 years from the date of creation, whichever expires first.

Generally, the copyright is owned by the person (or persons) who creates the work. However, if the work is created by an employee within the scope of his or her employment, the employer owns the copyright because it is a "work for hire." The copyright law also includes another form of "work for hire": it applies only to certain types of works that are specially commissioned works. These works include audiovisual works, which will include most multimedia projects. In order to qualify the work as a "specially commissioned" work for hire, the creator must sign a written agreement stating that it is a "work for hire" prior to commencing development of the product.

Avoiding Copyright Infringement

Current technology makes it fairly easy to combine material created by others—film and television clips, music, graphics, photographs, and text—into a multimedia product. Just because you have the technology to copy these works does not mean you have the legal right to do so.

If you use copyrighted material owned by others without getting permission, you can incur liability for hundreds of thousands or even millions of dollars in damages. If you use copyrighted material in your multimedia project without getting permission, the owner of the copyright can prevent the distribution of your product and obtain damages from you for infringement, even if you did not intentionally include his or her material.

A number of misconceptions exist concerning the necessity of getting a license. Here are some of the most common misunderstandings:

- "If there is no copyright notice, then I am free to use it."

For works published on or after March 1, 1989, the use of copyright notice is optional. The fact that a work does not have a copyright notice does not mean that the work is not protected by copyright.

- "I am only going to use a small amount of the copyrighted work."

It is true that *de minimis* copying (copying a small amount) is not copyright infringement. However, there are no clear lines defining what constitutes a "small amount" of someone else's copyright. There is a myth of the thirty percent rule. That is, it is thought that if you use less than "thirty percent" of someone's work, you can avoid infringement charges. This is usually not true, and some people spend thousands of dollars finding this out.

- "My use of the copyrighted work will show off the author and will bring him or her attention."

Do not assume that a copyright owner will be happy to have you use his or her work. In 1993, ten freelance writers sued *The New York Times* and other publishers over the unauthorized publication of their work through online computer services. In 1997, due to a rarely used section of the copyright law, the court decided that the magazines had the right to publish the articles in certain databases. Also, consider the copyright controversy over the Napster programs. The recording industry is vigorously fighting to protect its copyrights in recorded songs.

- "I can copy anything I find on the Web without permission."

Again, while you are free to copy public domain material that you find on the Internet, generally you should not copy copyrighted material without getting permission from the copyright owner.

When You Do Not Need a License

You do not need a license to use a copyrighted work in three circumstances:

1. If your use is fair use
2. If the work you use is in the public domain
3. If the material you use is factual or an idea

Fair Use

There are certain limits to the copyright owner's exclusive rights in a work. One of the most important exceptions to a copyright owner's rights is the public's right to make "fair use"[8] of a copyrighted work. Fair use is a limited use of a copyrighted work without the copyright owner's permission. Fair use does not involve any liability for infringement. Fair use includes the use of a copyrighted work for purposes such as criticism, comment, parody, news reporting, teaching, scholarship, or research.

Public Domain

As a practical note, the public domain contains all works for which the statutory copyright period has expired. Consequently, the public is free to copy any work that is in the public domain and all works that were never protectable by copyright laws. Works enter the public domain in several ways:

- Because the term of the copyright expired
- Because the copyright owner failed to "renew" a copyright under the old Copyright Act of 1909
- Because the copyright owner failed to properly use copyright notice (of importance only for works created before March 1, 1989, at which time copyright notice became optional)

---

[8] 17 U.S.C.S. § 107.

Ideas or Facts

You do not need a license to copy facts from a protected work or to copy ideas from a protected work. The copyright on a work does not extend to the work's facts. This is because copyright protection is limited to original works of authorship, and no one can claim originality or authorship for facts. You are free to copy facts from a copyrighted work.

Special Web Site Issues

The use of copyrighted materials on a Web site poses a number of special issues. First, because of the international nature of the Internet, the licenses of third-party rights would have to be worldwide in scope. It may be difficult to obtain such broad rights, because different parties may own them. For example, many book publishers exclusively license or assign copyrights to different companies for distribution in different countries. Consequently, you would have to obtain clearances from several different companies for a single work. Second, you will need to license public display rights for text and photographs and public performance for video clips and music. You generally do not need those rights for a CD-ROM because it is used in the privacy of a home. However, you would need public performance rights to demonstrate the CD-ROM at trade shows. You would also need to license such rights if the CD-ROM is to be used in a school or company where the audience will be not be limited to family and friends. This is similar to the Ozzy Osborne lawsuit example noted earlier. The creation of a Web site requires careful attention to the legal as well as the technical aspects of the development. The online industry is so new that it has few or no traditions of the roles of the parties. A development contract should address the following issues:

- Ownership of the copyright and other rights in the completed Web site
- Responsibility for the Web site design, and definition of milestones in the development process
- Definition of Web site performance specifications
- Method for confirming that the Web site meets the performance specifications
- Responsibility for licensing third-party software
- Liability for the failure of the Web site to perform in accordance with the specifications
- The responsibility for continuing performance and updating the Web site
- Method and timing of payment
- Remedies for failure to perform
- Liability for infringement of third-party rights

Internet Research Scenario: Trademark Research

In this scenario, a client is considering an application for a new trademark and has requested some initial research on whether a similar mark already exists.

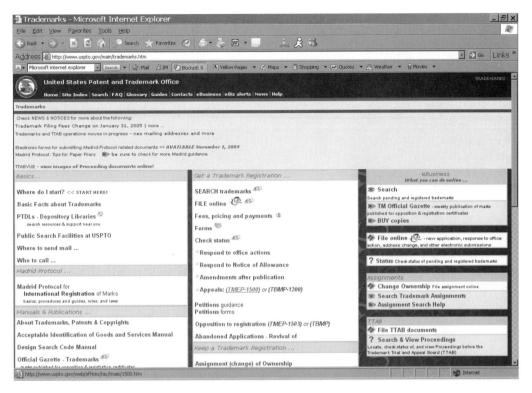

Figure 19-1   The Trademark Applications and Registrations Web site.

For this scenario, we will search for the mark "spam." To do so, go to the Trademark Applications and Registrations and Retrieval Homepage. A screenshot of the Trademark homepage is shown in Figure 19-1.

> Go to http://www.uspto.gov/main/trademarks.htm. At this Web site, select "Search pending & registered trademarks." Then select "New User Form Search (Basic)." Then, at the "Search Term" text box, type in the mark to be searched for. For instance, type in: spam. Then select the "Submit Query" button. This search generated "28 Records(s) found."

Intellectual Property Law Sites

The following topical links are sorted in alphabetical order, except that key federal sites are listed first, then other sites are listed. After selecting a site, type the Internet address (the URL), shown in the left column of the listing, into the browser software to get to the Internet site.

Intellectual Property Law Sites	
Patent and Trademark Fees http://www.uspto.gov/web/offices/ac/qs/ope	This site lists the fees for patent and trademark filings.
Patent and Trademark Forms http://www.uspto.gov/web/forms/index.html	This is the source for patent and trademark forms (in pdf format) and fees information.
Patent Cooperation Treaty (PCT) Index Page http://www.wipo.int/pct/en/index.html	The World Intellectual Property Organization (WIPO) sponsors this site with information about the PCT, which is an international standard for foreign patent filings.
Trademark Applications and Registrations Retrieval Homepage http://tarr.uspto.gov	The U.S. Patent and Trademark Office (USPTO) offers the opportunity to search for the current status of a U.S. trademark application or registration at this site. As with the other sites, this service is offered free of charge.
U.S. Copyright Office http://www.copyright.gov	The official site of the U.S. Copyright Office. The Library of Congress administers copyrights. This is why the site does not appear with the U.S. Patents and Trademark information. They are two separate agencies.
U.S. Copyright Office Information Circulars and Forms http://www.copyright.gov/pubs.html	The information circulars explaining U.S. copyright practice and the relevant forms with instructions may be found at this site.
U.S. Patent and Trademark Office General Information http://www.uspto.gov	This is the official site of the U.S. Patent and Trademark Office. It offers links to publicly available information on both patents and trademarks, including searchable databases (described next).
USPTO Patent Searching http://www.uspto.gov/patft/index.html	This is the public database sponsored by the U.S. Patent and Trademark Office for patents and may be searched free of charge.
USPTO Trademark Searching http://tess2.uspto.gov/bin/gate.exe?f=login&p_lang=english&p_d=trmk	This is the free public database sponsored by the U.S. Patent and Trademark Office for searching trademarks free of charge.

Other Sites

Center for Intellectual Property and Copyright in the Digital Environment[9] http://www.umuc.edu/distance/odell/cip	The Center for Intellectual Property and Copyright in the Digital Environment provides resources and information in the areas of intellectual property, copyright, and the emerging digital environment. The Center provides workshops, online training, and electronic and print publications, along with updates on legislative developments at the local, state, national, and international levels.
Copyright Clearance Center[10] http://www.copyright.com	This is the official site of one of the largest databases of licensed copyrights, particularly in the music and entertainment fields.
European Patent Office[11] http://www.european-patent-office.org/index.en.php	Information about the European Patent Office and international patent matters may be found at this site.
IANA Homepage[12] http://www.iana.org	This is the site for the Internet Assigned Numbers Authority (IANA), the supreme authority for assigning IP addresses at continental level. IANA delegates great blocks of IP addresses to regional registries, of which there are at present three[13] in the world.
IBM® Intellectual Property and Licensing[14] http://www.ibm.com/ibm/licensing	This is a patent site with images sponsored by IBM®. It is available free of charge.
ICANN-Accredited Registrars[15] http://www.icann.org/registrars/accredited-list.html	The Internet Corporation for Assigned Names and Numbers (ICANN) accredits registrars of domain names. The full list of accredited registrars may be found at this site.

(continued)

---

[9] Copyright © 1996–2005, University of Maryland University College.

[10] Copyright © 1995–2004, Copyright Clearance Center, Inc. All rights reserved.

[11] Copyright © 2005, European Patent Office.

[12] Copyright © 2004, The Internet Corporation for Assigned Names and Numbers. All rights reserved.

[13] The three current top-level domain-name registries are RIPE Network Coordination Center, which controls top-level domains for Europe; AP-NIC, which controls top-level domain names for the Asia-Pacific regions; and InterNIC, which controls top-level domain names for North America and the rest of the world.

[14] Copyright © 1994, 2004, IBM Corporation. All rights reserved.

[15] Copyright © 2003, The Internet Corporation for Assigned Names and Numbers. All rights reserved.

ICANN Uniform Dispute Resolution Policy[16] http://www.icann.org/udrp/udrp-policy-24oct99.htm	This site offers information and procedures for resolving domain-name disputes.
Lanham Act[17] http://www4.law.cornell.edu/uscode/15/ch22.html	The text of the U.S. Trademark Act (Lanham Act, 15 U.S.C. §§ 1051–1127) is searchable at this site.
National Intellectual Property Law Institute http://www.nipli.org	This is the homepage for the NIPLI, which researches and analyzes developments in significant areas of intellectual property.
Network Solutions Domain Name "WHOIS" Lookup[18] http://www.networksolutions.com/en_US/whois/index.jhtml	Network Solutions still maintains the universal database for all registered domain name even though it is no longer the sole registrars of domain names. Information on all registered domain names may be found by a search at this site, but it may be necessary to contact the individual registrars for additional information.
The TEACH Toolkit: An Online Resource for Understanding Copyright and Distance Education[19] http://www.lib.ncsu.edu/scc/legislative/teachkit	The TEACH Toolkit is an online resource to the Technology, Education, and Copyright Harmonization Act (TEACH Act). The act updates copyright law in the area of digital distance education and, if numerous requirements are met, facilitates the use of copyrighted materials in digital distance education efforts without having to obtain prior permission from the copyright owner.
Wacky Patent of the Month[20] http://colitz.com/site/wacky.htm	A fun site to see what some people have patented over the years.
World Intellectual Property Organization http://wipo.org	The official site of the World Intellectual Property Organization (WIPO) offers information about international patents, trademarks, and copyright laws and enforcement.

---

[16] Copyright © 2003, The Internet Corporation for Assigned Names and Numbers. All rights reserved.
[17] Copyright © 2005, Cornell University.
[18] Copyright © 2005, Network Solutions. All rights reserved.
[19] Copyright © 2002, Peggy E. Hoon.
[20] Copyright © 1997, Michael J. Colitz, Jr.

DISCUSSION QUESTIONS

1. What are the basic differences in patent, trademark, and copyright law? As to the Internet, do these basic differences change? What other factors come into play when the Internet is involved? Explain.
2. What types of issues should you consider when determining if you should take content from a Web site and use it for yourself? Are there times when copying may be done without permission?
3. Why are copyright forms not listed on the USPTO Web site with the other forms?
4. Where can you find more information about the implementation of electronic filing of patents and trademarks?
5. Where would you go to find out information about an individual who has registered a domain name through Register.Com? What would be the difficulties involved?

PROJECTS

1. Locate on the Internet and print a copy of the Copyright Act from the online U.S.C.
2. Find the Declaration for Utility or Design Application Using an Application Data Sheet form on the responsible agency's Internet site. Be sure to select the "Fillable PDF" form. Complete that form as far as you can for the following facts:

   - Title of Invention: Useful Widget.
   - We are attaching the Application.
   - Craig Johnsign of the USA is the inventor.
   - No other inventors.

CHAPTER 20

International Law Internet Sources and Sites

SUMMARY

This chapter provides a brief introduction to the international law practice area and provides descriptions of and links to related Internet Web sites with documents and useful resources.

OBJECTIVES

- The student will learn about the international law practice area.
- The student will be introduced to practice area related Internet Web sites.

International Law

There is a wide variety of sites about international law and information. For instance, the Central Intelligence Agency provides an Internet copy in full text of its *World Fact Book,* which contains facts and figures for countries and regions around the world. It is a good resource for general international information. Besides primary sources of international laws and regulations, the full text of international treaties and conventions is found easily on line. Embassies and consulates around the world are on the Internet, in some cases providing detailed visa and travel information for business and pleasure. Often the travel application forms are available on line.

Internet Research Scenario: Doing Business in China

In this scenario, the firm has a large corporate client that is considering doing business in the People's Republic of China (PRC). The question is whether there are sources for Chinese law and regulations that would govern business transactions on the Internet. To answer this question, we would go to the Foreign and International Law page at the Washburn University School of Law. A screenshot of the WashLaw homepage is shown in Figure 20-1.

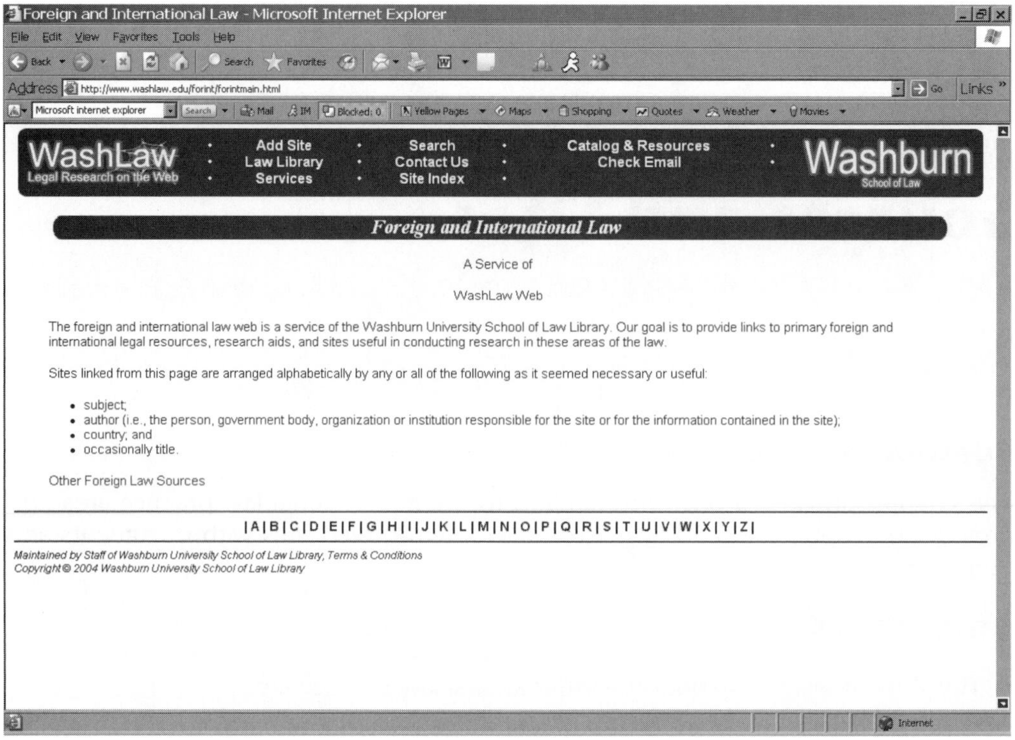

Figure 20-1 The Foreign and International Law page at the Washburn University School of Law's WashLaw Web site.
Reprinted with permission. Copyright © 2004, Washburn University School of Law Library.

Go to http://www.washlaw.edu/forint/forintmain.html. Select the index link to "C" resources, and then use the find tool (<Ctrl><F>) to search quickly for the section dealing with China. Select the "China" link. Here there are various resources and Web sites listed for finding Chinese law and regulations.

International Law Sites

The following topical links are sorted in alphabetical order, except that key federal sites are listed first, then other sites are listed. After selecting a site, type the Internet address (the URL), shown in the left column of the listing, into the browser software to get to the Internet site.

International Law Sites	
CIA's World Fact Book http://www.odci.gov/cia/ publications/factbook/index.html	This is an astounding compilation of facts and figures for countries and regions around the world.

International Judicial Assistance (IJA) http://travel.state.gov/law/info/judicial/judicial_702.html	This is an official United States Department of State site. The IJA site offers information concerning appropriate judicial procedures and documents in foreign nations. Information is provided regarding service of process, obtaining evidence, and enforcement of judgments in criminal and family matters. The information is presented by subject and country. Foreign attorneys in U.S. embassies abroad are listed in addition to guidelines for retaining their services. The IJA Web site also links to treaty, United Nations, and other international information Web sites.
Laws of Canada http://laws.justice.gc.ca/en/index.html	This site by the Canadian Department of Justice provides the searchable full text of the consolidated laws and regulations.
United States Court of International Trade http://www.cit.uscourts.gov	This site provides full-text slip opinions of the Court for 1999 and 2000 in pdf file format. The text of the rules governing the Court's procedure and amendments to the rules are also available. Other resources include a court calendar, a directory of court-affiliated personnel, and biographical information about some of the Court's judges.
United States Government Electronic Commerce Policy http://www.technology.gov/digeconomy/examples.htm	This site provides U.S. documents on electronic commerce policy, along with national and international news releases, reports, articles, and links relating to e-commerce and U.S. government and international policy.

Other Sites

Buffalo Criminal Law Center—Criminal Law Resources on the Internet http://wings.buffalo.edu/law/bclc/resource.htm	This site provides access to criminal law materials from the United States and throughout the world, including criminal codes, criminal procedure codes, and enforcement codes.
EISIL: Electronic Information System for International Law[1] http://www.eisil.org	The EISIL site provides a developing database of international legal materials. It is a tool for finding primary documents, Web sites, and research guides.

(continued)

---

[1] Copyright © 2005, American Society of International Law.

Foreign and International Law, Washburn University School of Law[2] http://www.washlaw.edu/forint/forintmain.html	This is a good collection of links to international law and lawyer resources.
Hong Kong Legal Information Institute[3] http://www.hklii.org	The Hong Kong Legal Information Institute Web site includes court decisions from various levels of Hong Kong courts, legislation, and the full text of Hong Kong laws.
International Chamber of Commerce—International Court of Arbitration[4] http://www.iccwbo.org/index_court.asp	This site is the homepage for the International Court of Arbitration, which is sponsored by the International Chamber of Commerce (ICC). It provides information concerning international dispute resolution, including the ICC Rules of Arbitration that are available in full text, in pdf file format, in English, Arabic, Chinese, French, and German. Also available at the site are statistics and an "arbitration cost calculator."
LLRX International Law Guides[5] http://www.llrx.com/international_law.html	The Law Library Resource Xchange, LLC provides comprehensive guides to foreign law collections on the Internet.
Multilaterals Project[6] http://fletcher.tufts.edu/multilaterals.html	This site by the Fletcher School of Law and Diplomacy provides the full text of international treaties and conventions.
North Atlantic Treaty Organization http://www.nato.int	This site provides up-to-date information and articles on hot spots around the world. Also, it allows for registration to an e-mail list for NATO news releases and provides international links.
North American Free Trade Agreement (NAFTA) http://www.sice.oas.org/trade/nafta.asp	This site provides the full text of the NAFTA agreement and its annexes and related agreements.

---

[2] Copyright © 2004, Washburn University School of Law.
[3] Copyright © 2004, HKLII. HKLII is a project of China IT & Law Centre, a centre jointly established by Department of Computer Science and Faculty of Law of the University of Hong Kong. HKLII has obtained the kind assistance of the Australasian Legal Information Institute (AustLII) in its development.
[4] Copyright © 2005, International Chamber of Commerce. All rights reserved.
[5] Copyright © 1996–2005, Law Library Resource Xchange, LLC. All rights reserved.
[6] Copyright © 2004, The Fletcher School, Tufts University.

Organization of American States[7] http://www.oas.org	This is the site for the Organization of American States (OAS), which "is playing a central role in working toward many of the goals that are shared by the countries of North, Central and South America and the Caribbean." The site provides full-text documents and publications on the organization and its purposes.
Proceedings of the Old Bailey, London 1674 to 1834[8] http://www.oldbaileyonline.org	The Old Bailey Proceedings Online Project describes its site as "a fully searchable online edition of the largest body of texts detailing the lives of non-elite people ever published, containing accounts of over 100,000 criminal trials held at London's central criminal court."

DISCUSSION QUESTIONS

1. If you received a question about shipping and customs information for a client who was considering new business in Canada, where would you look for the answers?
2. If a client or a relative (of yours) had a criminal problem in a foreign country, would you be able to find helpful information on the Internet to assist him or her?

PROJECT

1. Research the environmental law in Canada. Print a list of the applicable laws.

---

[7] Copyright © 2005, Organization of American States, Office of Public Information. All rights reserved.
[8] Copyright © 2003, The Old Bailey Proceedings Online.

CHAPTER 21

Labor and Employment Law Internet Sources and Sites

SUMMARY

This chapter provides a brief introduction to the labor and employment law practice area and provides descriptions of and links to related Internet Web sites with documents and useful resources.

OBJECTIVES

- The student will learn about the labor and employment law practice area.
- The student will be introduced to practice area related Internet Web sites.

Labor and Employment Law

It is easy to find a large number of Web sites about labor and employment law. For instance, one U.S. Department of Labor (DOL) Web site provides an interactive e-laws site. A major feature of this site is the "Poster Advisor" that allows businesses to determine what posters they need to display. The site also allows free downloads of the posters. Besides the Poster Advisor, the site has twenty four other advisors, including versions from the Employment Standards Administration, Mine Safety and Health Administration, Occupational Safety and Health Administration, Pension and Welfare Administration, and Veterans' Employment and Training Service. Another federal site provides the full text of the National Labor Relations Board (NLRB) administrative decisions, NLRB forms, and policy and guidance documents for NLRB practice.

Internet Research Scenario: EEOC Cases

In this scenario, it is not a firm client but a friend of the family who has contacted you. He believes his employer has discriminated against him. You quickly point out that legal counsel is required but that for general information your friend may review helpful information about his potential case at the U.S. Equal Employment Opportunity Commission's Web site. A screenshot of the EEOC.gov homepage is shown in Figure 21-1.

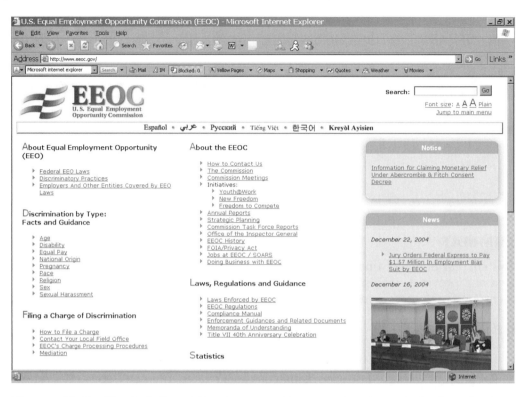

Figure 21-1 The U.S. Equal Employment Opportunity Commission's Web site.

Go to http://www.eeoc.gov. At this Web site, at the top of the page, are listed a couple of immediately helpful materials:

- Federal laws prohibiting job discrimination: Q&A
- How to file a charge of employment discrimination
- Other useful information for employees

This site, again, is an example of the federal government making available, in user-friendly format, information and documents that really are an asset and an aid to the public at large.

Labor and Employment Law Sites

The following topical links are sorted in alphabetical order, except that key federal sites are listed first, then other sites follow. After selecting a site, type the Internet address (the URL), shown in the left column of the listing, into the browser software to get to the Internet site.

Labor and Employment Law Sites	
America's Job Bank http://www.ajb.org	This is the site for the U.S. DOL's job listing database, containing thousands of job listings. This site is useful for finding job comparables and requirements.

Employment Laws Assistance for Workers and Small Businesses http://www.dol.gov/elaws	This U.S. Department of Labor Web site is an interactive e-laws site. One major feature is the "Poster Advisor" that allows businesses to determine what posters they need to display. Besides the Poster Advisor, the site has twenty-four other advisors.
National Labor Relations Board http://www.nlrb.gov	This is the homepage for the National Labor Relations Board (NLRB). The site provides the full text of NLRB administrative decisions, NLRB forms, and policy and guidance documents for NLRB practice.
Office of Administrative Law Judges http://www.oalj.dol.gov	This is the homepage for the U.S. Department of Labor's Office of Administrative Law Judges. The DOL's administrative law judges preside over formal hearings concerning many labor-related matters.
U.S. Department of Labor http://www.dol.gov	This site provides links to all related DOL bureaus and agencies. According to the DOL, it is "responsible for the administration and enforcement of over 180 federal statutes. These legislative mandates and the regulations produced to implement them cover a wide variety of workplace activities for nearly 10 million employers and well over 100 million workers, including protecting workers' wages, health and safety, employment and pension rights; promoting equal employment opportunity; administering job training, unemployment insurance, and workers' compensation programs; strengthening free collective bargaining; and collecting, analyzing, and publishing labor and economic statistics."
U.S. Department of Labor's Program on Alternative Dispute Resolution http://www.dol.gov/asp/programs/adr/main.htm	This is the Department of Labor's site for its Alternative Dispute Resolution Program. The DOL "has experimented with ADR in a number of areas." The DOL site provides full text of its ADR policies and links to other documents.
U.S. Equal Employment Opportunity Commission http://www.eeoc.gov	This is the homepage for the U.S. Equal Employment Opportunity Commission (EEOC). The site provides laws, regulations, policy and guidance, and manuals for Commission practice.

(continued)

Other Sites	
Child Labor Legislative Database[1] http://www.childlaborlaws.org	The Child Labor Legislative Database is an undertaking of The University of Iowa Center for Human Rights Child Labor Research Initiative to collect child labor laws from around the world and to make them available in searchable form via the Internet. Legislation can be searched by keyword and is available in English and the original language.
Cornell Law School's Legal Information Institute Page on Labor Law[2] http://www.law.cornell.edu/topics/labor.html	This site provides the full text of labor laws, regulations, and cases.
FindLaw's® Labor & Employment Law[3] http://www.findlaw.com/01topics/27labor/gov_laws.html	This site provides links to the full text of laws and regulations, and other government documents.
Seyfarth Shaw Labor and Employment Links[4] http://www.seyfarth.com/practice/links.asp?groupid=5	This is an especially good resource of links to labor and employment sites, including federal agency sites; sources of cases, laws, and regulations; statistical sites; and human resource sites.

DISCUSSION QUESTION

1. If your client was faced with employment litigation, say in a wrongful termination suit, which Internet sites would you suggest that the litigation team use to do its initial case legal research and factual information gathering? Would further research be appropriate on the for-pay databases such as Westlaw®?

PROJECT

1. Prepare a Freedom of Information Act request for any documents held by the EEOC (at your local office) that concern a former employee of our client. [NOTE: Look at the Freedom of Information Act link right on the EEOC's homepage!]

---

[1] Copyright © 2002–2005, The University of Iowa Center for Human Rights. All rights reserved.
[2] Copyright © 2005, Cornell University.
[3] Copyright © 1994–2005, FindLaw.
[4] Copyright © 2005, Seyfarth Shaw LLP.

CHAPTER 22

Litigation, Personal Injury, and Tort Internet Sources and Sites

SUMMARY

This chapter provides a brief introduction to the litigation practice area and provides descriptions of and links to related Internet Web sites with documents and useful resources.

OBJECTIVES

- The student will learn about the litigation practice area.
- The student will be introduced to practice area related Internet Web sites.

Litigation

Sources relating to litigation have become increasingly abundant on the Internet. For instance, one site has links to more than 700 sources for state and federal court rules, forms, and dockets. The Federal Rules of Civil Procedure are provided by the Legal Information Institute at Cornell University, which notes that "these rules govern the conduct of all civil actions brought in federal district courts. While they do not apply to suits in state courts, the rules of many states have been closely modeled on these provisions." Another site has links to federal and state rules of court—especially helpful when out-of-state or district rules are needed.

Internet Research Scenario: Finding Registered Agents for Service

In this case, the firm is preparing to bring suit against a company, but the company's registered agent for legal service is unknown. To locate that information:

> Go to the "State Web Locator" at the Villanova Center for Information Law and Policy, at http://www.infoctr.edu/swl, and follow the link to the state in which the suit is to be brought.
> Sometimes a state homepage will have a link to "Agencies and Departments." Follow that link, and select the Secretary of State's (SOS) office. In this example, follow the link for the state of Illinois, which goes to http://www.state.il.us.

At the Illinois homepage, there is a link to "Government" sites. Follow that link, and then select the link to "Agencies, Boards and Commissions." Once there, select the link to the SOS's office (http://www.sos.state.il.us). A screenshot of the Illinois SOS's homepage is shown in Figure 22-1.

On the SOS's homepage is a link for "Services for Business." Follow that link, and then select "Corporation Search." At this page, researchers may access and search for domestic and foreign corporations and their agents in the state of Illinois. Queries may be run on company names or partial names by selecting the "Search the Corporate/LLC Database" link.

For "Step One," select "Both Corp and LLC search." For "Step Two," select "Search Database by Key Word." For "Step Three," "Enter Your Search" in the text box provided.

Run this search for the company name, and see what variations of the company names are returned.

Litigation Resource Sites

The following topical links are sorted in alphabetical order, except that key federal sites are listed first, then other sites are listed. After selecting a site, type the Internet address (the URL), shown in the left column of the listing, into the browser software to get to the Internet site.

Figure 22-1   The Illinois Secretary of State's Web site.

Litigation Resource Sites	
Department of Justice Homepage http://www.usdoj.gov	The homepage for the U.S. Department of Justice.
Federal Judiciary Homepage http://www.uscourts.gov	This site is a first-place-to-look site for recent federal court opinions.
PACER Docket System http://pacer.psc.uscourts.gov	"Public Access to Court Electronic Records (PACER) is an electronic public access service that allows users to obtain case and docket information from Federal Appellate, District and Bankruptcy courts, and from the U.S. Party/Case Index." *See also* PACER FAQs at http://pacer.psc. uscourts.gov/faq.html.
U.S. Consumer Product Safety Commission http://www.cpsc.gov	This is the official site of the CPSC, an independent federal regulatory agency, whose purpose is to help keep American families safe by reducing the risk of injury or death from consumer products. It includes its prompt to consumers to "report unsafe products."
Other Sites	
American Tort Reform Association[1] http://www.atra.org	This site is for the American Tort Reform Association (ATRA), "a broad-based, bipartisan coalition of more than 300 businesses, corporations, municipalities, associations, and professional firms who support civil justice reform." The ATRA publishes weekly updates by e-mail to its paid membership, and the site provides links to state and national civil justice organizations and entities.
Class Action Litigation Information[2] http://www.classactionlitigation. com	"This page contains answers to common questions asked about class action litigation." It also provides numerous links to courts, documents, and resources.
Court Rules, Forms and Dockets[3] http://www.llrx.com/courtrules	"This site includes links to over 700 sources for state and federal court rules, forms and dockets. You can browse to find the resource you need, or search by keyword."

(continued)

[1] Copyright © 2002, The American Tort Reform Association.
[2] Copyright © 1998–2005, Timothy E. Eble. All rights reserved.
[3] Copyright © 1996–2005, Law Library Resource Xchange, LLC. All rights reserved.

CrimeLynx® http://www.crimelynx.com	This site was developed for criminal defense attorneys as a crime and criminal justice portal. It consists of hyperlinks to legal resources, forensic research, investigative tools, and crime policy materials.
Directory of Expert Witnesses and Consultants[4] http://www.expertpages.com	This is a searchable directory listing of over 300 categories and thousands of experts and consultants.
e-DICTA[5] http://www.edicta.org	This site provides law and insurance resources for the ABA's Tort Trial & Insurance Section.
Expert Witness Internet Resources http://www.nocall.org/experts.htm	The site, put together by the Northern California Association of Law Libraries, is a collection of links to experts and to other collections of expert witnesses lists and links.
Federal Rules of Civil Procedure by Cornell University[6] http://www.law.cornell.edu/rules/frcp/overview.htm	This site, provided by the Legal Information Institute at Cornell University, notes that "these rules govern the conduct of all civil actions brought in federal district courts. While they do not apply to suits in state courts, the rules of many states have been closely modeled on these provisions."
Litigation Support Service Links[7] http://marketcenter.findlaw.com/scripts/search.pl?vendor=7&ac=110&pa=110&search=state&direction=1	This site provides a comprehensive listing of nationwide litigation support service providers.
Litigator's Internet Resource Guide to the Rules of Court[8] http://www.llrx.com/columns/litigat.htm	This site has links to federal and state rules of court. It is especially helpful when out-of-state or district rules are needed.

---

[4] Expert Pages® is a registered trademark. Copyright © 1995–2005, ExpertPages.com, a unit of Advice Company.

[5] Copyright © 2004, eDICTA.org.

[6] Copyright © 2005, Cornell University.

[7] Copyright © 1994–2005, FindLaw.

[8] Copyright © 1996–2005, Law Library Resource Xchange, LLC. All rights reserved.

Pleading Index[9] http://www.law.fsu.edu/library/faculty/gore/index.html	This is a model index of pleadings, which is useful for students to see how to prepare one. Links are provided to the actual underlying pleadings.
Prosecuting Attorneys, District Attorneys, Attorneys General, and U.S. Attorneys[10] http://www.eatoncounty.org/prosecutor/proslist.htm	This site, compiled by the state of Michigan's Eaton County Prosecuting Attorney, provides links to government attorneys across the nation.
Tobacco Control Resource Center/Tobacco Products Liability Project[11] http://www.tobacco.neu.edu	The Northeastern University School of Law in Boston provides news on lawsuits against the major tobacco manufacturers, including post-verdict developments, court opinions, documents such as complaints and stipulations, helpful "media backgrounders," and information about the distribution of the awards.
Web Guide to U.S. Supreme Court Research[12] http://www.llrx.com/features/supremectwebguide.htm	This site provides a selection of annotated links to the most reliable, substantive sites for U.S. Supreme Court research.

DISCUSSION QUESTIONS

1. What potential uses of the Internet do you see for support of litigation? Research? Practice/case management? Others? Explain.
2. How would you set out to find and then actually use information obtained from the Internet in the evaluation of opposing expert witnesses? Explain.

PROJECT

1. Our client has called and wants to know what sorts of environmental cases the U.S. EPA has recently brought and/or won. Where specifically on the Internet would you go for this particular information? Would you go to more than one site for this information?

---

[9] Copyright © 2005, Florida State University College of Law and other copyrights. All rights reserved.
[10] Copyright © 1997–2005, Eaton County Prosecuting Attorney, Jeffrey L. Sauter; and Copyright © 1997–2005, Eaton County Information Systems.
[11] Copyright © 2004, Tobacco Control Resource Center, Inc.
[12] Copyright © 1996–2005, Law Library Resource Xchange, LLC. All rights reserved.

CHAPTER 23

Occupational Safety and Health Law Internet Sources and Sites

SUMMARY

This chapter provides a brief introduction to the occupational safety and health law practice area and provides descriptions of and links to related Internet Web sites with documents and useful resources.

OBJECTIVES

- The student will learn about the occupational safety and health law practice area.
- The student will be introduced to practice area related Internet Web sites.

Occupational Safety and Health Law

This chapter lists Internet sites in the occupational health and safety law practice area. In 1970 the U.S. Congress, through the Occupational Safety and Health Act of 1970, established the Occupational Safety and Health Administration (OSHA). As defined in its enabling legislation, OSHA's mission is to "assure so far as possible every working man and woman in the Nation safe and healthful working conditions." This mandate involved the OSHA's development of regulations, standards, compliance assistance documents, and enforcement authorities to assist certain employers—in regulated SIC (standard industrial classification) code categories—to maintain safe and healthful workplaces. All of these OSHA documents are available on the Internet.

The Occupational Safety and Health Administration, in partnership with state governments, regulates 6.5 million employers, in ensuring the safety of more than 100 million working men and women. The administration and its state partners have approximately 2100 inspectors, plus complaint discrimination investigators, engineers, physicians, educators, standards writers, and other technical and support personnel spread over more than 200 offices throughout the country. Most of the inspection reports, or at least summaries of the inspections, are available on the Internet.

Internet Research Scenario: The Responsible Agency in Indiana?

In this case, the supervising attorney has asked: "What is the agency responsible for OSHA-type matters in Indiana?" The firm's client has requested that a Freedom of Information Act (FOIA)–type request be made to that agency. If you work in this area (OSHA practice), or if you have reviewed the following links, you know that OSHA has a Web site that lists the several states that have authority to run their own programs; the site also has links to the states' related local Web sites. So, to find this answer:

Go to the OSHA Web site for "State Occupational Safety and Health Plans," at http://www.osha.gov/fso/osp/index.html, and there, select the link to the Indiana program.

That link brings up detailed address and telephone information for IOSHA and also lists and links to the IOSHA Web site (http://www.in.gov/labor/iosha/index.html). A screenshot of the IOSHA homepage is shown in Figure 23-1.

In this case, follow the IOSHA link to review its site for FOIA-type contact lists and addresses. The IOSHA page does not provide a direct link to FOIA information, but it does contain an "IOSHA FAQs" page. Following that link brings up a list of questions, one being: "How do I get copies of IOSHA case files or

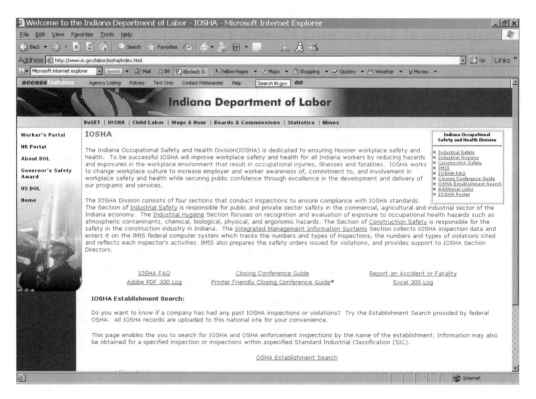

Figure 23-1   The Indiana Department of Labor—IOSHA's Web site.

company histories?" Follow that link to the information on reviewing and obtaining IOSHA case files or histories. That brings up the following:

Indiana Department of Labor—IOSHA
Case History Request
402 West Washington Street
Room W195
Indianapolis, IN 46204
Fax a written request to:
IOSHA Case History Request
317-233-3790

Occupational Safety and Health Sites

The following topical links are sorted in alphabetical order, except that key federal sites are listed first, then other sites are listed. After selecting a site, type the Internet address (the URL), shown in the left column of the listing, into the browser software to get to the Internet site.

Occupational Safety and Health Sites	
OSHA Homepage http://www.osha.gov	The main page for the U.S. Occupational Safety and Health Administration's (OSHA's) Internet domain. Check here first for all OSHA issues.
Chemical Safety and Hazard Investigation Board (CSB) http://www.csb.gov	This site publishes the full text of its investigative reports. A library of chemical hazard and other information is also available through the site's comprehensive links.
National Institute for Occupational Safety and Health (NIOSH) http://www.cdc.gov/niosh	The National Institute for Occupational Safety and Health (NIOSH) is the federal agency responsible for conducting research and making recommendations for the prevention of work-related disease and injury. The Institute is part of the Centers for Disease Control and Prevention (CDC).
NIOSH Pocket Guide to Chemical Hazards http://www.cdc.gov/niosh/ npg/npg.html	This is the site for the *NIOSH Pocket Guide to Chemical Hazards*.
OSHA Inspections [Establishments] Search Page http://www.osha.gov/cgi-bin/ est/est1	This page enables the user to search for OSHA enforcement inspections by the name of the establishment or facility or company. Information may also be obtained for a specified inspection or inspections within a specified SIC.

(continued)

| **State Occupational Safety and Health Plans** http://www.osha.gov/fso/osp/index.html | This site provides links to the state OSHA-equivalent/approved agencies that administrate the OSHA program in selected states. |
| **Work-Related Injury Statistics Query System (Work-RISQS)** http://www2.cdc.gov/risqs | Work-RISQS provides a Web-based public access query system for obtaining national estimates (number of cases) and rates (number of cases per hours worked) for nonfatal occupational injuries and illnesses treated in U.S. hospital emergency departments. Users may interactively query based on demographic characteristics, nature of injury/illness, and incident circumstances for the years 1998 and 1999. |

Other Sites

DMOZ Open Directory Project: Occupational Health and Safety Topics[1] http://dmoz.org/Health/Occupational_Health_and_Safety	This site provides a comprehensive directory of the Web relating to OSHA topics. It relies on volunteer editors.
Occupational Safety and Health Act of 1970 http://www.osha.gov/pls/oshaweb/owasrch.search_form?p_doc_type=OSHACT&p_toc_level=0&p_keyvalue=	This site, put up by OSHA, provides the full text of the OSH Act of 1970.
Occupational Safety and Health Administration's Regulations http://www.access.gpo.gov/cgi-bin/cfrassemble.cgi?title=200429	This is the Government Printing Office's site for Internet access to the full text of OSHA's regulations, 29 C.F.R. Parts 1900 to 2000.
Seyfarth Shaw OSHA Links[2] http://www.seyfarth.com/practice/links.asp?groupid=4	This is an especially good resource of links to OSHA and OSHA-related sites, including federal agency sites, sources of cases, laws, and regulations.
United States Code, Title 29, Chapter 15, Occupational Safety and Health[3] http://www4.law.cornell.edu/uscode/29/ch15.html	This site, by the Legal Information Institute, Cornell Law School, provides the full text of the OSHA federal law.

[1] Copyright © 1998–2005, Netscape.
[2] Copyright © 2005, Seyfarth Shaw LLP.
[3] Copyright © 2005, Cornell University.

DISCUSSION QUESTION

1. Search the OSHA Establishments page for an employer with which you are familiar. Were there any records? What significance does that have (1) generally? (2) in a transaction concerning the company?

PROJECT

1. We understand that NIOSH has some sort of ergonomics guidelines. Exactly what ergonomics guidelines does NIOSH have?

CHAPTER 24

Real Estate Law Internet Sources and Sites

SUMMARY

This chapter provides a brief introduction to the real estate law practice area and provides descriptions of and links to related Internet Web sites with documents and useful resources.

OBJECTIVES

- The student will learn about the real estate law practice area.
- The student will be introduced to practice area related Internet Web sites.

Real Estate Law

How many of us who have achieved majority (over eighteen years old) have not had dealings with real estate? For instance, just renting or subleasing an apartment involves leasing forms. We who have actually purchased (and probably mortgaged) a home are amazed at the number of forms and documents that are involved in a real estate transaction.

Forms are a big part of real estate practice, and forms are a big part of the real estate Internet sources and sites available. There are "boilerplate" forms for sales and purchase agreements, mortgages, leases, and many others. Of course, the huge resources for laws, regulations, and case law are out there too.

Internet Research Scenario: Information About Real Estate on the Internet

In this scenario, as a prospective homeowner, you are considering purchasing a home without an agent or broker. What you need is some good background information in order to educate yourself and see if purchasing without an agent is even a good idea. What you need is, in this case, a review of the comprehensive materials on the U.S. Department of Housing and Urban Development's Web site. A screenshot of the Web site is shown in Figure 24-1.

Go to HUD, at http://www.hud.gov. A screenshot of the HUD.gov homepage is shown in Figure 24–1. Follow the links to Home "Buying," "Selling," and "Owning." Review the materials there carefully.

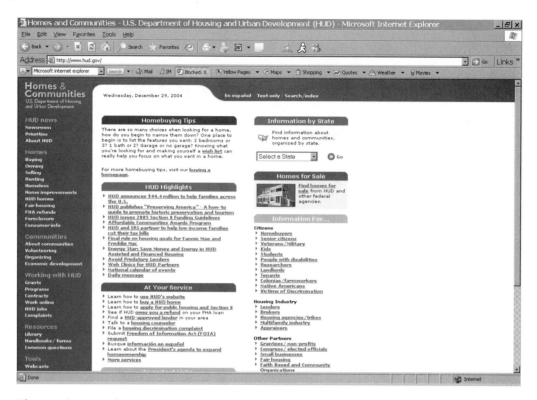

Figure 24-1 The U.S. Department of Housing and Urban Development's Web site.

Real Estate Law Sites

The following topical links are sorted in alphabetical order, except that key federal sites are listed first, then other sites are listed. After selecting a site, type the Internet address (the URL), shown in the left column of the listing, into the browser software to get to the Internet site.

Real Estate Law Sites	
U.S. Department of Housing and Urban Development http://www.hud.gov	This is HUD's homepage. It provides many consumer-friendly documents, like the "buyer's kit." It also provides information on the federal mortgage programs that can help people buy homes. The site is also a considerable resource for businesses with real estate interests. In addition, the site explains to the consumer how to prepare complaints, such as for housing discrimination or regarding deceptive contractors. The site also provides a reading room with extensive links.

Other Sites	
Bankrate.com[1] http://www.bankrate.com	This site provides current mortgage rates and financial calculators to estimate a monthly mortgage payment.
Cornell Law School's Legal Information Institute Page on Real Estate Transaction Law[2] http://www.law.cornell.edu/topics/real_estate.html	This site provides the full text of real estate transaction laws, regulations, and cases.
FannieMae[3] http://www.fanniemae.com	The Fannie Mae Web site provides online mortgage and lending information and documents, and it provides descriptions of its corporate charter and financial purposes. Congress created it in 1938 to bolster the housing industry during the Depression. In 1968 Fannie Mae became a private company operating with private capital on a self-sustaining basis. Its role was expanded to buy mortgages beyond traditional government loan limits, reaching out to a broader cross-section of Americans. Today, Fannie Mae operates under a congressional charter that directs the availability and affordability of homeownership for low-, moderate-, and middle-income Americans.
The Home Buyer's Handbook http://www.ag.state.mn.us/consumer/housing/HmBuyers/Default.htm	This handbook, by the Office of the State of Minnesota Attorney General, is "a step-by-step guide with simple explanations of the confusing terms, easy-to-use worksheets and expert tips for avoiding common pitfalls. It will take some of the mystery—and some of the misery—out of the process."
'Lectric Law Library's Business & General Forms[4] http://www.lectlaw.com/formb.htm	These sites provide free-to-copy basic boilerplate language for litigation and business forms and agreements.

(continued)

---

[1] Copyright © 2005, Bankrate Inc. All rights reserved.
[2] Copyright © 2005, Cornell University.
[3] Copyright © 1998–2005, Fannie Mae.
[4] Copyright © 2005, 'Lectric Law Library.

Legal Forms[5] http://www.legalwiz.com/forms.htm	This site provides sample ("pdf") boilerplate language for forms and agreements.
Legal Resource Center[6] http://resources.lawinfo.com/index.cfm?action=faq&act=form&i=b	This site for boilerplate language for forms allows a search for the particular topical area and for the state for which forms are needed.
Real Estate Self-Help Law Center[7] http://www.nolo.com/resource.cfm/catID/B610DF8A-B9F2-429A-8B9B77A2E203513F/213/243	This site provides the basics on real estate transactions.
Real Estate News and Advice[8] http://realtytimes.com/consumer.htm	This site provides realty news, information, and tools.

DISCUSSION QUESTIONS

1. What real estate forms can you find on the Web? Is it appropriate to use those forms for your clients?
2. In considering Internet intellectual property, would a particular law office be able to download and then give away the Minnesota Attorney General's *The Home Buyer's Handbook?* Why or why not? Explain.

PROJECT

1. Use an Internet Web site to get today's mortgage rate for a thirty-year fixed-rate loan, and calculate out the estimated monthly payment for a $200,000 mortgage loan.

---

[5] Copyright © 2003–2005, Legalwiz Publications. All rights reserved.
[6] Copyright © 1995–2005, LawInfo.com.
[7] Copyright © 2005, Nolo.
[8] Copyright © 2005, Realty Times®. All rights reserved.

CHAPTER 25

Tax, Probate, Trusts, and Estates Law Internet Sources and Sites

SUMMARY

This chapter provides a brief introduction to the tax, probate, trusts, and estates law practice area and provides descriptions of and links to related Internet Web sites with documents and useful resources.

OBJECTIVES

- The student will learn about the tax, probate, trusts, and estates law practice area.
- The student will be introduced to practice area related Internet Web sites.

Tax, Probate, Trusts and Estates Law

Sources of materials relating to tax, probate, trusts, and estates law are prolific on the Internet. For example, the *Internal Revenue Code* itself, embodied as Title 26 of the *United States Code*, is easily found. In fact, the Internal Revenue Service (IRS) has made the entire tax law—with its regulations, interpretations, instructions, and forms—accessible at the IRS Web site. The IRS's *The Digital Daily* Web site provides forms, instructions, regulations, interpretations, and tax news.

One of the oldest taxes is the taxation of property held by an individual at the time of death. This tax is known as estate tax, which is levied on the estate before any other transfers. An estate tax is a charge on the decedent's entire estate. Another form of death tax is an inheritance tax, which is a tax levied on individuals receiving property from an estate. Taxes imposed upon death provide incentives to the living to transfer assets from the estate before death. The probate law governs the passing of property at a death generally, but that may be affected if the deceased left a last will and testament. Gift tax laws are generally designed to prevent tax avoidance in this way. Generally, a gift tax applies to transfers made without receiving any value in return.

Internet Web sites provide links to various state statutes and codes affecting the planning and administering of trusts and estates. Also, information on questions about planning for death, from writing a basic will to organ donation, is easily found on line.

Internet Research Scenario: Finding Needed Tax Forms

In this scenario, you have to file your individual income tax forms by April 15. It is April 14, and you do not even have the forms that are needed.

Go to the IRS Web site, at http://www.irs.gov. A screenshot of the IRS.gov homepage is shown in Figure 25-1. Follow the link to "Forms and Publications."
At this screen there is another link to "Forms and Instructions." Follow that link to download the needed forms in "pdf" format, which can then be filled in by hand or with an old-fashioned typewriter. Select the needed forms from the list.
Note that the IRS is providing many of its forms as "Fillable." These allow you to complete the forms by typing directly onto the downloaded forms.

Tax, Probate, Trusts, and Estates Law Sites

The following topical links are sorted in alphabetical order, except that key federal sites are listed first, then other sites are listed. After selecting a site, type the Internet address (the URL), shown in the left column of the listing, into the browser software to get to the Internet site.

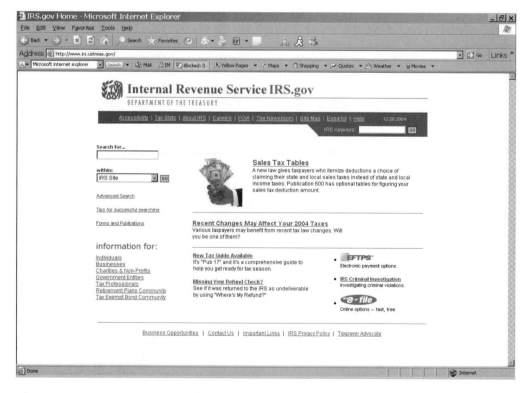

Figure 25-1   The IRS Web site.

Tax, Probate, Trusts, and Estates Law Sites

Internal Revenue Bulletins http://www.irs.gov/pub/irs-irbs	This site is a directory that provides links to the *Internal Revenue Bulletins* by their document numbers (e.g., Bulletin No. 1999–9 is listed as "irb99-09.pdf").
Internal Revenue Manual http://www.irs.gov/irm/part20/index.html	This site provides the IRS *Internal Revenue Manual.* The purpose of the *Manual* is to provide guidance to all areas of the IRS for all penalties imposed by the *Internal Revenue Code.* It reviews procedures both for assessing and abating penalties and contains discussions on topics such as various types of relief from the penalties.
U.S. Internal Revenue Service (IRS) Homepage http://www.irs.gov	The IRS homepage provides online forms, information, and assistance.
United States Tax Court http://www.ustaxcourt.gov	The U.S. Tax Court provides a judicial forum in which affected persons may dispute tax deficiencies determined by the Commissioner of Internal Revenue prior to payment of the disputed amounts. The jurisdiction of the Tax Court includes the authority to hear a wide variety of tax disputes. The Tax Court is composed of nineteen appointed members. All of the judges have expertise in the tax laws. Although the Court is physically located in Washington, D.C., the judges travel nationwide to conduct trials in various designated cities.

Other Sites

Cornell Law School's Legal Information Institute Page on Estate and Gift Tax Law[1] http://fatty.law.cornell.edu/topics/estate_gift_tax.html	This site provides the full text of estate and gift tax laws, regulations, and cases.
Cornell Law School's Legal Information Institute Page on Income Tax Law[2] http://www.law.cornell.edu/topics/income_tax.html	This site provides the full text of income tax laws, regulations, and cases.

(continued)

---

[1] Copyright © 2005, Cornell University.
[2] Copyright © 2005, Cornell University.

Estate Planning, Trust & Probate Law[3] http://www.calbar.ca.gov/state/calbar/calbar_generic.jsp?sCategoryPath=/Home/Attorney%20Resources/Sections/Trusts%20and%20Estates	This site provides resource materials relating to estate planning generally and for California specifically.
Internet Law Library— Trusts and Estates[4] http://www.lawmoose.com/internetlawlib/112.htm	This site provides links to various state statutes and codes affecting the planning and administering of trusts and estates.
Tax History Project[5] http://www.taxhistory.org	The Tax History Project was established to provide scholars, policymakers, students, the media, and citizens with information about the history of American taxation. The Project pursues its mission through a program of Web-based documentary publications and original historical research. The Project's main focus is the creation of a detailed chronology of American tax history.
Tax Policy Center[6] http://www.taxpolicycenter.org	The Tax Policy Center (TPC) researches tax issues for the benefit of policymakers, journalists, researchers, and the public. A joint venture of the Urban Institute and the Brookings Institution, the TPC provides analysis and commentary on federal and state tax and budget policies.
U.S. Tax Code On-Line[7] http://www.fourmilab.ch/ustax/ustax.html	This site provides access to the complete text of the U.S. *Internal Revenue Code*. Hyperlinks have been embedded in the *Code* to permit users to follow cross-references between sections with a simple mouse click.
Wills & Estate Planning Self-Help Law Center[8] http://www.nolo.com/resource.cfm/catID/FD1795A9–8049–422C-9087838F86A2BC2B/309	This site purports to answer your questions about everything from planning for death to writing a basic will to organ donation.

---

[3] Copyright © 2005, The State Bar of California.
[4] Copyright © 1999–2003, Pritchard Law Webs. All rights reserved.
[5] Copyright © 2005, Tax Analysts. All rights reserved.
[6] Copyright © 2005, Urban Institute, Brookings Institution, and individual authors. All rights reserved.
[7] This site, at the *Index Librorum Liberorum*, at Fourmilab, in Switzerland, is compiled by John Walker.
[8] Copyright © 2005, Nolo.

Yahoo!® Finance Tax Center[9] http://taxes.yahoo.com	This site provides links to useful tax tools, such as forms, calculators, articles and interpretations, the tax code, and such.

DISCUSSION QUESTIONS

1. Do you think that the accessibility of the tax law on the Internet has made understanding of the *Code* easier and brought greater compliance?
2. What estate planning forms can you find on the Web? Is it appropriate to use those forms for your clients?

PROJECT

1. Find and print a copy of Internal Revenue Bulletin No. 2000–24, dated June 12, 2000.

Bibliography

Bacal, Glenn S., J. D., M.B.A., *The Practical Litigator's 1999 Guide to Internet Research,* formerly on the Internet at http://www.ali-aba.org/aliaba/intro.htm (1999).

BLACK, PETER MCNAUGHTON, INFORMATICA 1.0: ACCESS TO THE BEST TOOLS FOR MASTERING THE INFORMATION REVOLUTION (Random House 2000).

CADENHEAD, ROGERS, HOW TO USE THE INTERNET (5th ed. Sams 2000).

Cohen, Laura, *Conducting Research on the Internet, at* http://library.albany.edu/internet/research.html (2000).

CROWDER, DAVID, TEACH YOURSELF THE INTERNET (IDG Books Worldwide 1999).

Department of Education, Employment & Training, State of Victoria, *Using the Internet: Research on the Net,* Initiative of the SOFWeb Project©, *at* http://www.sofweb.vic.edu.au/internet/research.htm (2002).

DOING INTERNET RESEARCH: CRITICAL ISSUES AND METHODS FOR EXAMINING THE NET (Steve Jones ed., Sage Publications 1999).

DOWNING, DOUGLAS, ET AL., DICTIONARY OF COMPUTER AND INTERNET TERMS (Barron's 2003).

Harris, Robert, *Evaluating Internet Research Sources, at* http://www.virtualsalt.com/evalu8it.htm (1997).

HEALTH CARE RESOURCES ON THE INTERNET: A GUIDE FOR LIBRARIANS AND HEALTH CARE CONSUMERS (Sandra M. Wood ed., Haworth Information Press 2000).

THE INTERNET AND TECHNOLOGY GUIDE FOR MICHIGAN LAWYERS (Mary Ellen LeBlanc ed., Institute of Continuing Education 1999).

Internet Help: Guides and Tutorials, at http://www.refdesk.com/help.html (2005).

KASSER, BARBARA, PRACTICAL INTERNET (Que 2000).

LAW OF THE SUPERSEARCHERS: THE ONLINE SECRETS OF THE TOP LEGAL RESEARCHERS (T. R. Halvorson & Reva Basch eds., CyberAge Books 2000).

LAWSON, JERRY, THE COMPLETE INTERNET HANDBOOK FOR LAWYERS (American Bar Association 1999).

LEVINE, JOHN R., CAROL BAROUDI, & MARGARET LEVINE YOUNG, THE INTERNET FOR DUMMIES STARTER KIT (7th ed. IDG Books Worldwide, Inc. 2000).

MALONE, BILL, & ANDREW WOLFE, 1001 INTERNET TIPS (Jamsa Press 2000).

Martin, Peter W., *Five Reasons for Lawyers and Law Firms to Be on the Internet, at* http://www.law.cornell.edu/papers/5reasons.html (April 22, 1994).

Neibauer, Alan R., Internet!: I Didn't Know You Could Do That (Sybex 2000).

Schlein, Alan M., et al., Find It Online: The Complete Guide to Online Research (Facts on Demand Press 2003).

Sterne, Jim, World Wide Web Marketing: Integrating the Web into Your Marketing Strategy (2d ed. John Wiley & Sons 1999).

Tutorial: Guide to Effective Searching of the Internet, at http://www.brightplanet.com/deepcontent/tutorials/Search/index.asp (2005).

Vander Hook, Sue, Internet (Smart Apple Media 2000).

Wolinsky, Art, The History of the Internet and the World Wide Web (Enslow Publishers 1999).

Zimmerman, Jan, Marketing on the Internet (4th ed. Maximum Press 2000).

Internet Terms, Concepts, and Acronyms

To assist the aspiring Internet research professional in maximizing the value of the Internet, this appendix provides definitions and explanations of Internet terms, concepts, and acronyms. For each term, concept, or acronym listed,[1] an explanation is provided, along with examples where appropriate.

Active Server Page or asp	A new type of program-enabled active page that is rapidly replacing "htm" files.
Address	An Internet location of an index, resource file, or e-mail. A typical commercial Web address looks like this: http://www.seyfarth.com. An e-mail address lists first the user name and then, after the "@" sign, lists the Internet domain. CSimonsen@seyfarth.com is an example.
Address and Routing Parameter Area Domain or arpa	The arpa domain is designated to be used exclusively for Internet-infrastructure purposes. It is administered by the IANA in cooperation with the Internet technical community under the guidance of the Internet Architecture Board.
Advanced Communications Technology Satellite or ACTS	Part of a joint NASA–ARPA NREN collaboration that will provide high-speed ATM/SONET transmission and will provide interface and operations experience in mating high-speed terrestrial communications systems with high-speed satellite communications systems.
Advanced Research Projects Agency Network or ARPANET	"ARPANET" is an acronym for the network developed by the Advanced Research Projects Agency.

[1] Users are encouraged to submit other Internet terms, concepts, and acronyms—or to comment on those listed—to the author for inclusion in updates to this volume. Submit to csimonsen@seyfarth.com.

America Online® or AOL®[2]	A large Internet service provider with millions of users around the world.
Anchor	Either the starting point or the destination of a hyperlink.
Anonymous FTP	An anonymous FTP site allows Internet users to log on to its site and download files without having to register and receive a private user name and password.
APNIC or National Informatics Centre—Andhra Pradesh [India]	One of three current top-level, regional domain-name registries in the world. Its area of authority is for the Asia-Pacific regions.
Applet	A program that is downloaded over a network and launched on the user's computer.
ASCII File	An American Standard Code for Information Interchange file is a plain-text file. The opposite would be a formatted file, such as WordPerfect® (wpd), Microsoft® Word (doc), or Adobe® (pdf).
Avi	A common file format for video files (.avi). See also "mov" and "mpg."
Binary File	An executable or digital type of computer file. Binary files are typically "exe," "com," or other non-text-based (graphical or multimedia).
Bitmap File	An image file format (bmp).
Bits per Second or "bps"	A measurement of the speed that data travel through a modem. Typical modem speeds are over 56K bps (56,000 bits per second).
Bookmarks	Links to a user's favorite Internet sites. Internet browsers support bookmarks or "favorite places" so that users may return to them easily.
Browser	A computer program that runs through an Internet service provider to access sites and files on the Internet. Examples are Netscape®, Microsoft® Internet Explorer, and Mosaic®.
CALR or Computer-Aided Legal Research	Computer-aided legal research (CALR) is defined simply as the use of computers to automate the search for legal and factual information.
Catalog	A database compiled and used by a search engine that uses the spider or crawler software technology.
Chat	A method for online, interactive, and instantaneous communication between Internet users.
Client	The name of a specific machine within a larger domain. A computer that relies on another computer (the host) for some or all of its resources. The host computer communicates with the client computer to exchange data through a data transmission device, such as a modem.

[2] America Online and AOL are registered trademarks of America Online, Inc.

Com	Either (1) a file name suffix that indicates a type of executable file, or (2) an Internet top-level domain for commercial sites.
Commercial Software	Copyrighted software that is developed specifically for commercial sale.
Common Gateway Interface or CGI	A category of languages, including PERL, a language used to manipulate text files with information in them. It also provides a direct link to Unix commands. Unix is the operating system used on most Internet servers. PERL is the most popular CGI language in the world today.
Compressed	Data files available for download from the Internet are often compacted or compressed in order to save file space on the computer and to reduce the transfer times. Examples of compressed files are "zip" and "mim" files.
Computer-Aided Legal Research or CALR	See CALR.
Confidence Score	A search engine's estimate of how closely a returned site meets the search parameters.
Cookie	A message from a Web server computer, sent to and stored on a local computer. The main use for cookies is to provide customized Web pages according to a profile of the user's interests. When the user selects "customize" on a Web page and fills in the user name and other information, this may result in a cookie being placed on the user's computer (as a "txt" file) that the Web site will access on future visits to appear to "know" the user and will provide information that is "user friendly," such as "Your Local Weather." Completing these Web site forms may also initiate the receipt of e-mail and other unwanted solicitation independent of cookies.
Crawler	A synonym for a spider software that visits Internet sites and builds indexes for use by the search engine.
Database	A collection of related information or documents. An example is the index to all the books in a library. Where as, under the "old way," a card system was used to search manually by "author," "subject," or "title", now, with a database, researchers can still search by "author," "subject," or "title" but also by keyword, by date, by publisher, or by any number of other fields or types of information.
db	A file name suffix that indicates a type of database file.

Dial-Up Connection	A connection to the Internet via phone and modem.
Direct Connection	A connection (usually much faster than dial-up) made directly to the Internet through a cable or satellite system. Could be a T1 or T3 connection.

Directory	A subject directory is a site on the Web that catalogs or categorizes Web sites by subject and also manually indexes the sites, often providing a brief description of content. Yahoo!® is the most well-known directory site: a catalog or listing of linked topics related to a particular Internet site; for instance, the Centers for Disease Control and Prevention (at http://www.cdc.gov) has the following listing as its directory:
	    Contents
	    In the News
	    Travelers Health
	    Health Topics A-Z
	    Publications, Software & Products
	    Data & Statistics
	    Training
	    Employment
	    Subscriptions
	    Other Sites
	    Visitor Survey

Discussion Group	An Internet area that is typically dedicated to a particular subject of interest. Also known as a newsgroup.
Domain	The Internet is divided into smaller sets of computers known as domains, including "com" (commercial and business) sites, "gov" (government) sites, "edu" (educational) sites, and many others.
Domain Name	Domain names represent addresses for places to go, such as Web sites on the Internet. In the same way that a street address represents the location of a destination in the physical world, a domain name is used to represent a location on the Internet. In the physical world, we rely on both street addresses and the postal system to send information back and forth between individuals and organizations. On the Internet, we rely on domain names and the Domain-Name System (DNS).
Domain-Name System (DNS)	The Domain-Name System plays a critical role in the process that computers and people use to communicate on the Internet. The DNS is a distributed database containing information about domains and the hosts, or computers, within those domains.

Download	The process of copying computer file(s) from a remote computer to a local (your) computer. See also "upload."
E-Commerce	The act of setting up a Web site for the particular purpose of promoting commerce.
edu	An Internet top-level domain for educational organizations.
E-Mail	Electronic, computer mail.
E-Messaging	Involves two or more computer users connected through the Internet and sending instantaneous or live messages between each other.
exe	A file name suffix that indicates a type of executable file.
Extensible Markup Language or XML	A superset of HTML; Extensible Markup Language allows the user to tag various parts of a document with user-defined tags and extends the HTML language for greater flexibility and reusability.
Favorite Places	Links to a user's favorite Internet sites. Internet browsers support favorite places or bookmarks so that users may return to sites easily.
File Transfer Protocol or FTP	A set of rules for exchanging files between computers over the Internet.
Framing	A Web page design that places other and linked pages within the current page. The appearance is that the surfer never leaves the current site, when the material being reviewed in a "frame" is straight off of another page. You either love them or you hate them!
Freeware	Copyrighted software that is available for downloading at essentially no cost to the recipient. Typically, the author retains the copyright and so freeware is not necessarily in the public domain, and its distribution may be controlled by the copyright owner.
Frequently Asked Questions or FAQs	A collection of questions and answers on a particular subject and associated with a particular Web site. This is an excellent starting point for users to learn about features of a particular site.
Gateway	Computer hardware and software that allow users to connect from one network to another.
gif	See Graphic Interchange Format.
Google™	A good example of an Internet site with an excellent search engine.
Gopher	A file search system that allows users to search for files through menus and directory structures. Most Gopher sites have been replaced by Web pages.

Graphic Interchange Format or gif	A common image format (gif). Many images seen on Web pages are gif files.
gov	An Internet top-level domain for government offices and agencies.
High-Performance Computing and Communications or HPCC	Part of the High-Performance Computing and Communications Program.
High-Performance Computing and Communications Program or HPCC Program	The federal program that is an effort of the government to accelerate the development of high-performance computing and communications technologies and for the diffusion of these technologies to improve U.S. competitiveness and the well-being of citizens.
Hit	A site returned by a search request.
Homepage	The first page of a Web site or the Web site that automatically loads each time you launch your browser.
Host	The name of a specific machine within a larger domain. The source of records or information sought (by a client) on the Internet. The host computer communicates with the client computer to exchange data through a data transmission device, such as a modem.
HotJava®	A Web browser developed by Sun Microsystems that takes full advantage of applets written in the Java™[3] programming language.
htm or html	A file name suffix that indicates a Hypertext Markup Language file.
Hyperlink	A connection between two anchors. Clicking on one anchor will take you to the other anchor, perhaps within the same document or page or in two totally different documents.
Hypertext	An Internet-ready document that contains links to other documents, commonly seen in Web pages and e-mail files.
Hypertext Link	Appears on the Internet as a highlighted word or graphic image. Selecting a hypertext link will transfer to the user a document or file from the current computer or from another computer anywhere in the world.
Hypertext Markup Language or HTML	A fairly simple Internet programming language.
Hypertext Transfer Protocol or HTTP	The form for writing an Internet address to acquire access to its files and resources. Technically, it is a set of instructions for communication between a local computer and an Internet client.

---

[3] Java is a registered trademark of Sun Microsystems, Inc.

Index	A searchable database of documents created automatically or manually by a search engine; a Web page that contains links to other Web pages of a specific category; the means by which a search engine catalogs a Web site; or the main or starting page of a Web site.
int	An Internet top-level domain for international databases and organizations established by international treaties.
Integrated Services Digital Network or ISDN	A fast data transmission system that allows the simultaneous delivery of audio, video, and data.
Internet	The worldwide network of computers communicating through an agreed-on set of protocols. As defined by the Federal Networking Council (FNC), the term "Internet" refers to the global information system that (i) is logically linked together by a globally unique address space based on the Internet Protocol (IP) or its subsequent extensions/follow-ons; (ii) is able to support communications using the Transmission Control Protocol/Internet Protocol (TCP/IP) suite or its subsequent extensions/follow-ons, and/or other IP-compatible protocols; and (iii) provides, uses or makes accessible, either publicly or privately, high-level services layered on the communications and related infrastructure described herein.[4]
Internet Assigned Number Authority or IANA	The authority for assigning IP addresses. The IANA delegates blocks of IP addresses to the regional registries.
Internet Protocol Address or IP Address	Every computer on the Internet has a unique identifying number, like 232.1.33.5.
Internet Service Provider or ISP	A company or organization that provides an Internet connection.
Internetwork	A network is made up of two or more computers that are connected so that they can exchange messages and share information. An internetwork is two or more networks that are connected so that they can exchange messages and share information. The Internet is the world's largest internetwork.
InterNIC[5]	One of three current, top-level, regional domain-name registries in the world. InterNIC's area of authority is for North America and other areas

[4] FNC Resolution, *Definition of Internet,* formerly on the internet *at* http://www.fnc.gov/Internet_res.html (Oct. 24, 1995).

[5] InterNIC is a registered service mark of the U.S. Department of Commerce.

	of the world besides the Asia-Pacific regions (APNIC) and Europe (RIPE Network Coordination Centre One).
Java™	A programming language created by Sun Microsystems for developing applets that are capable of running on any computer regardless of the operating system.
Joint Photographic Experts Group or JPEG	A common image format (jpg) used especially in art and photographic applications.
LAN	See Local Area Network.
Link	Another name for a hyperlink.
Listserv	An electronic mailing list. After subscribing to a listserv, the user receives periodic e-mail messages about the subject topic. An example is the frequent e-mails from the U.S. Environmental Protection Agency of its daily news releases.
Local Area Network or LAN	A network of computers confined within a small area, such as in a small business.
Lynx	A popular text (nongraphical) based Internet browser.
Mailing List	A list of e-mail addresses used to send e-mail to users that have the same interest. For instance, all members of a working group. A user typically must join a mailing list or give permission to have its address used or published, though some lists are compiled illicitly and then sold in commerce for spam mailings.
Metatag	A bit of descriptive information placed into the html coding of a page to assist search engines in properly indexing a page. Metatags are placed in the head section of a page, and each metatag contains two elements or properties: (1) its name and (2) its content. For example: <meta name="name or key words" content="key word one, key word two, etc">.
Microsoft®	Short for Microsoft Corporation, the biggest supplier of operating systems and other software for IBM PC compatible computers. Other software products include MS-DOS, Microsoft® Windows®, Windows® NT®, Windows® XP®, and Microsoft® Office, which includes Word®, Access®, Excel®, Outlook®, and PowerPoint®.
Microsoft® Internet Explorer®	Software that provides a set of Web browsing technologies for navigating the Internet.
Mid	A high-quality audio file format (mid).
Mil	An Internet top-level domain for the U.S. military.

Mirror Site	An Internet site set up as a "mirror image" of a site; contains copies of all the files stored at the primary location.
Modem	A host computer communicates with a client computer to exchange data through a data transmission device, such as a modem. Basic telecommunication hardware consists of a host computer, the host's transmitting modem, a client's receiving modem, a client computer, and telephone lines in between.
Mosaic	One of the first Internet browsers developed at NCSA.
mov	A common file format for video files (mov).
mp3	A high-quality audio file. Requires proprietary software to play.
MPEG or mpg	A common file format for video files (mpg).
Multimedia	A combination of media types on a single document, including text, graphics, animation, audio, and video.
Multipurpose Internet Mail Extensions or MIME	An Internet compression utility that allows e-mail messages to attach numerous compressed files in a single file (mime). For instance, the AOL® e-mail system automatically converts multifile attachments received in Internet e-mail and creates a single mim file that the AOL® user must then "unzip" or uncompress in order to access the attached files.
Musical Instrument Digital Interface or MIDI	A hardware interface card that is designed specifically to interface with electronic musical instruments.
National Center for Supercomputing Applications or NCSA	The National Center for Supercomputing Applications (NCSA) at the University of Illinois at Urbana-Champaign is the leading-edge site for the National Computational Science Alliance (Alliance). In this capacity, NCSA anchors all Alliance teams and oversees the administration of all Alliance programs. NCSA leads the Alliance in its mission to maintain American preeminence in science and technology.
National Research and Education Network or NREN	The realization of an interconnected gigabit computer network system devoted to HPCC. NREN is also a component of the HPCC Program.
National Science Foundation Network or NSFNET	NSFnet was one of the Internet's backbone networks. It had been funded by the National Science Foundation.
Netiquette	Slang for Internet etiquette.
Netscape® Navigator®	One of several Internet browser programs that share the Internet browser market.

Network	A group of connected computers. A LAN is a smaller form of a network, in contrast to the Internet, which is a worldwide network of computers.
Newsgroups	An Internet Usenet area that is typically dedicated to a particular subject or interest; an electronic discussion in which information and opinions are shared with people all over the world. Within each newsgroup are articles on a given subject. Usenet newsgroups allow readers to reply to articles read and to publish (post) articles for others to read.
Offline Computing	Processing data while not connected to a host computer. The time spent communicating with a host computer is called "connect" or "online" time.
Online Computing	When a computer is connected to an online service, such as AOL®, or to the Internet, it is "on line."
Online Service	Services, such as America Online®, CompuServe®[6], Prodigy®[7], and the Microsoft®[8] Network, which provide information content to subscribers along with connections to the Internet.
org	An Internet top-level domain for organizations that do not fall under other Internet top-level domains.
Page	An HTML document, or an Internet site.
Pixel	Short for picture element. A unit of resolution or measurement on a computer monitor.
Plug-In	An application that extends the built-in capabilities of another program, such as the Web browser. Examples include Macromedia's Shockwave, providing animation, and RealAudio, offering streamed sound files over the Internet.
Portable Document Format or pdf	A formatted file that provides a "what you see is what you get" image of paper documents.
Portal	A gateway to the Internet, such as a search engine or directory Web site. Examples include Google™, AltaVista®, Excite™, Yahoo!®, and AOL®. A starting point for Internet surfing.

---

[6] CompuServe is a registered trademark of America Online, Inc.

[7] Prodigy, the Prodigy globe logo, Prodigy High, the Prodigy Interactive Personal Service logo, Prodigy Internet, and Prodigy Plus are registered trademarks of Prodigy Communications L.P.

[8] Microsoft, Windows, Windows NT, MSN, The Microsoft Network, Home Essentials, HomeAdvisor, Expedia, Encarta, Bookshelf, PowerPoint, BackOffice, Outlook, FrontPage, Computing Central, MapPoint, CarPoint, Hotmail, WebTV, Advisor FYI, ZoneMatch, ZoneMessage, and/or other Microsoft products referenced herein are either trademarks or registered trademarks of Microsoft Corporation.

Protocol	An agreed-on set of rules by which computers exchange information.
Provider	An Internet Service Provider, or ISP.
QuickTime®	A common Internet video file format (qt or mov), created by Apple Computer®.[9]
RIPE (Réseaux IP Européens) Network Coordination Centre	One of three current, top-level, regional domain-name registries in the world. Its area of authority is Europe.
Search Engine	A Web program or service that allows you to query a database for keywords and then returns matching Web pages. Popular search engines include Google.com and Yahoo.com.
Server	One-half of the client-server protocol runs on a networked computer and responds to requests submitted by the client. Your World Wide Web browser is a client of a World Wide Web server.
Shareware	Shareware is copyrighted software that is available for downloading on a free, limited trial basis. If users like the shareware and decide to use it, they are expected to register with the author and pay a small fee. Registering the software usually enables a user to be eligible for technical assistance and updates from the author.
Signature	A personal tag or message automatically appended to an e-mail message.
Site	A collection of related Web pages.
Snail Mail	Plain old paper U.S. Postal Service mail.
Spam	Sometimes unwelcome e-mail messages that promote a commercial product or Web site. Hormel Foods Corporation, the commercial manufacturer of the edible SPAM®[10], has stated: "You've probably seen, heard or even used the term 'spamming' to refer to the act of sending unsolicited commercial e-mail (UCE), or "SPAM" to refer to the UCE itself . . . . We do not object to the use of this slang term to describe UCE, although we do object to the use of our product image in association with that term. Also, if the term is to be used, it should be used in all lowercase letters to distinguish it from our trademark SPAM®, which should be used with all uppercase letters."
Spider	Software that visits Internet sites and builds indexes for use by a related search engine.

[9] Apple, the Apple logo, FireWire, GeoPort, HyperCard, Light Bulb logo, ImageWriter, LaserWriter, Mac, Mac logo, Macintosh, MessagePad, Newton, OpenDoc, Power Macintosh, PowerBook, QuickTake, QuickTime, QuickTime logo, and StyleWriter are trademarks of Apple Computer, Inc.

[10] SPAM is a registered trademark of Hormel Foods Corporation.

Standard General Markup Language or SGML	A standard for Internet markup languages. STML is one version of HTML.
Subscribe	To become a member or subscriber to a mailing list, a newsgroup, an online service, or an Internet Service.
Tag Image File Format or tif	A popular graphic image file format (tif).
TCP/IP	See Transmission Control Protocol/Internet Protocol.
Telecommunication	One of the most useful and widely used methods of data communication. Basic telecommunication hardware consists of a host computer, the host computer's transmitting modem, a client computer's receiving modem, a client computer, and telephone lines in between.
Telnet	A protocol for logging on to remote computers from anywhere on the Internet.
Thread	An ongoing message-based conversation on a single subject.
Top-Level Domain or TLD	A domain name consists of two parts: (1) a nomenclature, "gte," followed by (2) a generic abbreviation, ".com," which identifies the type of organization and/or country. The generic abbreviation (.com) is known as the TLD and the preceding nomenclature (gte) is referred to as the second-level domain.
Transmission Control Protocol/Internet Protocol or TCP/IP	The foundational protocol of the Internet; an agreed-on set of rules for computers (and their programmers) on how to exchange information with each other. Other Internet protocols, such as FTP, Gopher, and HTTP, run on top of TCP/IP.
txt	A plain-text ASCII file. May be unformatted or may be formatted for importation into another application, such as "delimited text," which can be easily imported into database or spreadsheet files.
Uniform Resource Locator or URL	The form by which Internet sites are addressed. An example is http://www.seyfarth.com.
Unix	The operating system used on many of the networked machines of the Internet. World Wide Web servers frequently run on Unix. Unix files are case sensitive.
Upload	The process for copying a file from a local (your) computer connected to the Internet to a remote computer. See also "download."
Usenet	Describes a set of machines that exchange articles tagged with one or more universally recognized labels, called newsgroups (or "groups" for short). Usenet encompasses government agencies, large universities, high schools, businesses of all sizes, home computers of all descriptions, and so on.

Virtual Library	A Web site that is set up for the specific purpose of collecting and disseminating particular types or groups of documents and information.
Virtual Reality Modeling Language or VRML	A growing language used to create virtual reality worlds. In the future, Web pages will most likely only be used after flying to a place in a virtual world and accessing a document from a virtual book.
Vortal	Short for vertical portal. A portal Web site that specializes in a particular industry and that is directed toward business rather than consumers. These sites provide in-depth "vertical information" relating to special interests rather than the "horizontal" information provided at most general portal sites. A typical vortal provides news, research and statistics, documents, and a specialized topical search engine. An example of a vortal is http://www.FindLaw.com.
Waveform Audio or wav	A common audio file format (wav) for DOS and Microsoft® Windows computers.
Web site	An http address or location that is on the Internet.
Winsock	A Microsoft® Windows DLL file that provides the interface to TCP/IP services, through which Windows is able to use Web browsers, FTP programs, and such.
wks or wk1	A common spreadsheet (IBM Lotus) format file.
World Wide Web or WWW	Or simply, the "Web." A subset of the Internet that uses a combination of text, graphics, audio, and video (multimedia) to provide information to users.
xls	A common spreadsheet (Microsoft® Excel) format file.
Yahoo!®	A good example of an Internet site with an extensive directory.
zip	A compressed file format (zip) used by many ISPs and their users to compress or "zip" large and multiple files in order to reduce storage space and transfer times. See also Multipurpose Internet Mail Extensions.

The Domain-Name System

Christian R. Andersen

A question often asked is "Where or how does an Internet address (such as 'hot-dog.com') get registered?" There is a science to what in the Internet are known as **domain names.** This appendix provides an overview of the **Domain-Name System (DNS),** which is the system for the establishment and operation of individual domains. The operation of a domain name is illustrated, and examples of domain-name servers and resolutions of domain-name issues are covered. Future trends in domain-name registration and administrative domain-name challenges are discussed. Simply put, domain names represent the addresses for places on the Internet. In the same way that a street address represents the location of a destination in the physical world, a domain name represents a location of a destination on the Internet. In the physical world, we rely on both street addresses and the postal system to send information back and forth between individuals and organizations. On the Internet, we rely on domain names (the addresses) and the DNS (the electronic postal system). The DNS plays a critical role in the process that computers and people use to communicate on the Internet. Consequently, a smoothly functioning DNS is extremely important. While it is not necessary to understand all the technical intricacies of the DNS, this overview offers both an understanding of an important element of Internet communication and an explanation of why the DNS is important to domain-name registrants.

How a Domain Name Operates

The Internet is the network of connected Transmission Control Protocol/ Internet Protocol (TCP/IP) computers that can "talk" to each other over telecommunications networks by using the numeric **Internet Protocol addresses (IP addresses).** Internet Protocol addresses are numbers that must be assigned to every computer or server that is directly connected to the Internet. The authority for assigning IP addresses is the **Internet Assigned Number Authority (IANA).** The IANA delegates blocks of IP addresses to the regional registries. Currently, there are three[1] regional registries in the world.

---

[1] The three top-level domain-name registries are the RIPE Network Coordination Centre, which controls top-level domains for Europe; APNIC, which controls top-level domain names for the Asia-Pacific regions; and InterNIC, which controls top-level domain names for North America and the rest of the world.

Domain names, such as "seyfarth.com," are alphabetic representations of underlying Internet addresses. A domain name consists of two parts: (1) a nomenclature, "seyfarth," followed by (2) a generic abbreviation, ".com," that identifies the type of organization and/or country. The generic abbreviation (.com) is known as the **top-level domain (TLD)** and the preceding nomenclature (seyfarth) is referred to as the *second-level domain.*

Through the DNS, Internet-connected computers use a numeric addressing system to locate other computers on the network. This numeric addressing system requires that each computer connected to the Internet have its own, unique numeric address—an Internet Protocol (IP) address. Internet Protocol addresses are thirty-two-bit addresses that are represented by a string of numbers separated by periods, for example, 198.41.0.108.

Machines such as computers, of course, have no problem remembering and using numerical addresses. Humans, in contrast, generally find it easier to remember addresses if they are familiar, relational, or hierarchical. For instance, a commercial wholesaler of hotdog products wants an Internet address that sells hotdogs. It will be easier for customers to remember "hotdogs.com" than it will be to remember a string of numbers such as "182.31.432.122."

The global computer network, however, must use the numeric IP address. Therefore, when an Internet user types in the domain name hotdogs.com, an intermediary system is needed to translate the domain name typed by the Internet user to the corresponding IP address. The DNS is the system that enables this translation to occur.

Characteristics of the DNS

The DNS has several key characteristics: it is hierarchical, distributed, interdependent, and requires unique addresses.

It Is Hierarchical

The DNS uses a hierarchical structure. At the very top of the hierarchy is the root, which is also technically called the "." (dot). Beneath the root level of the hierarchy are the top-level domains, for example, *.com, .net, .org, .edu,* and *.gov.* Other examples of top-level domains (TLDs) include those for countries, which use the International Standards Organization's ISO 3166 standard—for example, *.us* for the United States of America, *.fr* for France, and *.de* for Germany. Beneath each of these top-level domains are subdomains that are commonly referred to as second-level domains. The TLDs are currently divided into regional top-level domains and global top-level domains.

Regional domains consist of multiple designations to the right of the first "." such as *.com.de,* which designates a German regional top-level domain. Global TLDs consist of only one designation. The standard global TLDs managed by various IANA delegated registries are

- **.edu** for educational organizations
- **.com** for commercial entities
- **.net** for computers of network providers such as InterNIC

- **.int** for international databases and organizations established by international treaties
- **.org** for other organizations
- **.gov** for federal government offices and agencies
- **.mil** for the U.S. military

See Chapter 4 concerning the addition of new global TLDs in November 2000.

The IANA is now creating new players by delegating new global top-level domains to new registries. For example, the Cocos (Keeling) Islands have been given the approval to make their national designation ".cc", a global top-level domain (see http://www.enic.cc). Entities that were unable to secure any of the standard global TLDs are flocking to this new registry. This has caused the Internet equivalent of a gold rush to register names in an island that is about 24 times the size of The Mall in Washington and has just over 600 residents. The IANA is also currently working on adding global TLDs. Other DNS providers are waiting in the wings. Alternative top-level domain companies are waiting for approval from the IANA.

Recently, the IANA has also been allowing most regional registries to act as global TLDs. In several instances, this has led to the subletting of registries to entrepreneurs for profit. For example, the small nation of Tuvalu sublet its *.tv* global TLD designation to a Canadian company funded by a venture capital company in California. To return to our example, hotdogs.com, "hotdogs" represents a second-level domain within the top-level domain of ".com." Beneath the second-level domains are subdomains, the next level of the hierarchy. For example, an organization using the domain name "hotdogs.com" might create a subdomain called "mustard.hotdogs.com" to represent a separate site devoted to mustard information for hotdogs.

It is important to remember that subdomains are assigned by the owners of the domain names and not by the registry that assigned the original domain name. Domain-name registries cannot exercise any control over what precedes a domain name. Although "www" is still the most common prefix, it is not mandated and can be replaced by any prefix.

This has led to the practice of domain-name sharing. This occurs when more than one group makes use of a single domain. An example of domain sharing would be when the wheat and barley growers of America decided to have separate sites sharing a domain like *grains.com*. The wheat group could have *wheat.grains.com* and the barley group could use *barley.grains.com*. In this example, the owner of the domain name *grains.com* has agreed to let two different groups share its domain name.

The domain-name system has been compared to an inverted tree, with the root (dot) at the top, branches (the top-level domains) stemming from the root, and the second-level domains beneath each branch representing sprouts on the branches. A domain name represents a specific and unique portion of the domain-name space, which is the total number of computers and resources that can be described and located via the domain-name system.

Thus, a domain name appears as a string of alphanumeric characters separated into segments by periods. Each segment of the name represents a different level of the hierarchy. When reading a domain name, the rightmost segment of the domain name will represent the highest level of the hierarchy; as you move left, each segment will represent increasingly lower levels of the hierarchy.

It Is Distributed

The DNS is actually a distributed database containing information about domains and the hosts, or computers, within those domains. By "distributed," we mean that the database is actually split up among multiple computers that are scattered across the global computer network commonly called the *Internet*. Each of these computers is running a program called a *name server*. Each of the name server computers controls or has authority over the particular portion of the database that it contains. The portion of the database that a name server has authority over is called a *zone*. The entire Internet can access the information held by each of the name servers. This ability to exchange information is essential to the functioning of the DNS.

This distributed framework means that there is no central authority that takes responsibility for administering all of the data on all of the domains in the world. The control over a specific portion of the database will reside with those closest to the information contained in that portion of the database. This is similar to the situation you may have in tackling a large project. One way to handle the situation would be to split the project into a group of smaller tasks and then distribute the tasks to various people. Then you can delegate the control or authority over each task to the person you assigned to the task. Each person working on the project will hold information essential to the project's completion. By exchanging their information, the people involved will be able to work together to complete the project.

Using this analogy, the project would be the database, the tasks represent the portions of the database, the people delegated the tasks would be the computers running the name server programs, and the tasks over which one person has authority would represent a zone. Everyone working together and exchanging information to complete the project would represent the DNS at work.

It Is Interdependent

The information used by the DNS—and the control over this information—is distributed among name servers. Therefore, it is extremely important that these name servers run smoothly and maintain current information in their areas of authority. The actual data that represent a name server's area of authority are also known as *zone files*. If one of the name servers experiences a problem, it is very likely that the rest of the network will also encounter problems with the portion of the database or zone controlled by that name server.

Under this model, it would seem as though a simple problem with one local name server could pose significant problems of global proportions for communicating on the Internet. If the name server that contains the authoritative information—that is, the information needed to translate *example.com* to its corresponding IP address—failed to operate or contained incorrect information, it would be impossible to reach any people or information in *example.com*. For all intents and purposes, everything within the domain *example.com* would be unreachable.

The DNS uses several techniques to protect against such possibilities, but the interdependent nature of the system still demands the smooth operation and careful management of the machines, software, and data that constitute the DNS.

It Requires Uniqueness of Each Internet Address

As with most addressing systems, it is necessary for each domain name to be unique. Just as postal addresses describe specific and unique locations in the physical world, domain names describe specific and unique locations within the domain-name space. Think for a moment about the postal address "123 Main Street, Any Town, Texas, 12345." This type of address is just as hierarchical as a domain name. It is easy to see how duplication at any level of the address—e.g., more than one Texas; more than one Any Town in Texas; more than one Main Street in Any Town, Texas, more than one 123 Main Street, and so on—would pose problems. A unique address leaves no doubt where a letter is supposed to be delivered.

The DNS is no different. At each level in the DNS hierarchy, a domain name must be unique. For example, at the top of the hierarchy, there can be only one root; among top-level domains, there can be only one *.com;* within *.com,* there can only be one *example.com.*

Of course, in the physical world, it is *possible* to come across two towns in Texas named Any Town. The postal system is able to rely on humans to sort out the confusion and come up with the correct destination. The DNS, however, relies on automation and cannot use human intervention to resolve confusion. Consequently, it is even more critical that domain names remain unique.

Domain-Name Servers and Resolution of Domain-Name Issues

Have you ever wondered what really happens when you type in a URL or an e-mail address? Domain-name system name resolution occurs when a client queries a name server to obtain the IP address with which it wants to connect. If a name server in the local domain cannot resolve a client's request, it queries other servers to locate a server that can. There are two types of name resolution, namely, by iteration and by recursion.

Iteration

By default, a name server queries iteratively (or nonrecursively). This means that it queries several name servers in turn until it finds an answer. It starts by consulting a known name server within the domain hierarchy that contains the destination machine. If it does not already know of a suitable server to ask, it first asks a server in the root domain.

In turn, each server responds by referring to a name server in the domain-name hierarchy that is closer to the one containing the destination machine. The local server then repeats its query to the name server whose name and IP address it has just been given. In this way, the local server traverses the domain-name space until it reaches a name server for the domain that contains the destination machine.

When you type in a URL or an e-mail address, a series of queries takes place between your computer and name server computers. Say that you wanted to locate the computer at http://www.example.com. In the following example, the hierarchical, distributed, and interdependent nature of the DNS is illustrated.

The first query would be sent to your local name server. Your local name server most likely has information about your domain, as well as information about any other domains within its area of authority. Chances are, however, that the domain name you entered is not within your local name server's zone of authority. The response is: "I don't know, so I'll ask the root server."

Your local name server will then send a query to the root server. The root server will not have the specific information needed to translate http://www.example.com to the proper IP address, but the root server knows where to find the name server that contains authoritative information for the *.com* zone. The root server will provide your local name server with the information it needs to contact the name server for the *.com* top-level domain.

The next step is to send a query to the name server for the *.com* top-level domain. The *.com* name server will not have specific information about the IP address of the machine http://www.example.com, but the *.com* name server will know where to find the local name server for *example.com* and will send this information to your local name server. In the last step, your local name server sends a query to the local name server for *example.com*. The local name server for *example.com* will be able to tell your computer the IP address for http://www.example.com, your local name server will send the address of http://www.example.com to your machine, and your computer will make the connection. This entire process normally takes only a few seconds.

Technically, the queries are exchanged not between users and computers but between software programs. We have already mentioned name server programs that enable a machine to store a part of the DNS data, accept queries about domains and hosts, and send responses. Resolver software acts as a client of the name server program, asking questions and waiting for the name server to return the authoritative answer. It is the name servers that do most of the work, however, sending the queries, accepting referrals, asking more questions, and interpreting the information returned by other name servers.

Recursion

Alternatively, a domain name or e-mail address may be resolved or "found" by a recursive query. With a recursive query, a name server behaves like a client and asks another name server to either provide it with the answer to its query or to return an error because it cannot supply an answer. Unlike an iterative query, the name server that is queried will not reply with a referral to a different name server.

Index to Internet Domains

Infrastructure Domain	
.arpa	Exclusively for Internet-infrastructure purposes

Generic Top-Level Domains (GTLDs)	
.aero	For airlines and related industries
.biz	For businesses
.com	For commercial entities
.coop	For business cooperatives
.edu	For educational organizations
.info	For general information sites
.int	For international databases and organizations established by international treaties
.mil	For the U.S. military
.museum	For accredited museums
.name	For individual names
.net	For international network providers, such as InterNIC
.org	For miscellaneous entities
.pro	For individuals who belong to a profession; still being established

Specific Country Domains	
.ac	Ascension Island
.ad	Andorra
.ae	United Arab Emirates
.af	Afghanistan
.ag	Antigua and Barbuda
.ai	Anguilla
.al	Albania
.am	Armenia
.an	Netherlands Antilles
.ao	Angola
.aq	Antarctica

(continued)

.ar	Argentina
.as	American Samoa
.at	Austria
.au	Australia
.aw	Aruba
.az	Azerbaijan
.ba	Bosnia and Herzegowina
.bb	Barbados
.bd	Bangladesh
.be	Belgium
.bf	Burkina Faso
.bg	Bulgaria
.bh	Bahrain
.bi	Burundi
.bj	Benin
.bm	Bermuda
.bn	Brunei Darussalam
.bo	Bolivia
.br	Brazil
.bs	Bahamas
.bt	Bhutan
.bv	Bouvet Island
.bw	Botswana
.by	Belarus
.bz	Belize
.ca	Canada
.cc	Cocos (Keeling) Islands
.cd	Zaire
.cf	Central African Republic
.cg	Congo
.ch	Switzerland
.ci	Côte d'Ivoire
.ck	Cook Islands
.cl	Chile
.cm	Cameroon
.cn	China
.co	Colombia
.cr	Costa Rica
.cu	Cuba
.cv	Cape Verde
.cx	Christmas Island
.cy	Cyprus
.cz	Czech Republic
.de	Germany
.dj	Djibouti
.dk	Denmark
.dm	Dominica
.do	Dominican Republic

.dz	Algeria
.ec	Ecuador
.ee	Estonia
.eg	Egypt
.eh	Western Sahara
.er	Eritrea
.es	Spain
.et	Ethiopia
.fi	Finland
.fj	Fiji
.fk	Falkland Islands
.fm	Micronesia
.fo	Faroe Islands
.fr	France
.ga	Gabon
.gb	United Kingdom
.gd	Grenada
.ge	Georgia
.gf	French Guiana
.gg	Guernsey
.gh	Ghana
.gi	Gibraltar
.gl	Greenland
.gm	Gambia
.gn	Guinea
.gp	Guadeloupe
.gq	Equatorial Guinea
.gr	Greece
.gs	South Georgia and the South Sandwich Islands
.gt	Guatemala
.gu	Guam
.gw	Guinea-Bissau
.gy	Guyana
.hk	Hong Kong
.hm	Heard and McDonald Islands
.hn	Honduras
.hr	Croatia
.ht	Haiti
.hu	Hungary
.id	Indonesia
.ie	Ireland
.il	Israel
.im	Isle of Man
.in	India
.io	British Indian Ocean Territory
.iq	Iraq
.ir	Iran

(continued)

.is	Iceland
.it	Italy
.je	Jersey
.jm	Jamaica
.jo	Jordan
.jp	Japan
.ke	Kenya
.kg	Kyrgyzstan
.kh	Cambodia
.ki	Kiribati
.km	Comoros
.kn	Saint Kitts and Nevis
.kr	Korea, Republic of
.kw	Kuwait
.ky	Cayman Islands
.kz	Kazakhstan
.la	Lao People's Democratic Republic
.lb	Lebanon
.lc	Saint Lucia
.li	Liechtenstein
.lk	Sri Lanka
.lr	Liberia
.ls	Lesotho
.lt	Lithuania
.lu	Luxembourg
.lv	Latvia
.ly	Libyan Arab Jamahiriya
.ma	Morocco
.mc	Monaco
.md	Moldova
.mg	Madagascar
.mh	Marshall Islands
.mk	Macedonia
.ml	Mali
.mm	Myanmar
.mn	Mongolia
.mo	Macau
.mp	Northern Mariana Islands
.mq	Martinique
.mr	Mauritania
.ms	Montserrat
.mt	Malta
.mu	Mauritius
.mv	Maldives
.mw	Malawi
.mx	Mexico
.my	Malaysia
.mz	Mozambique
.na	Namibia

.nc	New Caledonia
.ne	Niger
.nf	Norfolk Island
.ng	Nigeria
.ni	Nicaragua
.nl	The Netherlands
.no	Norway
.np	Nepal
.nr	Nauru
.nu	Niue
.nz	New Zealand
.om	Oman
.pa	Panama
.pe	Peru
.pf	French Polynesia
.pg	Papua New Guinea
.ph	Philippines
.pk	Pakistan
.pl	Poland
.pm	St. Pierre and Miquelon
.pn	Pitcairn
.pr	Puerto Rico
.pt	Portugal
.pw	Palau
.py	Paraguay
.qa	Qatar
.re	Reunion
.ro	Romania
.ru	Russia
.rw	Rwanda
.sa	Saudi Arabia
.sb	Solomon Islands
.sc	Seychelles
.sd	Sudan
.se	Sweden
.sg	Singapore
.sh	St. Helena
.si	Slovenia
.sj	Svalbard and Jan Mayen Islands
.sk	Slovakia
.sl	Sierra Leone
.sm	San Marino
.sn	Senegal
.so	Somalia
.sr	Surinam
.st	Sao Tome and Principe
.su	USSR (former)
.sv	El Salvador

(continued)

.sy	Syrian Arab Republic
.sz	Swaziland
.tc	The Turks & Caicos Islands
.td	Chad
.tf	French Southern Territories
.tg	Togo
.th	Thailand
.tj	Tajikistan
.tk	Tokelau
.tm	Turkmenistan
.tn	Tunisia
.to	Tonga
.tp	East Timor
.tr	Turkey
.tt	Trinidad and Tobago
.tv	Tuvalu
.tw	Taiwan
.tz	Tanzania
.ua	Ukraine
.ug	Uganda
.uk	United Kingdom
.um	United States Minor Outlying Islands
.us	United States
.uy	Uruguay
.uz	Uzbekistan
.va	Holy See (Vatican City State)
.vc	Saint Vincent and the Grenadines
.ve	Venezuela
.vg	Virgin Islands British
.vi	Virgin Islands U.S.
.vn	Vietnam
.vu	Vanuatu
.wf	Wallis and Futuna Islands
.ws	Samoa
.ye	Yemen
.yt	Mayotte
.yu	Yugoslavia
.za	South Africa
.zm	Zambia
.zr	Zaire
.zw	Zimbabwe

Netiquette

There are certain norms and proper etiquette when communicating over the Internet, which are collectively dubbed "**netiquette.**" It is simply being professional, polite, and considerate of others in electronic correspondences. If a few basic guidelines are followed, professional work product will be the result.

The rules of e-mail netiquette[1] are generally:

- Never give your user ID or password to another person.
- Never assume that your e-mail messages are private or that they can be read by only yourself or the recipient.
- Keep paragraphs and messages short and to the point.
- When quoting another person, edit out whatever is not directly applicable to your reply. Do not let your mailing or Usenet software automatically quote the entire body of messages you are replying to when it is not necessary. Take the time to edit any quotations down to the minimum necessary to provide context for a reply. Nobody likes reading a long message in quotes for the third or fourth time, only to be followed by a one-line response: "Yeah, me too."
- Focus on one subject per message and always include a pertinent subject title for the message. That way, the user can locate the message quickly.
- Include your signature at the bottom of e-mail messages when communicating with people who may not know you personally or when broadcasting to a dynamic group of recipients.
- Your e-mail signature should include your name, position, affiliation, and Internet addresses and should not exceed four or five lines. Optional information could include your address and phone number.
- Capitalize words only to highlight an important point or to distinguish a title or heading. Capitalizing whole words that are not titles is generally considered SHOUTING!

---

[1] These rules are from *The Net: User Guidelines and Netiquette, at* http://www.fau.edu/netiquette/net/elec.html. Copyright © 1998, Arlene Rinaldi and Florida Atlantic University. Used with permission.

- *Asterisks* surrounding a word can be used to make a stronger point.
- Use the underscore symbol before and after the title of a book, such as _The Wizard of Oz_.
- Because of the international nature of the Internet and the fact that most of the world uses an alternate format for listing dates (i.e., DD MM YY), avoid misinterpretation of dates by listing dates with the month spelled out, such as 24 JUN 1996.
- Follow chain-of-command procedures for corresponding with superiors. For example, do not send a complaint via e-mail directly to the "top" just because you can.
- Be professional and careful what you say about others. E-mail is easily forwarded.
- Cite all quotes, references, and sources. Respect copyright and license agreements.
- It is considered extremely rude to forward personal e-mail to mailing lists or Usenet without the original author's permission!
- Attaching return receipts to a message may be considered an invasion of privacy.
- Be careful when using sarcasm and humor. Without face-to-face communications, your joke may be viewed as criticism. When being humorous, use emoticons to express humor, such as :-) happy face for humor.
- Acronyms can be used to abbreviate when possible, but messages that are filled with acronyms can be confusing and annoying to the reader. For a list, see http://www.fau.edu/netiquette/net/acroynms.txt. (Yes, "acronyms" is spelled wrong in the Internet address.)

Netiquette and Usenet/Newsgroups

Usually at the end of a Usenet newsgroup message or articles, there is a small blurb called a **signature.** Many of the Usenet systems newsgroup lists automatically add a commenter's signature. It exists to provide information about how to get in touch with the person posting the article, including e-mail address, phone number, address, or where the poster is located. These days, though, some signatures have become the "graffiti" of the Internet. People put song lyrics, pictures, philosophical quotes, or even advertisements in their ".sigs." (Note, however, that advertising in your signature will more often than not get you flamed until you take it out.)

Netiquette dictates limiting the signature on Usenet sites to four lines. Some people make signatures that are ten lines or even more, including elaborate ASCII drawings of their handwritten signature or faces or even the space shuttle. This is not cute and will irritate people to no end.

Similarly, it is not necessary to include your signature. If you forget to append it to an article, do not worry about it. The article is just as good as it ever would be and contains everything you should want to say. Do not repost the article just to include the signature.

If, after reading a newsgroup post, a reply e-mail to a particular person does not make it through, avoid posting the message to the whole newsgroup.

Even if the likelihood of that person reading the group is very high, all of the other people reading the articles do not care what you have to say to a particular individual. Simply wait for the person to post again and double-check the address, or get in touch with the system administrator and see if there is a problem with local e-mail delivery. It may also turn out that the recipient's site is down or is having problems, in which case it is necessary to wait until things return to normal before contacting the recipient.

In the interests of privacy, it is considered extremely bad taste to post any e-mail that someone else (a third party) may have sent, unless you have explicit permission from the sender to redistribute it. While the legal issues can be heavily debated, most users agree that e-mail should be treated privately.

Many people, particularly new users, want to try out posting before actually taking part in discussions. Often the mechanics of getting messages out is the most difficult part of Usenet. To this end, many, many users find it necessary to post their tests to "normal" groups (for example, news.admin or comp.mail.misc). This is considered a major netiquette faux pas in the Usenet world. There are a number of groups available, called *test groups*, that exist solely for the purpose of trying out a news system, reader, or even a new signature. They include: *alt.test, gnu.gnusenet.test,* and *misc.test.* Some of these test groups will generate automatic replies to your posts to let you know they made it through. There are certain denizens of Usenet that frequent the test groups to help new users out. They respond to the posts, often including the article so the poster can see how it got to the person's site.

Authors of articles occasionally say that readers should reply by mail and they will summarize. Accordingly, readers should reply via mail. Responding with a follow-up article to such an article defeats the intention of the author. The author, in a few days, may post one article containing the highlights of all the responses received. If a reader posted a follow-up to the whole group, the original author may not have read what was posted separately.

When creating a summary of the replies to a post, try to make it as reader friendly as possible. Avoid putting all of the messages received into one big file. Rather, take some time and edit the messages into a form that contains the essential information that would interest other readers. Sometimes people will respond but request to remain anonymous. One example is the employees of a corporation who feel the information is not proprietary but at the same time want to protect themselves from political backlash. Summaries should honor this request accordingly by listing the "From:" address as "anonymous" or "Address withheld by request."

When following up to an article, many newsreaders provide the facility to quote the original article with each line prefixed by >. When you quote another person, include only those quotes that speak to the points you are addressing. By including the entire article, you only annoy those reading it.

Avoid being tedious with responses; rather than pick apart an article, address it in parts or as a whole. Addressing practically each and every word in an article suggests that the person responding has absolutely nothing better to do with his or her time.

If a dispute starts (insults and personal comments get thrown back and forth), take it into e-mail. Exchange e-mail with the person with whom you are arguing. No one enjoys watching people bicker incessantly.

One should avoid posting "recent" events: sports scores, a plane crash, or whatever people will see on the evening news or read in the morning paper. By the time the article has propagated across all of Usenet, the "news" value of the article has become stale.

How you write and present yourself in your articles is important. Keep a dictionary nearby. If you have trouble with grammar and punctuation, get a book on English grammar and composition (found in many bookstores and at garage sales). Pay attention to what you say; it makes you who you are on the Internet.

Try to be clear in what you ask. Ambiguous or vague questions often lead to no response at all, leaving the poster discouraged. Give as much essential information as you feel is necessary to let people help you, but keep it within limits.

Index